Adobe® Photoshop® CS6

CLASSROOM IN A BOOK

The official training workbook from Adobe Systems

Adobe

WHAT'S ON THE DISC

Here is an overview of the contents of the Classroom in a Book disc.

The *Adobe Photoshop CS6 Classroom in a Book* disc includes the lesson files that you'll need to complete the exercises in this book, as well as other content to help you learn more about Adobe Photoshop CS6 and use it with greater efficiency and ease. The diagram below represents the contents of the disc, which should help you locate the files you need.

Lesson files

Each lesson has its own folder inside the Lessons folder. You will need to copy these lesson folders to your hard drive before you can begin each lesson.

Online resources

Links to Adobe Community Help, product Help and Support pages, Adobe Press, Adobe certification programs, Adobe TV, and other useful online resources can be found inside a handy HTML file. Just open it in your web browser and click the links, including a special link to this book's product page where you can access updates and bonus material.

Learn by Video bonus tutorials

A bonus 2-hour set of "Adobe Photoshop CS6: Learn by Video" tutorials is included on this disc, from video2brain and Adobe Press. "Learn by Video" is one of the most critically acclaimed training products on Adobe software and is the only Adobe-approved video courseware for the Adobe Certified Associate Level certification.

CONTENTS

GETTING STARTED   **1**

About Classroom in a Book.................................... 1

What's new in this edition.................................... 2

What's in Photoshop Extended............................. 2

Prerequisites 3

Installing Adobe Photoshop................................. 3

Starting Adobe Photoshop................................... 4

Copying the Classroom in a Book files 4

Restoring default preferences 4

Additional resources 6

Adobe certification 7

1   GETTING TO KNOW THE WORK AREA   **8**

Starting to work in Adobe Photoshop 10

Using the tools 14

Using the options bar and other panels.................... 22

Undoing actions in Photoshop 26

Customizing the workspace................................ 33

Finding resources for using Photoshop 37

Checking for updates 37

2   BASIC PHOTO CORRECTIONS   **44**

Strategy for retouching 46

Resolution and image size 47

Getting started 48

Adjusting the color in Camera Raw 49

Straightening and cropping the image in Photoshop 51

Replacing colors in an image. 53

Adjusting saturation with the Sponge tool. 54

Repairing areas with the Clone Stamp tool 55

Using the Spot Healing Brush tool 57

Applying a content-aware patch. 58

Applying the Unsharp Mask filter 60

Saving the image for four-color printing 61

3   WORKING WITH SELECTIONS   66

About selecting and selection tools 68

Getting started 69

Using the Quick Selection tool 69

Moving a selected area 70

Manipulating selections 71

Using the Magic Wand tool. 78

Selecting with the lasso tools 80

Rotating a selection. 81

Selecting with the Magnetic Lasso tool 82

Cropping an image and erasing within a selection 84

4   LAYER BASICS   90

About layers. 92

Getting started 92

Using the Layers panel. 93

Rearranging layers. 98

Applying a gradient to a layer 108

Applying a layer style 109

Adding an adjustment layer. 113

Updating layer effects 115

Adding a border 116

Flattening and saving files 118

5 CORRECTING AND ENHANCING DIGITAL PHOTOGRAPHS   **124**

Getting started 126

About camera raw files. 129

Processing files in Camera Raw 129

Applying advanced color correction 141

Correcting digital photographs in Photoshop. 151

Correcting image distortion. 155

Adding depth of field 158

6 MASKS AND CHANNELS   **166**

Working with masks and channels. 168

Getting started 168

Creating a mask 169

Refining a mask. 170

Creating a quick mask. 174

Manipulating an image with Puppet Warp 177

Working with channels 178

7 TYPOGRAPHIC DESIGN   **186**

About type 188

Getting started 188

Creating a clipping mask from type. 189

Creating type on a path 194

Warping point type 196

Designing paragraphs of type. 197

8 VECTOR DRAWING TECHNIQUES   **206**

About bitmap images and vector graphics. 208

About paths and the Pen tool 209

Getting started 209

Using paths with artwork 210

Creating vector objects for the background. 218

Working with defined custom shapes 224

Importing a Smart Object. 227

9 ADVANCED COMPOSITING   **232**

Getting started 234

Assembling a montage of images 234

Applying filters 243

Hand-coloring selections on a layer 246

Applying Smart Filters 252

Adding drop shadows and a border 254

Matching color schemes across images. 256

Automating a multistep task 258

Stitching a panorama 262

Finishing the image. 264

10 EDITING VIDEO   **268**

Getting started 270

Creating a new video project. 271

Animating text with keyframes. 274

Creating effects. 276

Adding transitions 281

Adding audio. 282

Muting unwanted audio 283

Rendering video. 284

11 PAINTING WITH THE MIXER BRUSH   **288**

About the Mixer Brush 290

Getting started 290

Selecting brush settings 291

Mixing colors 295

Creating a custom brush preset 298

Mixing colors with a photograph. 300

12 WORKING WITH 3D IMAGES   **308**

Getting started 310

Creating a 3D shape from a layer 310

Manipulating 3D objects. 312

Adding 3D objects. 314

Merging 3D layers to share the same 3D space 318

Positioning objects in a scene 319

Applying materials to 3D objects 326

Lighting a 3D scene 332

Rendering a 3D scene 334

13 PREPARING FILES FOR THE WEB   **338**

Getting started 340

Creating slices 343

Exporting HTML and images 349

Using the Zoomify feature 354

Creating a web gallery 355

14 PRODUCING AND PRINTING CONSISTENT COLOR   **360**

About color management 362

Getting started 364

Specifying color-management settings .364

Proofing an image 365

Identifying out-of-gamut colors 366

Adjusting an image and printing a proof 368

Saving the image as a CMYK EPS file 370

Printing 371

INDEX   **374**

GETTING STARTED

Adobe® Photoshop® CS6, the benchmark for digital imaging excellence, provides strong performance, powerful image-editing features, and an intuitive interface. Adobe Camera Raw, included with Photoshop CS6, offers flexibility and control as you work with raw images as well as TIFF and JPEG images. Photoshop CS6 pushes the boundaries of digital image editing and helps you turn your dreams into designs more easily than ever before.

About Classroom in a Book

Adobe Photoshop CS6 Classroom in a Book® is part of the official training series for Adobe graphics and publishing software, developed with the support of Adobe product experts. The lessons are designed to let you learn at your own pace. If you're new to Adobe Photoshop, you'll learn the fundamental concepts and features you'll need to master the program. And if you've been using Adobe Photoshop for a while, you'll find that Classroom in a Book teaches many advanced features, including tips and techniques for using the latest version of the application and preparing images for the web.

Although each lesson provides step-by-step instructions for creating a specific project, there's room for exploration and experimentation. You can follow the book from start to finish, or do only the lessons that match your interests and needs. Each lesson concludes with a review section summarizing what you've covered.

What's new in this edition

This edition covers many new features in Adobe Photoshop CS6, such as intuitive video editing tools, which make it easy to create and add effects to video clips and still images; the Content-Aware Move tool, which lets you remove unwanted objects or replicate existing portions of an image; simpler and more powerful 3D controls (Photoshop CS6 Extended only); and the all-new Crop tool, providing greater flexibility in cropping, straightening, and skewing an image. In addition, these lessons introduce you to erodible brush tips, new vector layers, lens-aware adjustments, paragraph styles, and more.

New exercises and lessons cover:

- Using the Timeline panel, keyframes, and motion effects to create movie files from video clips and still images within Photoshop.

- Creating and applying paragraph styles to text.

- Painting more realistic effects with erodible brush tips.

- Creating, positioning, and adding effects to objects in a 3D scene (Photoshop CS6 Extended only).

This edition is also chock-full of extra information on Photoshop features and how best to work with this robust application. You'll learn best practices for organizing, managing, and showcasing your photos, as well as how to optimize images for the web. And throughout this edition, look for tips and techniques from one of Adobe's own experts, Photoshop evangelist Julieanne Kost.

What's in Photoshop Extended

This edition of *Adobe Photoshop CS6 Classroom in a Book* works with the 3D features in Adobe Photoshop CS6 Extended—a version with additional functions for professional, technical, and scientific users, intended for those creating special effects in video or in architectural, scientific, or engineering images.

Photoshop Extended features include:

- The ability to import 3D images and to edit individual frames or image sequence files by painting, cloning, retouching, or transforming them.

- Support for 3D files including the U3D, 3DS, OBJ, KMZ, and Collada file formats created by programs such as Adobe Acrobat® 9 Professional and Google Earth. See Lesson 12, "Working with 3D Images," to learn about these features.

- Support for specialized file formats, such as DICOM, the most common standard for receiving medical scans; MATLAB, a high-level technical computing language and interactive environment for developing algorithms, visualizing and analyzing data, and computing numbers; and 32-bit high-resolution images, including a special HDR Color Picker and the capability to paint and layer these 32-bit HDR images.

Prerequisites

Before you begin to use *Adobe Photoshop CS6 Classroom in a Book*, you should have a working knowledge of your computer and its operating system. Make sure that you know how to use the mouse and standard menus and commands, and also how to open, save, and close files. If you need to review these techniques, see the documentation included with your Microsoft® Windows® or Apple® Mac® OS X documentation.

Installing Adobe Photoshop

Before you begin using *Adobe Photoshop CS6 Classroom in a Book*, make sure that your system is set up correctly and that you've installed the required software and hardware. You must purchase the Adobe Photoshop CS6 software separately. For system requirements and complete instructions on installing the software, see the Adobe Photoshop CS6 Read Me file on the application DVD or on the web at www.adobe.com/support. Note that some Photoshop CS6 Extended features, including all 3D features, require a video card that supports OpenGL 2.0.

Photoshop and Bridge use the same installer. You must install these applications from the Adobe Photoshop CS6 application DVD (you cannot run the programs from the disc), or from the installation files you downloaded from Adobe, onto your hard drive. Follow the onscreen instructions.

Make sure that your serial number is accessible before installing the application.

Starting Adobe Photoshop

You start Photoshop just as you do most software applications.

To start Adobe Photoshop in Windows: Choose Start > All Programs > Adobe Photoshop CS6.

To start Adobe Photoshop in Mac OS: Open the Applications/Adobe Photoshop CS6 folder, and double-click the Adobe Photoshop program icon.

Copying the Classroom in a Book files

The *Adobe Photoshop CS6 Classroom in a Book* DVD includes folders containing all the electronic files for the lessons in the book. Each lesson has its own folder; you must copy the folders to your hard drive to complete the lessons. To save room on your hard drive, you can install only the folder necessary for each lesson as you need it, and remove it when you're done.

To install the lesson files, do the following:

1 Insert the *Adobe Photoshop CS6 Classroom in a Book* DVD into your disc drive.

2 Browse the contents and locate the Lessons folder.

3 Do one of the following:

- To copy all the lesson files, drag the Lessons folder from the DVD onto your hard drive.

- To copy only individual lesson files, first create a new folder on your hard drive, and name it **Lessons**. Then, drag the lesson folder or folders that you want to copy from the DVD into the Lessons folder on your hard drive.

● **Note:** As you complete each lesson, you will preserve the start files. In case you overwrite them, you can restore the original files by recopying the corresponding Lesson folder from the *Adobe Photoshop CS6 Classroom in a Book* DVD to the Lessons folder on your hard drive.

Restoring default preferences

The preferences file stores information about panel and command settings. Each time you quit Adobe Photoshop, the positions of the panels and certain command settings are recorded in the preferences file. Any selections you make in the Preferences dialog box are also saved in the preferences file.

To ensure that what you see onscreen matches the images and instructions in this book, you should restore the default preferences as you begin each lesson. If you prefer to preserve your preferences, be aware that the tools, panels, and other settings in Photoshop CS6 may not match those described in this book.

If you have custom-calibrated your monitor, save the calibration settings before you start work on this book. To save your monitor-calibration settings, follow the simple procedure described below.

To save your current color settings:

1 Start Adobe Photoshop.

2 Choose Edit > Color Settings.

3 Note what is selected in the Settings menu:

   • If it is anything other than Custom, write down the name of the settings file, and click OK to close the dialog box. You do not need to perform steps 4–6 of this procedure.

   • If Custom is selected in the Settings menu, click Save (*not* OK).

The Save dialog box opens. The default location is the Settings folder, which is where you want to save your file. The default file extension is .csf (color settings file).

4 In the File Name field (Windows) or Save As field (Mac OS), type a descriptive name for your color settings, preserving the .csf file extension. Then click Save.

5 In the Color Settings Comment dialog box, type any descriptive text that will help you identify the color settings later, such as the date, specific settings, or your workgroup.

6 Click OK to close the Color Settings Comment dialog box, and again to close the Color Settings dialog box.

To restore your color settings:

1 Start Adobe Photoshop.

2 Choose Edit > Color Settings.

3 In the Settings menu in the Color Settings dialog box, select the settings file you noted or saved in the previous procedure, and click OK.

Additional resources

Adobe Photoshop CS6 Classroom in a Book is not meant to replace documentation that comes with the program or to be a comprehensive reference for every feature. Only the commands and options used in the lessons are explained in this book. For comprehensive information about program features and tutorials, refer to these resources:

Adobe Community Help: Community Help brings together active Adobe product users, Adobe product team members, authors, and experts to give you the most useful, relevant, and up-to-date information about Adobe products.

To access Community Help, press F1 or choose Help > Photoshop Help.

Adobe content is updated based on community feedback and contributions. You can add comments to both content and forums (including links to web content), publish your own content using Community Publishing, or contribute Cookbook Recipes. Find out how to contribute at www.adobe.com/community/publishing/download.html.

See community.adobe.com/help/profile/faq.html for answers to frequently asked questions about Community Help.

Adobe Photoshop Help and Support: www.adobe.com/support/photoshop is where you can find and browse Help and Support content on Adobe.com.

Adobe Forums: forums.adobe.com lets you tap into peer-to-peer discussions, questions, and answers on Adobe products.

Adobe TV: tv.adobe.com is an online video resource for expert instruction and inspiration about Adobe products, including a How To channel to get you started with your product.

Adobe Design Center: www.adobe.com/designcenter offers thoughtful articles on design and design issues, a gallery showcasing the work of top-notch designers, tutorials, and more.

Adobe Developer Connection: www.adobe.com/devnet is your source for technical articles, code samples, and how-to videos that cover Adobe developer products and technologies.

Resources for educators: www.adobe.com/education offers a treasure trove of information for instructors who teach classes on Adobe software. Find solutions for education at all levels, including free curricula that use an integrated approach to teaching Adobe software and can be used to prepare for the Adobe Certified Associate exams.

Also check out these useful links:

Adobe Marketplace & Exchange: www.adobe.com/cfusion/exchange is a central resource for finding tools, services, extensions, code samples, and more to supplement and extend your Adobe products.

Adobe Photoshop CS6 product home page: www.adobe.com/products/photoshop.

Adobe Labs: labs.adobe.com gives you access to early builds of cutting-edge technology, as well as forums where you can interact with both the Adobe development teams building that technology and other like-minded members of the community.

Adobe certification

The Adobe training and certification programs are designed to help Adobe customers improve and promote their product-proficiency skills. There are four levels of certification:

*   Adobe Certified Associate (ACA)

*   Adobe Certified Expert (ACE)

*   Adobe Certified Instructor (ACI)

*   Adobe Authorized Training Center (AATC)

The Adobe Certified Associate (ACA) credential certifies that individuals have the entry-level skills to plan, design, build, and maintain effective communications using different forms of digital media.

The Adobe Certified Expert program is a way for expert users to upgrade their credentials. You can use Adobe certification as a catalyst for getting a raise, finding a job, or promoting your expertise.

If you are an ACE-level instructor, the Adobe Certified Instructor program takes your skills to the next level and gives you access to a wide range of Adobe resources.

Adobe Authorized Training Centers offer instructor-led courses and training on Adobe products, employing only Adobe Certified Instructors. A directory of AATCs is available at partners.adobe.com.

For information on the Adobe Certified programs, visit www.adobe.com/support/certification/main.html.

1 GETTING TO KNOW THE WORK AREA

Lesson overview

In this lesson, you'll learn how to do the following:

- Open Adobe Photoshop files.

- Select and use some of the tools in the Tools panel.

- Set options for a selected tool using the options bar.

- Use various methods to zoom in on and out from an image.

- Select, rearrange, and use panels.

- Choose commands in panel and context menus.

- Open and use a panel in the panel dock.

- Undo actions to correct mistakes or to make different choices.

- Customize the workspace.

- Find topics in Photoshop Help.

 This lesson will take about 90 minutes to complete. Copy the Lesson01 folder into the Lessons folder that you created on your hard drive for these projects (or create it now), if you haven't already done so. As you work on this lesson, you'll preserve the start files. If you need to restore the start files, copy them from the *Adobe Photoshop CS6 Classroom in a Book* DVD.

As you work with Adobe Photoshop, you'll discover that you can often accomplish the same task in several ways. To make the best use of the extensive editing capabilities in Photoshop, you must first learn to navigate the work area.

Starting to work in Adobe Photoshop

The Adobe Photoshop work area includes menus, toolbars, and panels that give you quick access to a variety of tools and options for editing and adding elements to your image. You can also add commands and filters to the menus by installing third-party software known as *plug-ins*.

Photoshop works with bitmapped, digitized images (that is, continuous-tone images that have been converted into a series of small squares, or picture elements, called *pixels*). You can also work with vector graphics, which are drawings made of smooth lines that retain their crispness when scaled. You can create original artwork in Photoshop, or you can import images from many sources, such as:

*   Photographs from a digital camera

*   Commercial CDs of digital images

*   Scans of photographs, transparencies, negatives, graphics, or other documents

*   Captured video images

*   Artwork created in drawing programs

Starting Photoshop and opening a file

● **Note:** Typically, you won't need to reset defaults when you're working on your own projects. However, you'll reset the preferences before working on each lesson in this book to ensure that what you see onscreen matches the descriptions in the lessons. For more information, see "Restoring default preferences" on page 4.

To begin, you'll start Adobe Photoshop and reset the default preferences.

1 On the desktop, double-click the Adobe Photoshop icon to start Adobe Photoshop, and then immediately hold down Ctrl+Alt+Shift (Windows) or Command+Option+Shift (Mac OS) to reset the default settings.

If you don't see the Photoshop icon on your desktop, choose Start > All Programs > Adobe Photoshop CS6 (Windows) or look in either the Applications folder or the Dock (Mac OS).

2 When prompted, click Yes to confirm that you want to delete the Adobe Photoshop Settings file.

The Photoshop work area appears as shown in the following illustration.

A. Menu bar
B. Options bar
C. Tools panel
D. Mini Bridge tab
E. Timeline tab
F. Workspaces menu
G. Panels

● **Note:** This illustration shows the Mac OS version of Photoshop. The arrangement is similar on Windows, but operating system styles may vary.

The default workspace in Photoshop consists of the menu bar and options bar at the top of the screen, the Tools panel on the left, and several open panels in the panel dock on the right. When you have documents open, one or more image windows also appear, and you can display them at the same time using the tabbed interface. The Photoshop user interface is very similar to the one in Adobe Illustrator®, Adobe InDesign®, and Adobe Flash®—so learning how to use the tools and panels in one application means that you'll know how to use them in the others.

There is one main difference between the Photoshop work area on Windows and that on Mac OS: On Mac OS, you can work with an application frame, which contains the Photoshop application's windows and panels within a frame that is distinct from other applications you may have open; only the menu bar is outside the application frame. The application frame is enabled by default; to disable the application frame, choose Window > Application Frame.

On Mac OS, the application frame keeps the image, panels, and menu bar together.

3 Choose File > Open, and navigate to the Lessons/Lesson01 folder that you copied to your hard drive from the *Adobe Photoshop CS6 Classroom in a Book* DVD.

4 Select the 01A_End.psd file, and click Open. Click OK if you see the Embedded Profile Mismatch dialog box.

The 01A_End.psd file opens in its own window, called the *image window*. The end files in this book show you what you are creating in each project. In this file, an image of a vintage car has been enhanced without overexposing the headlight.

5 Choose File > Close, or click the close button on the title bar of the image window. (Do not close Photoshop.)

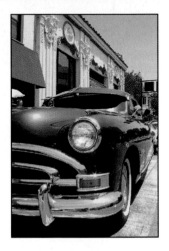

Opening a file with Adobe Bridge

In this book, you'll work with different start files in each lesson. You may make copies of these files and save them under different names or locations, or you may work from the original start files and then copy them from the DVD again if you want a fresh start. This lesson includes three start files.

In the previous exercise, you used the Open command to open a file. Now you'll open another file using Adobe Bridge, a visual file browser that helps take the guesswork out of finding the image file that you need.

1 Choose File > Browse In Bridge. If you're prompted to enable the Photoshop extension in Bridge, click OK.

Adobe Bridge opens, displaying a collection of panels, menus, and buttons.

2 Select the Folders tab in the upper left corner, and then browse to the Lessons folder you copied from the DVD onto your hard disk. The Lessons folder appears in the Content panel.

3 Select the Lessons folder, and choose File > Add To Favorites. Adding files, folders, application icons, and other assets that you use often to the Favorites panel lets you access them quickly.

4 Select the Favorites tab to open the panel, and click the Lessons folder to open it. Then, in the Content panel, double-click the Lesson01 folder.

Thumbnail previews of the folder contents appear in the Content panel.

5 Double-click the 01A_Start.psd thumbnail in the Content panel to open the file, or select the thumbnail and choose File > Open.

The 01A_Start.psd image opens in Photoshop. Leave Bridge open; you'll use it to locate and open files later in this lesson.

Using the tools

Photoshop provides an integrated set of tools for producing sophisticated graphics for print, web, and mobile viewing. We could easily fill the entire book with details on the wealth of Photoshop tools and tool configurations. While that would certainly be a useful reference, it's not the goal of this book. Instead, you'll start gaining experience by configuring and using a few tools on a sample project. Every lesson will introduce you to more tools and ways to use them. By the time you finish all the lessons in this book, you'll have a solid foundation for further explorations of the Photoshop toolset.

Selecting and using a tool from the Tools panel

The Tools panel is the long, narrow panel on the far left side of the work area. It contains selection tools, painting and editing tools, foreground- and background-color selection boxes, and viewing tools.

● **Note:** For a complete list of the tools in the Tools panel, see the Tools panel overview at the end of this lesson.

You'll start by using the Zoom tool, which also appears in many other Adobe applications, including Illustrator, InDesign, and Acrobat.

1 Click the double arrows just above the Tools panel to toggle to a double-column view. Click the arrow again to return to a single-column Tools panel and use your screen space more efficiently.

2 Examine the status bar at the bottom of the work area (Windows) or image window (Mac OS), and notice the percentage that appears on the far left. This represents the current enlargement view of the image, or zoom level.

3 Move the pointer over the Tools panel, and hover it over the magnifying-glass icon until a tool tip appears. The tool tip displays the tool's name (Zoom tool) and keyboard shortcut (Z).

4 Click the Zoom tool (🔍) in the Tools panel, or press Z to select it.

5 Move the pointer over the image window. The pointer now looks like a tiny magnifying glass with a plus sign in the center of the glass (🔍).

6 Click anywhere in the image window.

The image enlarges to a preset percentage level, which replaces the previous value in the status bar. The location you clicked when you used the Zoom tool is centered in the enlarged view. If you click again, the zoom advances to the next preset level, up to a maximum of 3200%.

7 Hold down the Alt key (Windows) or Option key (Mac OS) so that the Zoom tool pointer appears with a minus sign in the center of the magnifying glass (🔍), and then click anywhere in the image. Then release the Alt or Option key.

● **Note:** You can use other methods to zoom in and out. For example, when the Zoom tool is selected, you can select the Zoom In or Zoom Out mode on the options bar. You can choose View > Zoom In or View > Zoom Out. Or, you can type a new percentage in the status bar and press Enter or Return.

● **Note:** Scrubby Zoom is available only if Use Graphics Processor is enabled in the Performance panel of the Photoshop Preferences dialog box. (Choose Edit > Preferences > Performance or Photoshop > Preferences > Performance to open the dialog box.)

Now the view zooms out to a lower preset magnification, so that you can see more of the image, but in less detail.

8   If Scrubby Zoom is selected in the options bar, click anywhere on the image and drag the Zoom tool to the right. The image enlarges. Drag the Zoom tool to the left to zoom out. When Scrubby Zoom is selected, you can drag the Zoom tool across the image to zoom in and out.

9   Deselect Scrubby Zoom in the options bar if it's selected. Then, using the Zoom tool, drag a rectangle to enclose the area of the image that includes the headlight.

The image enlarges so that the area you enclosed in your rectangle now fills the entire image window.

You have now used four methods with the Zoom tool to change the magnification in the image window: clicking, holding down a keyboard modifier while clicking, dragging to zoom in and out, and dragging to define a magnification area. Many of the other tools in the Tools panel can be used with keyboard combinations and options, as well. You'll have opportunities to use these techniques in various lessons in this book.

Selecting and using a hidden tool

Photoshop has many tools you can use to edit image files, but you will probably work with only a few of them at a time. The Tools panel arranges some of the tools in groups, with only one tool shown for each group. The other tools in the group are hidden behind that tool.

A small triangle in the lower right corner of a button is your clue that other tools are available but hidden under that tool.

1 Position the pointer over the second tool from the top in the Tools panel until the tool tip appears. The tool tip identifies the Rectangular Marquee tool (⬚) with the keyboard shortcut M. Select that tool.

2 Select the Elliptical Marquee tool (⬭), which is hidden behind the Rectangular Marquee tool, using one of the following methods:

- Press and hold the mouse button over the Rectangular Marquee tool to open the pop-up list of hidden tools, and select the Elliptical Marquee tool.

- Alt-click (Windows) or Option-click (Mac OS) the tool button in the Tools panel to cycle through the hidden marquee tools until the Elliptical Marquee tool is selected.

- Press Shift+M, which switches between the Rectangular and Elliptical Marquee tools.

3 Move the pointer over the image window, to the upper left side of the headlight. When the Elliptical Marquee tool is selected, the pointer becomes cross-hairs (+).

4 Drag the pointer down and to the right to draw an ellipse around the headlight, and then release the mouse button.

An animated dashed line indicates that the area inside it is *selected*. When you select an area, it becomes the only editable area of the image. The area outside the selection is protected.

5 Move the pointer inside your elliptical selection so that the pointer appears as an arrow with a small rectangle (⬚).

6 Drag the selection so that it is accurately centered over the headlight.

When you drag the selection, only the selection border moves, not pixels in the image. When you want to move the pixels in the image, you'll need to use a different technique. You'll learn more about making different kinds of selections and moving the selection contents in Lesson 3, "Working with Selections."

Using keyboard combinations with tool actions

Many tools can operate under certain constraints. You usually activate these modes by holding down specific keys as you move the tool with the mouse. Some tools have modes that you choose in the options bar.

The next task is to make a fresh start at selecting the headlight. This time, you'll use a keyboard combination that constrains the elliptical selection to a circle that you'll draw from the center outward instead of from the outside inward.

1 Make sure that the Elliptical Marquee tool (⬭) is still selected in the Tools panel, and then deactivate the current selection by doing one of the following:

- In the image window, click anywhere outside the selected area.

- Choose Select > Deselect.

- Use the keyboard shortcut Ctrl+D (Windows) or Command+D (Mac OS).

2 Position the pointer in the center of the headlight.

● **Note:** If you accidentally release the Alt or Option key prematurely, the tool reverts to its normal behavior (drawing from the edge). If you haven't yet released the mouse button, you can just press the key again, and the selection changes back. If you have released the mouse button, simply start again at step 1.

3 Press Alt+Shift (Windows) or Option+Shift (Mac OS) and drag outward from the center of the headlight until the circle completely encloses the headlight. The Shift key constrains the ellipse to a perfect circle.

4 Carefully release first the mouse button and then the keyboard keys.

If you aren't satisfied with the selection circle, you can move it: Place the pointer inside the circle and drag, or click outside the selection circle to deselect it, and then try again.

5 Select the Zoom tool, and then click the Fit Screen button in the options bar so that you can see the entire image.

Notice that the selection remains active even after you change the view.

Applying a change to a selected area

In most cases, you'd change the area within the selection. But in order to spotlight the headlight, you'll want to darken the rest of the image, not the area inside the current selection. To protect that area, you'll invert the selection, so that everything *but* the headlight is selected in the image.

Selected   Unselected
(editable)   (protected)
area   area

1 Choose Select > Inverse.

Although the animated selection border around the headlight looks the same, notice that a similar border appears all around the edges of the image. Now everything in the image is selected except the area within the circle. The unselected area (the headlight) cannot be changed while the selection is active.

▶ **Tip:** The keyboard shortcut for this command, Ctrl+Shift+I (Windows) or Command+Shift+I (Mac OS), appears by the command name in the Select menu. In the future, you can just press that keyboard combination to invert a selection.

2 In the Adjustments panel, click the Curves icon to add a Curves adjustment layer. The Curves options appear in the Properties panel.

3 In the Properties panel, drag the control point in the upper right corner of the graph straight across to the left until the Input value is approximately 204. The Output value should remain 255. (If you don't see the Input and Output values, drag the triangle at the lower right corner of the Properties panel to extend the panel downward.)

As you drag, highlights are brightened in the selected area of the image.

4 Adjust the Input value up or down until you are satisfied with the results.

5 In the Layers panel, examine the Curves adjustment layer. (If the Layers panel isn't open, click its tab or choose Window > Layers.)

Adjustment layers let you make changes to your image, such as adjusting the brightness of the highlights in this car, without affecting the actual pixels. Because you've used an adjustment layer, you can always return to the original image by hiding or deleting the adjustment layer—and you can edit the adjustment layer at any time. You'll use adjustment layers in several lessons in this book.

6 Do one of the following:

- To save your changes, choose File > Save, click OK if you see the Photoshop Format Options dialog box, and then choose File > Close.

- To revert to the unaltered version of the file, choose File > Close, and click No or Don't Save when you're asked if you want to save your changes.

- To save changes without affecting the original file, choose File > Save As, rename the file or save it to a different folder, and click OK. Click OK in the Photoshop Format Options dialog box. Then choose File > Close.

You don't have to deselect, because closing the file cancels the selection.

Congratulations! You've just finished your first Photoshop project. Although a Curves adjustment layer is actually one of the more sophisticated methods of altering an image, it isn't difficult to use, as you have seen. You'll learn more about making adjustments to images in many other lessons in this book. Lessons 2 and 6, in particular, address techniques like those used in classic darkroom work, such as adjusting for exposure, retouching, and correcting colors.

Zooming and scrolling with the Navigator panel

The Navigator panel is another speedy way to make large changes in the zoom level, especially when the exact percentage of magnification is unimportant. It's also a great way to scroll around in an image, because the thumbnail shows you exactly what part of the image appears in the image window. To open the Navigator panel, choose Window > Navigator.

The slider under the image thumbnail in the Navigator panel enlarges the image when you drag to the right (toward the large mountain icon) and reduces it when you drag to the left.

The red rectangular outline represents the area of the image that appears in the image window. When you zoom in far enough that the image window shows only part of the image, you can drag the red outline around the thumbnail area to see other areas of the image. This is also an excellent way to verify which part of an image you're working on when you work at very high zoom levels.

Using the options bar and other panels

You've already had some experience with the options bar. When you selected the Zoom tool in the previous project, you saw that the options bar contained options that change the view of the current image window. Now you'll learn more about setting tool properties in the options bar, as well as using panels and panel menus.

Previewing and opening another file

The next project involves a promotional postcard for a community project. First, preview the end file to see what you're aiming to do.

1 Click the Mini Bridge tab at the bottom of the application window to open the Mini Bridge panel.

You can access many of the features of Adobe Bridge without leaving Photoshop. The Mini Bridge panel lets you browse, select, open, and import files while you're working with your image in Photoshop.

2 Choose Favorites from the pop-up menu on the left side of the panel. Then double-click the Lessons folder, and double-click the Lesson01 folder.

3 Select the 01B_End.psd file in the Content area, and press the spacebar to see a full-screen preview of the image.

Notice the text that is set against the sandy area across the lower part of the image.

Beach photo: Amana Stock Photography

4   Press the spacebar again to return to the thumbnail view.

5   Double-click the 01B_Start.psd file in the Content area to open it in Photoshop.

6   Double-click the Mini Bridge tab to hide the panel so you can see the image window clearly.

Setting tool properties in the options bar

With the 01B_Start.psd file open in Photoshop, you're ready to select the text properties and then to type your message.

1   In the Tools panel, select the Horizontal Type tool (T).

The buttons and menus in the options bar now relate to the Type tool.

2   In the options bar, select a font you like from the first pop-up menu. (We used Garamond, but you can use another font if you prefer.)

3   Specify **38 pt** for the font size.

You can specify 38 points by typing directly in the font-size text box and pressing Enter or Return, or by scrubbing the font-size menu label. You can also choose a standard font size from the font-size pop-up menu.

▶ **Tip:** You can place the pointer over the labels of most numeric settings in the tool options bar, in panels, and in dialog boxes in Photoshop to display a "scrubby slider." Dragging the pointing-finger slider to the right increases the value; dragging to the left decreases the value. Alt-dragging (Windows) or Option-dragging (Mac OS) changes the values in smaller increments; Shift-dragging changes them in larger increments.

4 Click once anywhere on the left side of the image, and type **Monday is Beach Cleanup Day.**

The text appears with the font and font size that you selected.

5 In the Tools panel, select the Move tool (▸✢). It's the first tool.

6 Position the Move tool pointer over the text you typed, and drag the text onto the sand, centering it over the bench.

● **Note:** Don't select the Move tool using the V keyboard shortcut, because you're in text-entry mode. Typing V will add the letter to your text in the image window.

 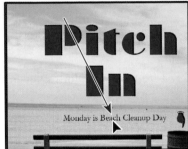

Using panels and panel menus

The text color in your image is the same as the Foreground Color swatch in the Tools panel, which is black by default. The text in the end-file example was a magenta shade that made the text stand out. You'll color the text by selecting it and then choosing another color.

1 In the Tools panel, select the Horizontal Type tool (T).

2 Drag the Horizontal Type tool across the text to select all the words.

3 Click the Swatches tab to bring that panel forward, if it's not already visible.

4 Select any swatch.

● **Note:** When you move the pointer over the swatches, it temporarily changes into an eyedropper. Set the tip of the eyedropper on the swatch you want, and click to select it.

The color you select appears in three places: as the Foreground Color in the Tools panel, in the text color swatch in the options bar, and in the text you selected in the image window. (Select any other tool in the Tools panel to deselect the text so that you can see the color applied to it.)

That's how easy it is to select a color, although there are other methods in Photoshop. However, you'll use a specific color for this project, and it's easier to find it if you change the Swatches panel display.

5 Select another tool in the Tools panel, such as the Move tool (▶⊹), to deselect the Horizontal Type tool. Then, click the menu button (▾☰) on the Swatches panel to open the panel menu, and choose Small List.

6 Select the Type tool and reselect the text, as you did in steps 1 and 2.

7 In the Swatches panel, scroll about halfway down the list to find the Pastel Violet Magenta swatch, and then select it.

Now the text appears in the lighter violet color.

8 Select the Hand tool (✋) to deselect the text. Then click the Default Foreground And Background Colors button in the Tools panel to make Black the foreground color.

Resetting the default colors does not change the color of the text in the image, because that text is no longer selected.

9 You've finished the task, so close the file. You can either save it, close it without saving, or save it under a different name or location.

It's as simple as that—you've completed another project. Nice job!

Undoing actions in Photoshop

In a perfect world, you'd never make a mistake. You'd never click the wrong object. You'd always perfectly anticipate how specific actions would bring your design ideas to life exactly as you imagined them. You'd never have to backtrack.

For the real world, Photoshop gives you the power to step back and undo actions so that you can try other options. The next project provides you with an opportunity to experiment freely, knowing that you can reverse the process.

This project also introduces you to layering, which is one of the fundamental and most powerful features in Photoshop. Photoshop includes many kinds of layers, some of which contain images, text, or solid colors, and others that simply interact with layers below them. The file for this next project has both kinds of layers. You don't have to understand layers to complete this project successfully, so don't worry about that right now. You'll learn more about layers in Lesson 4, "Layer Basics," and Lesson 9, "Advanced Compositing."

Undoing a single action

Even beginning computer users quickly come to appreciate the familiar Undo command. Once again, you'll begin this project by looking at the final result.

1 Click the Mini Bridge tab to open the Mini Bridge panel again. It displays the contents of the Lesson01 folder.

2 Look at the thumbnails for the 01C_End.psd file and the 01C_Start.psd file. In the start file, the tie is solid; in the end file, it is patterned.

3 In the Content panel, double-click the 01C_Start.psd file thumbnail to open it in Photoshop.

4 Double-click the Mini Bridge tab to close the panel.

5 In the Layers panel, select the Tie Designs layer.

Notice the arrow in the Tie Designs layer in the Layers panel. The Tie Designs layer is a *clipping mask*. A clipping mask works somewhat like a selection in that it restricts the area of the image that can be altered. With the clipping mask in place, you can paint a design over the tie without worrying about any stray brush strokes disturbing the rest of the image. You've selected the Tie Designs layer because it's the layer you'll be editing now.

6 In the Tools panel, select the Brush tool (✐), or press B to select it by its keyboard shortcut.

7 In the options bar, click the brush size to display brush options. Then, move the Size slider to 65 pixels. In the list of brushes, select the Soft Round Pressure Size brush. (The name will appear as a tool tip if you hover the pointer over a brush.)

If you want to try a different brush, that's OK, but select a brush that's reasonably close to 65 pixels—preferably between 45 and 75 pixels.

8 Move the pointer over the image so that it appears as a circle the same diameter as the brush. Then draw a stripe anywhere in the orange tie. You don't have to worry about staying within the lines, because the brush won't paint anything outside the tie clipping mask.

Illustration: Pamela Hobbs

Oops! Your stripe may be very nice, but the design calls for dots, so you'll need to remove the stripe you just painted.

9 Choose Edit > Undo Brush Tool, or press Ctrl+Z (Windows) or Command+Z (Mac OS) to undo the Brush tool action.

The tie is again a solid orange color, with no stripe.

● **Note:** You'll get more experience with clipping masks in Lesson 6, "Masks and Channels" and Lesson 7, "Typographic Design."

Undoing multiple actions

The Undo command reverses only one step. This is a practicality, because Photoshop files can be very large, and maintaining multiple Undo steps can tie up a lot of memory, which tends to degrade performance. You could use the Step Backward command to undo additional steps one at a time. However, it's faster and easier to step back through multiple actions using the History panel.

1 Using the same Brush tool settings, click once over the (unstriped) orange tie to create a soft dot.

2 Click several more times in different areas on the tie to create a pattern of dots.

3 Choose Window > History to open the History panel. Then drag a corner of the History panel to resize it so that you can see more steps.

The History panel records the recent actions you've performed in the image. The current state is selected, at the bottom of the list.

4 Click an earlier action in the History panel, and notice how the image changes. Several actions are undone.

5 In the image window, create a new dot on the tie with the Brush tool.

Notice that the History panel has removed the dimmed actions that were listed after the selected history state and has added a new one.

6 Choose Edit > Undo Brush Tool or press Ctrl+Z (Windows) or Command+Z (Mac OS) to undo the dot you created in step 5.

Now the History panel restores the earlier listing of dimmed actions.

7 Select the state at the bottom of the History panel list.

The image is restored to the condition it was in when you finished step 2 of this exercise.

By default, the Photoshop History panel retains only the last 20 actions. This is a compromise, striking a balance between flexibility and performance. You can change the number of levels in the History panel by choosing Edit > Preferences > Performance (Windows) or Photoshop > Preferences > Performance (Mac OS) and entering a different value for History States.

Using a context menu

Context menus are short menus that contain commands and options appropriate to specific elements in the work area. They are sometimes referred to as "right-click" or "shortcut" menus. Usually, the commands on a context menu are also available in some other area of the user interface, but using the context menu can save time.

1   If the Brush tool (✏) is not still selected in the Tools panel, select it now.

2   In the image window, right-click (Windows) or Control-click (Mac OS) anywhere in the image to open the Brush tool context menu.

Context menus vary with their context, of course, so what appears can be a menu of commands or a panel-like set of options, which is what happens in this case.

3   Select a finer brush, such as the Hard Round brush, and change the size to **9** pixels. You may need to scroll up or down the list in the context menu to find the right brush.

4   In the image window, use the selected brush to create smaller dots on the tie.

● **Note:** Clicking anywhere in the work area closes the context menu. If the tie area is hidden behind the Brush tool context menu, click another area or double-click your selection in the context menu to close it.

5   As it suits you, use the Undo command and the History panel to backtrack through your painting actions to correct mistakes or make different choices.

6   When you finish making changes to your tie design, choose File > Save if you want to save your results, choose File > Save As if you want to save the file in another location or with a different name, or close the file without saving.

Give yourself a pat on the back for finishing another project.

More about panels and panel locations

Photoshop panels are powerful and varied. Rarely would you need to see all panels simultaneously. That's why they're in panel groups, and why the default configurations leave some panels unopened.

The complete list of panels appears in the Window menu, with check marks by the names of the panels that are open at the front of their panel groups. You can open a closed panel or close an open one by selecting the panel name in the Window menu.

You can hide all panels at once—including the options bar and Tools panel—by pressing the Tab key. To reopen them, press Tab again.

You already used panels in the panel dock when you used the Layers and Swatches panels. You can drag panels to or from the panel dock. This is convenient for bulky panels or ones that you use only occasionally but want to keep handy.

● **Note:** When panels are hidden, a thin, semitransparent strip is visible at the edge of the document. Hovering the pointer over the strip displays its contents.

You can arrange panels in other ways, as well:

- To move an entire panel group, drag the title bar to another location in the work area.

- To move a panel to another group, drag the panel tab into that panel group so that a blue highlight appears inside the group, and then release the mouse button.

- To dock a panel or panel group, drag the title bar or panel tab onto the top of the dock.

- To undock a panel or panel group so that it becomes a floating panel or panel group, drag its title bar or panel tab away from the dock.

Expanding and collapsing panels

You can resize panels to use screen space more efficiently and to see fewer or more panel options, either by dragging or clicking to toggle between preset sizes:

- To collapse open panels to icons, click the double arrow in the title bar of the dock or panel group. To expand a panel, click its icon or the double arrow.

- To change the height of a panel, drag its lower right corner.

- To change the width of the dock, position the pointer on the left edge of the dock until it becomes a double-headed arrow, and then drag to the left to widen the dock, or to the right to narrow it.

- To resize a floating panel, move the pointer over the right, left, or bottom edge of the panel until it becomes a double-headed arrow, and then drag the edge in or out. You can also pull the lower right corner in or out.

- To collapse a panel group so that only the dock header bar and tabs are visible, double-click a panel tab or panel title bar. Double-click again to restore it to the expanded view. You can open the panel menu even when the panel is collapsed.

Notice that the tabs for the panels in the panel group and the button for the panel menu remain visible after you collapse a panel.

Special notes about the Tools panel and options bar

The Tools panel and the options bar share some characteristics with other panels:

- You can drag the Tools panel by its title bar to a different location in the work area. You can move the options bar to another location by dragging the grab bar at the far left end of the panel.

- You can hide the Tools panel and options bar.

However, some panel features are not available or don't apply to the Tools panel or options bar:

- You cannot group the Tools panel or options bar with other panels.

- You cannot resize the Tools panel or options bar.

- You cannot stack the Tools panel or options bar in the panel dock.

- The Tools panel and options bar do not have panel menus.

Customizing the workspace

It's great that Photoshop offers so many ways to control the display and location of the options bar and its many panels, but it can be time-consuming to drag panels around the screen so that you can see some panels for certain projects and other panels for other projects. That's why Photoshop lets you customize your work-space, controlling which panels, tools, and menus are available at any time. In fact, it comes with a few preset workspaces suitable for different types of workflows—tone and color correction, painting and retouching, and so on. You'll experiment with them.

● **Note:** If you closed 01C_Start.psd at the end of the previous exercise, open it—or open any other image file—to complete the following exercise.

1 Choose Window > Workspace > Painting. If prompted, click Yes to apply the workspace.

If you've been experimenting with opening, closing, and moving panels, you'll notice that Photoshop closes some panels, opens others, and stacks them neatly in the dock along the right edge of the workspace.

2 Choose Window > Workspace > Photography. If prompted, click Yes to apply the workspace. Different panels appear in the dock.

3 Click the Workspace Switcher in the options bar, and choose Essentials. Photoshop returns to the default workspace, which is arranged as you left it. (To return the Essentials workspace to its original configuration, choose Reset Essentials from the Workspace Switcher menu.)

You can choose workspaces from the Window menu or from the pop-up menu in the options bar.

For times when presets don't suit your purposes, you can customize the workspace to your specific needs. Say, for example, that you do lots of web design, but no digital video work. You can specify which menu items to display in the workspace.

4 Click the View menu, and choose Pixel Aspect Ratio to see the submenu.

This submenu includes several DV formats that many print and web designers don't need to use.

5 Choose Window > Workspace > Keyboard Shortcuts And Menus.

The Keyboard Shortcuts And Menus dialog box lets you control which application and panel menu commands are available, as well as create custom keyboard shortcuts for menus, panels, and tools. You can hide commands that you use infrequently, or highlight commonly used commands to make them easier to see.

6 Click the Menus tab in the Keyboard Shortcuts And Menus dialog box, and then choose Application Menus from the Menu For pop-up menu.

7 Expand the View menu commands by clicking the triangle next to View.

Photoshop displays the View menu commands and subcommands.

8 Scroll down to Pixel Aspect Ratio, and click the eye icon to turn off visibility for all of the DV and video formats—there are seven of them, beginning with D1/DV NTSC (0.91) and ending with DVCPro HD 1080 (1.5). Photoshop removes them from the menu for this workspace.

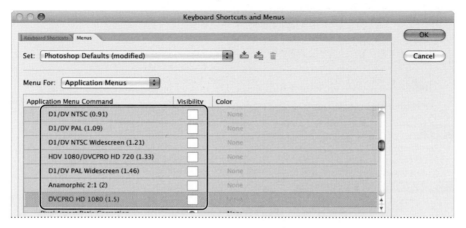

9 Expand the Image menu commands.

10 Scroll down to the Image > Mode > RGB Color command, and click None in the Color column. Choose Red from the pop-up menu to highlight this command in red.

11 Click OK to close the Keyboard Shortcuts And Menus dialog box.

12 Choose Image > Mode. RGB Color is now highlighted in red.

13 Choose View > Pixel Aspect Ratio. The DV and video formats are no longer included in this submenu.

14 To save a workspace, choose Window > Workspace > New Workspace. In the New Workspace dialog box, give your workspace a name, select the Keyboard Shortcuts and Menus options, and then click Save.

● **Note:** Selecting the Essentials workspace changes the panel configuration, but doesn't restore the menus to their defaults. You can do that now, or leave them altered. You'll reset defaults as you begin work on most lessons that follow.

The custom workspace you save is listed in the Window > Workspace submenu and in the Workspace Switcher on the options bar.

For now, return to the default workspace configuration.

15 Choose Essentials from the Workspace Switcher on the options bar. Don't save the changes in the current workspace.

Congratulations again. You've finished Lesson 1!

Now that you're acquainted with the basics of the Photoshop work area, you can begin learning how to create and edit images. Once you know the basics, you can complete the *Adobe Photoshop CS6 Classroom in a Book* lessons either in sequential order or according to the subjects you find most interesting.

Finding resources for using Photoshop

For complete and up-to-date information about using Photoshop panels, tools, and other application features, visit the Adobe website. To search for information in Photoshop Help and support documents, as well as other websites relevant to Photoshop users, choose Help > Photoshop Help. You can narrow your search results to view only Adobe Help and support documents.

For additional resources, such as tips and techniques and the latest product information, check out the Adobe Community Help page at community.adobe.com/help/main.

Checking for updates

Adobe periodically provides updates to software. You can easily obtain these updates through Adobe Application Manager, as long as you have an active Internet connection.

1 In Photoshop, choose Help > Updates. Adobe Application Manager automatically checks for updates available for your Adobe software.

2 In the Adobe Application Manager dialog box, select the updates you want to install, and then click to install them.

● **Note:** To set your preferences for future updates, click Preferences in the Adobe Application Manager. Select whether you want to be notified of updates, and which applications you want the Adobe Application Manager to check for. Click OK to accept the new settings.

Changing interface settings

By default, the panels, dialog boxes, and background in Photoshop CS6 are dark. You can lighten the interface or make other changes in the Photoshop Preferences dialog box.

To make changes:

1 Choose Edit > Preferences > Interface (Windows) or Photoshop > Preferences > Interface (Mac OS).

2 Select a different color theme, or make other changes.

When you select a different theme, you can see the changes immediately. You can also select specific colors for different screen modes and change other interface settings in this dialog box.

3 When you're satisfied with the changes, click OK.

Tools panel overview

Photoshop CS6 Tools panel

- Move (V)
- Rectangular Marquee (M)
- Lasso (L)
- Quick Selection (W)
- Crop (C)
- Eyedropper (I)
- Spot Healing Brush (J)
- Brush (B)
- Clone Stamp (S)
- History Brush (Y)
- Eraser (E)
- Gradient (G)
- Blur (R)
- Dodge (O)
- Pen (P)
- Horizontal Type (T)
- Path Selection (A)
- Rectangle (U)
- Hand (H)
- Zoom (Z)

The Move tool moves selections, layers, and guides.

The marquee tools make rectangular, elliptical, single row, and single column selections.

The lasso tools make free-hand, polygonal (straight-edged), and magnetic (snap-to) selections.

The Quick Selection tool lets you quickly "paint" a selection using an adjustable round brush tip.

The Magic Wand tool selects similarly colored areas.

The crop tools trim, straighten, and change the perspective of images.

The Eyedropper tool samples colors in an image.

The 3D Material Eyedropper tool loads selected material from a 3D object.

The Color Sampler tool samples up to four areas of the image.

The Ruler tool measures distances, locations, and angles.

The Note tool makes notes that can be attached to an image.

The Count tool counts objects in an image.

Tools panel overview (continued)

The Slice tool creates slices.

The Slice Select tool selects slices.

The Spot Healing Brush tool quickly removes blemishes and imperfections from photographs with a uniform background.

The Healing Brush tool paints with a sample or pattern to repair imperfections in an image.

The Patch tool repairs imperfections in a selected area of an image using a sample or pattern.

The Content-Aware Move tool recomposes and blends pixels to accommodate a moved object.

The Red Eye tool removes red eye in flash photos with one click.

The Brush tool paints brush strokes.

The Pencil tool paints hard-edged strokes.

The Color Replacement tool substitutes one color for another.

The Mixer Brush tool blends sampled color with an existing color.

The Clone Stamp tool paints with a sample of an image.

The Pattern Stamp tool paints with a part of an image as a pattern.

The History Brush tool paints a copy of the selected state or snapshot into the current image window.

The Art History Brush tool paints stylized strokes that simulate the look of different paint styles, using a selected state or snapshot.

The Eraser tool erases pixels and restores parts of an image to a previously saved state.

The Background Eraser tool erases areas to transparency by dragging.

The Magic Eraser tool erases solid-colored areas to transparency with a single click.

The Gradient tool creates straight-line, radial, angle, reflected, and diamond blends between colors.

The Paint Bucket tool fills similarly colored areas with the foreground color.

The 3D Material Drop tool drops the material loaded in the 3D Material Eyedropper tool onto the targeted area of a 3D object.

The Blur tool blurs hard edges in an image.

The Sharpen tool sharpens soft edges in an image.

The Smudge tool smudges data in an image.

Tools panel overview (continued)

The Dodge tool lightens areas in an image.

The Burn tool darkens areas in an image.

The Sponge tool changes the color saturation of an area.

The pen tools draw smooth-edged paths.

The type tools create type on an image.

The type mask tools create a selection in the shape of type.

The path selection tools make shape or segment selections showing anchor points, direction lines, and direction points.

The shape tools and Line tool draw shapes and lines in a normal layer or shape layer.

The Custom Shape tool makes customized shapes selected from a custom shape list.

The Hand tool moves an image within its window.

The Rotate View tool nondestructively rotates the canvas.

The Zoom tool magnifies and reduces the view of an image.

Review questions

1 Describe two types of images you can open in Photoshop.

2 How do you open image files using Adobe Bridge?

3 How do you select tools in Photoshop?

4 Describe two ways to change your view of an image.

5 What are two ways to get more information about Photoshop?

Review answers

1 You can scan a photograph, transparency, negative, or graphic into the program; capture a digital video image; or import artwork created in a drawing program. You can also import digital photos.

2 Choose File > Browse In Bridge in Photoshop to jump to Bridge. Then, locate the image file you want to open, and double-click its thumbnail to open it in Photoshop.

3 Click a tool in the Tools panel, or press the tool's keyboard shortcut. A selected tool remains active until you select a different tool. To select a hidden tool, either use a keyboard shortcut to toggle through the tools, or hold down the mouse button on the tool in the Tools panel to open a pop-up menu of the hidden tools.

4 Choose commands from the View menu to zoom in on or out from an image, or to fit it onscreen, or use the zoom tools and click or drag over an image to enlarge or reduce the view. You can also use keyboard shortcuts or the Navigator panel to control the display of an image.

5 The Photoshop Help system includes full information about Photoshop features plus keyboard shortcuts, task-based topics, and illustrations. Photoshop also includes a link to the Adobe Systems Photoshop web page for additional information on services, products, and tips pertaining to Photoshop.

2 BASIC PHOTO CORRECTIONS

Lesson overview

In this lesson, you'll learn how to do the following:

- Understand image resolution and size.

- Open and edit an image in Camera Raw.

- Adjust the tonal range of an image.

- Straighten and crop an image.

- Paint over a color with the Color Replacement tool.

- Adjust the saturation of isolated areas of an image using the Sponge tool.

- Use the Clone Stamp tool to eliminate an unwanted part of an image.

- Use the Spot Healing Brush tool to repair part of an image.

- Use the content-aware Patch tool to remove blemishes.

- Apply the Unsharp Mask filter to finish retouching photos.

- Save an image file for use in a page layout application.

 This lesson will take about an hour to complete. Copy the Lesson02 folder onto your hard drive if you haven't already done so. As you work on this lesson, you'll preserve the start files. If you need to restore the start files, copy them from the *Adobe Photoshop CS6 Classroom in a Book* DVD.

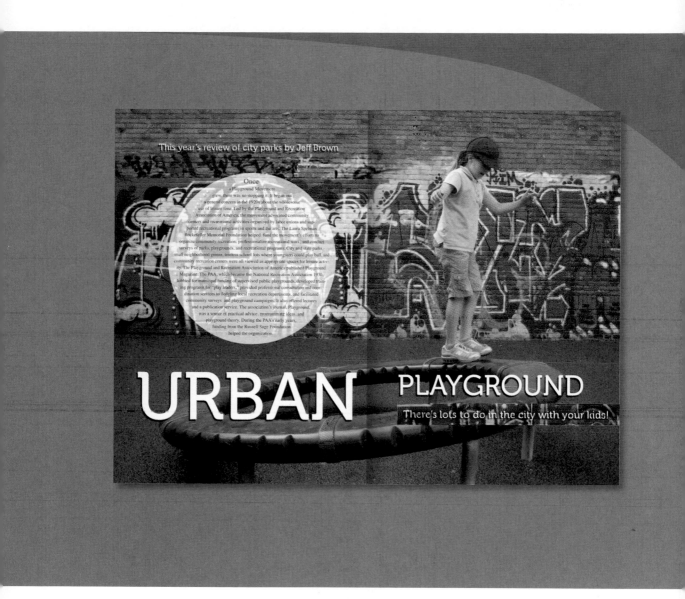

This year's review of city parks by Jeff Brown

Once
a Playground Movement
grew, there was no stopping it. It began out
a general concern in the 1920s about the wholesome
use of leisure time. Led by the Playground and Recreation
Association of America, the movement advocated community
centers and recreational activities organized by labor unions and supported recreational programs in sports and the arts. The Laura Spelman
Rockefeller Memorial Foundation helped fund the movement's efforts to
organize community recreation, professionalize recreational work, and conduct
surveys of parks, playgrounds, and recreational programs. City and state parks,
small neighborhood greens, treeless school lots where youngsters could play ball, and
community recreation centers were all viewed as appropriate spaces for leisure activ-
ity. The Playground and Recreation Association of America published Playground
Magazine. The PAA, which became the National Recreation Association 1930,
lobbied for municipal funding of supervised public playgrounds, developed training programs for "play leaders," provided professional consultation and coor-
dination services to fledgling local recreation departments, and facilitated
community surveys and playground campaigns. It also offered lectures
and a publication service. The association's journal, Playground,
was a source of practical advice, programming ideas, and
playground theory. During the PAA's early years,
funding from the Russell Sage Foundation
helped the organization.

URBAN PLAYGROUND
There's lots to do in the city with your kids!

Adobe Photoshop includes a variety of tools and commands for improving the quality of a photographic image. This lesson steps you through the process of acquiring, resizing, and retouching a photo intended for a print layout. The same basic workflow applies to web images.

Strategy for retouching

How much retouching you do depends on the image you're working on and your goals for it. For many images, you can achieve your desired outcome with just a few clicks in Adobe Camera Raw, which is installed with Adobe Photoshop. For others, you may start in Camera Raw to adjust the white point, for example, and then move on to Photoshop for more advanced retouching, such as applying filters to selected parts of an image.

Organizing an efficient sequence of tasks

Most retouching procedures follow these general steps:

- Duplicating the original image or scan; working in a copy of the image file makes it easy to recover the original later if necessary

- Ensuring that the resolution is appropriate for the way you'll use the image

- Cropping the image to final size and orientation

- Repairing flaws in scans of damaged photographs (such as rips, dust, or stains)

- Adjusting the overall contrast or tonal range of the image

- Removing any color casts

- Adjusting the color and tone in specific parts of the image to bring out highlights, midtones, shadows, and desaturated colors

- Sharpening the overall focus of the image

Usually, you should complete these processes in the order listed. Otherwise, the results of one process may cause unintended changes to other aspects of the image, making it necessary for you to redo some of your work.

● **Note:** In Lesson 1, you used an adjustment layer, which gives you great flexibility to experiment with different correction settings without risking damage to the original image.

Adjusting your process for different intended uses

The retouching techniques you apply to an image depend in part on how you'll use the image. Whether an image is intended for black-and-white publication on newsprint or for full-color online distribution affects everything from the resolution of the initial scan to the type of tonal range and color correction that the image requires. Photoshop supports the CMYK color mode for preparing an image to be printed using process colors, as well as RGB and other color modes for web and mobile authoring.

To illustrate one application of retouching techniques, this lesson takes you through the steps of correcting a photograph intended for four-color print publication.

For more information about CMYK and RGB color modes, see Lesson 14, "Producing and Printing Consistent Color."

Resolution and image size

The first step in retouching a photograph in Photoshop is to make sure that the image has an appropriate resolution. The term *resolution* refers to the number of small squares, known as *pixels,* that describe an image and establish its detail. Resolution is determined by *pixel dimensions*, or the number of pixels along the width and height of an image.

Pixels in a photographic image

In computer graphics, there are different types of resolution:

The number of pixels per unit of length in an image is called the *image resolution,* usually measured in pixels per inch (ppi). An image with a high resolution has more pixels (and therefore a larger file size) than an image of the same dimensions with a low resolution. Images in Photoshop can vary from high resolution (300 ppi or higher) to low resolution (72 ppi or 96 ppi).

The number of pixels per unit of length on a monitor is the *monitor resolution,* also usually measured in pixels per inch (ppi). Image pixels are translated directly into monitor pixels. In Photoshop, if the image resolution is higher than the monitor resolution, the image appears larger onscreen than its specified print dimensions. For example, when you display a 1x1-inch, 144-ppi image on a 72-ppi monitor, the image fills a 2x2-inch area of the screen.

4x6 inches at 72 ppi; file size 364.5 KB | 100% onscreen view | 4x6 inches at 200 ppi; file size 2.75 MB | 100% onscreen view

● **Note:** It's important to understand what "100% view" means when you work onscreen. At 100%, one image pixel = one monitor pixel. Unless the resolution of your image is exactly the same as the resolution of the monitor, the image size (in inches, for example) onscreen may be larger or smaller than the image size will be when printed.

The number of ink dots per inch (dpi) produced by a platesetter or laser printer is the *printer,* or *output, resolution*. Higher resolution images output to higher resolution printers generally produce the best quality. The appropriate resolution for a printed image is determined both by the printer resolution and by the *screen frequency,* or lines per inch (lpi), of the halftone screens used to reproduce images.

Keep in mind that the higher the image resolution, the larger the file size, and the longer the file takes to download from the web.

For more information on resolution and image size, see Photoshop Help.

Getting started

In this lesson, you'll prepare a scanned photograph to be placed in an Adobe InDesign layout for a fictitious magazine. The final image size in the print layout will be 3.5x2.5 inches.

You'll start the lesson by comparing the original scan to the finished image.

1 Start Adobe Bridge CS6 by choosing Start > All Programs > Adobe Bridge CS6 (Windows) or double-clicking Adobe Bridge CS6 in the Applications folder (Mac OS).

2 In the Favorites panel in the upper left corner of Bridge, click the Lessons folder. Then, in the Content panel, double-click the Lesson02 folder to see its contents.

3 Compare the 02Start.jpg and 02End.psd files. To enlarge the thumbnails in the Content panel, drag the Thumbnail slider at the bottom of the Bridge window to the right.

In the 02Start.jpg file, notice that the image is crooked, the colors are relatively dull, and the image has a red color cast. The dimensions are also larger than needed for the requirements of the magazine. You'll fix all of these problems in this lesson, and even change the color of the girl's cap. You'll start by addressing the color and tone of the image.

4 Select the 02Start.jpg thumbnail, and choose File > Open In Camera Raw.

The image opens in Camera Raw. As you make changes to the image, Camera Raw saves those changes in a separate file that is associated with your original image file. You can return to the original at any time when working in Camera Raw.

Adjusting the color in Camera Raw

You'll start by removing the color cast and adjusting the color and tone in the image.

● **Note:** You'll work with Camera Raw more extensively in Lesson 5.

1   Select the White Balance tool (✐) at the top of the Camera Raw dialog box.

Adjusting the white balance changes all the colors in the image. To set an accurate white balance, select an area that should be white or gray.

2   Click a white area of the graffiti. The color tone of the image changes dramatically.

3   Click the girl's white shoe. The color tone changes again.

In some images, adjusting the white balance is enough to remove a color cast and correct the tone of the image. Here, selecting a white balance is a good start. You'll use settings in the Basic panel to fine-tune the tone.

4 In the Basic panel, move the Temperature slider to **-53** and the Tint slider to **-54**.

5 In the next section of the Basic panel, move the sliders to the following values:

- Exposure: **-.50**

- Contrast: **+23**

- Blacks: **18**

6 In the bottom section of the Basic panel, move the sliders to the following values:

- Clarity: **+12**

- Vibrance: **+25**

- Saturation: **+5**

7 Deselect Preview at the top of the Camera Raw window to compare the edited version with the original image. Select Preview again to see how the changes affected it.

Preview selected

Preview deselected

You're ready to move the image into Photoshop to continue retouching it.

8 Click Open Image at the bottom of the Camera Raw window to open the image in Photoshop.

9 In Photoshop, choose File > Save As, rename the file **02Working.psd**, and click Save to save it in the Lesson02 folder.

Remember, when you're making permanent corrections to an image file, it's always wise to work on a copy rather than on the original. Then, if something goes horribly wrong, at least you'll be able to start over on a fresh copy of the original image.

Straightening and cropping the image in Photoshop

You'll use the Crop tool to straighten, trim, and scale the photograph so that it fits the space designed for it. You can use either the Crop tool or the Crop command to crop an image. By default, cropping is nondestructive, so you can change your mind and recover the original pixels later if you want to.

1 In the Tools panel, select the Crop tool (口).

2 In the options bar, choose Size & Resolution from the Preset Aspect Ratio menu. (Unconstrained is its default value.)

3 In the Crop Image Size & Resolution dialog box, enter **3.5** inches for the Width, **2.5** inches for the Height, and **200** pixels/inch for the Resolution. Click OK.

The Preset Aspect Ratio changes to reflect the preset you created, and a crop grid appears. A *cropping shield* covers the area outside the cropping selection. First, you'll straighten the image

4   Click Straighten in the options bar. The pointer changes to the Straighten tool.

5   Click at the top corner of the photo, and drag a straight line across the top edge of the photo.

Photoshop straightens the image, so that the line you drew is parallel with the top of the image area. You drew a line across the top of the photo but any line that defines either the vertical or horizontal axis of the image will work.

Now, you'll trim the white border and scale the image.

6   Drag the corners of the crop grid in to the corners of the photo, so that no white remains. Use the arrow keys if you need to nudge the photo up or down within the crop grid.

▶ **Tip:** You can choose Image > Trim to discard a border area around the edge of the image, based on transparency or edge color.

7   Press Enter or Return. The image is now cropped, and the cropped image fills the image window, straightened, sized, and cropped according to your specifications.

8   To see the image dimensions, choose Document Dimensions from the pop-up menu at the bottom of the application window.

9   Choose File > Save to save your work. Click OK if you see the Photoshop Format Options dialog box.

Replacing colors in an image

Use the Color Replacement tool to paint over one color with another. When you start painting with the Color Replacement tool, it analyzes the first pixels you paint over. Because it then only replaces pixels of a similar color, you don't have to be terribly precise as you paint. You can select settings that determine whether the tool paints over contiguous or discontiguous pixels, and how much color difference the tool accepts.

You'll use the Color Replacement tool to change the color of the child's cap in the image of the playground.

1   Zoom in to see the child's cap clearly.

2   Select the Color Replacement tool (🖌) in the Tools panel, hidden behind the Brush tool (🖌).

3   Click the Foreground Color swatch in the Tools panel. In the Color Picker, select a shade of green. We selected an RGB color with the values R=49, G=184, and B=6.

You'll paint the foreground color over the red hat.

4   In the options bar, open the Brush pop-up panel to view brush options.

5   Move the Size slider to **13** pixels, the Hardness slider to **40%**, and the Spacing slider to **25%**. Choose Off from the Size and Tolerance menus.

6 In the options bar, choose Hue from the Mode menu. Then click Sampling: Continous (<!-- -->) (the button next to the Hue menu). Choose Find Edges from the Limits menu, and set the Tolerance to **32%**. Make sure Anti-Alias is selected.

7 Begin painting in the middle of the hat, and paint out toward the edges.

8 Choose a smaller brush, if you like, and continue painting out towards the edges of the hat. You can zoom in if needed.

9 When the hat is green, save the file.

Adjusting saturation with the Sponge tool

When you change the saturation of a color, you adjust its strength or purity. The Sponge tool is useful for making subtle saturation changes to specific areas of an image. You'll use the Sponge tool to saturate the color of some of the graffiti.

1 Zoom out or scroll, if necessary, to see the colorful graffiti.

2 Select the Sponge tool (), hidden under the Dodge tool ().

3 In the options bar, do the following:

- In the Brush pop-up panel, move the Size slider to **150 px**, and then move the Hardness slider to **0%**.

- Choose Saturate from the Mode menu.

- For Flow, enter **40%**. The Flow value determines the intensity of the saturation effect.

4 Drag the sponge back and forth over the graffiti to the left of the girl to increase the saturation. The more you drag over an area, the more saturated the color becomes. Be careful not to oversaturate the graffiti.

5 Select the Move tool (⊹) to ensure you don't accidentally add saturation elsewhere.

6 Save your work.

Repairing areas with the Clone Stamp tool

The Clone Stamp tool uses pixels from one area of an image to replace the pixels in another part of the image. Using this tool, you can not only remove unwanted objects from your images, but you can also fill in missing areas in photographs you scan from damaged originals.

You'll start by replacing a bright white area of the wall—a hot spot—with cloned bricks from another area of the picture.

1 Select the Clone Stamp tool (🖫) in the Tools panel.

2 In the options bar, open the Brush pop-up menu, and set the size to **21** and the hardness to **0%**. Then, make sure that the Aligned option is selected.

3 Choose Window > Clone Source to open the Clone Source panel. This panel gives you greater control over the area you're cloning from (in this case, the bricks).

4 Select Show Overlay and Clipped in the Clone Source panel. Then, make sure Opacity is set to **100**%. The overlay lets you see what you're cloning before you stamp it.

5 Move the Clone Stamp tool over the darker bricks just to the right of the hot spot on the wall. (You may want to zoom in to see the area better.)

6 Alt-click (Windows) or Option-click (Mac OS) to start sampling that part of the image. (When you press Alt or Option, the pointer appears as target cross-hairs.)

7 Starting at the area just to the right of the girl's hat, drag the Clone Stamp tool to the right, over the hot spot on the bricks. The clone overlay lets you see what will appear there. This is particularly useful for keeping the bricks in a straight line.

8 Release the mouse button and move the pointer to another area in the hot spot, and then start dragging again.

Each time you click the Clone Stamp tool, it begins again with a new source point, in the same relationship to the tool as the first stroke you made. That is, if you begin painting further right, it samples from bricks that are further right than the original source point. That's because Aligned is selected in the options bar.

● Note: When the Aligned option is not selected, each time you make a stroke, you begin sampling from the same source point, regardless of where you place the tool.

9 Continue cloning the bricks until the entire hot spot is filled in.

If necessary to help make the bricks appear to blend in naturally with the rest of the image, you can adjust your cloning by resetting the sample area (as you did in step 6) and recloning. Or, you can try deselecting the Aligned option and cloning again.

10 When you're satisfied with the appearance of the bricks, close the Clone Source panel, and choose File > Save.

Using the Spot Healing Brush tool

The next task is to clean up some dark spots in the wall. You could do this with the Clone Stamp tool (🗸), but instead you'll use another technique. You'll use the Spot Healing Brush to clean up the wall.

The Spot Healing Brush tool quickly removes blemishes and other imperfections from photos. It paints with sampled pixels from an image or pattern and matches the texture, lighting, transparency, and shading of the sampled pixels to the pixels being healed. Unlike the Clone Stamp tool, the Spot Healing Brush doesn't require you to specify a sample spot. It automatically samples from around the retouched area.

● Note: The Healing Brush tool works similarly to the Spot Healing Brush tool, except that it requires you to sample source pixels before retouching an area.

The Spot Healing Brush is excellent for retouching blemishes in portraits, but will also work nicely in this image in the dark area of the wall, because the wall has a uniform, muted appearance to the right of the dark areas.

1 Zoom in or scroll to see the dark areas on the upper left corner of the image.

2 In the Tools panel, select the Spot Healing Brush tool ( ).

3 In the options bar, open the Brush pop-up panel, and specify a **100%** hard brush that is about **40** px in diameter.

4 In the image window, drag the Spot Healing Brush from right to left across the dark spots in the upper left corner of the image. You can use as many or as few strokes as you like; paint until you're satisfied with the results. As you drag, the stroke at first appears black, but when you release the mouse, the painted area is "healed."

5 Choose File > Save.

Applying a content-aware patch

Content-aware tools take blending a few steps further: Photoshop fills a selection with pixels that match the surroundings. Using the Patch tool in Content-Aware mode isn't like cloning, because you aren't copying part of the image to another part. Really, it's more like magic. You can fill any selection with content similar to the content around it, as if the object you selected never existed. You'll get a chance to see it for yourself as you touch up the brick wall, removing the large crack and the dark areas of the wall on the left. Because the wall varies in color, texture, and lighting, it would be challenging to successfully use the Clone Stamp tool to touch up these areas. Fortunately, the Patch tool makes this process easy.

1 In the Tools panel, select the Patch tool (▒), hidden beneath the Spot Healing Brush tool (✐).

2 In the options bar, choose Content-Aware from the Patch menu. Then make sure Medium is selected in the Adaptation menu, and that Sample All Layers is selected.

3 Drag the Patch tool around the crack in the wall to select it.

4 Click within the area you've just selected and drag it to the right.

The selection changes to match the area around it.

5 Choose Select > Deselect.

6 Use the Patch tool to select the darker area on the left edge of the wall. You can draw outside the photo to make sure the selection includes the very edge of the image.

7 Drag the selected area to the right.

8 Choose Select > Deselect.

Applying the Unsharp Mask filter

The last task you might want to do when retouching a photo is to apply the Unsharp Mask filter. The Unsharp Mask filter adjusts the contrast of the edge detail and creates the illusion of a more focused image.

1 Choose Filter > Sharpen > Unsharp Mask.

2 In the Unsharp Mask dialog box, make sure that Preview is selected so you can see the effect of settings you adjust in the image window.

You can drag inside the preview window in the dialog box to see different parts of the image, or use the plus and minus buttons below the thumbnail to zoom in and out.

▶ **Tip:** As you try different settings, toggle the Preview option on and off to see how your changes affect the image. Or, you can click and hold the mouse button on the preview window in the dialog box to temporarily toggle the filter off in the preview window. If your image is large, using the preview window can be more efficient, because only a small area is redrawn.

3 Drag the Amount slider to about **70%** to sharpen the image.

4 Drag the Radius slider to determine the number of pixels surrounding the edge pixels that will affect the sharpening. The higher the resolution, the higher the Radius setting should be. (We used the default value, 1.0 pixel.)

5 (Optional) Adjust the Threshold slider. This determines how different the sharpened pixels must be from the surrounding area before they are considered edge pixels and subsequently sharpened by the Unsharp Mask filter. The default Threshold value of 0 sharpens all pixels in the image. Try a different value, such as 2 or 3.

6 When you're satisfied with the results, click OK to apply the Unsharp Mask filter.

7 Choose File > Save.

About unsharp masking

Unsharp masking, or USM, is a traditional film-compositing technique used to sharpen edges in an image. The Unsharp Mask filter corrects blurring introduced during photographing, scanning, resampling, or printing. It's useful for images intended for both print and online viewing.

Unsharp Mask locates pixels that differ from surrounding pixels by the threshold you set and increases the pixels' contrast by the amount you specify. In addition, you can adjust the radius of the region to which each pixel is compared.

The effects of the Unsharp Mask filter are far more pronounced onscreen than they are in high-resolution output. If your final destination is print, experiment to determine which settings work best for your image.

Saving the image for four-color printing

Before you save a Photoshop file for use in a four-color publication, you must change the image to CMYK color mode. You'll use the Mode command to change the image color mode.

For more information about converting between color modes, see Photoshop Help.

1   Choose File > Save As, and save the file as **02_CMYK.psd**. Click OK if you see a Photoshop Format Options dialog box.

It's a good idea to save a copy of your original file before changing color modes, so that you can make changes in the original later, if necessary.

2   Choose Image > Mode > CMYK Color. Click OK when Photoshop displays an alert about the color management profile.

If you were preparing this image for a real publication, you'd want to confirm that you were using the appropriate CMYK profile. See Lesson 14, "Producing and Printing Consistent Color," to learn about color management.

▶ **Tip:** Most images include more than one layer. Choose Layer > Merge Visible before you change the color mode to ensure that all the changes you made are included in the CMYK image.

3 If you use Adobe InDesign to create your publications, simply choose File > Save. InDesign can import native Photoshop (PSD) files, so there is no need to convert the image to TIFF.

If you're using another layout application, choose File > Save As, and then proceed to step 4 to save the image as a TIFF file.

4 In the Save As dialog box, choose TIFF from the Format menu.

5 Click Save.

6 In the TIFF Options dialog box, select your operating system for the Byte Order, and click OK.

The image is now fully retouched, saved, and ready for placement in a page layout application.

For more information about file formats, see Photoshop Help.

You can combine Photoshop images with other elements in a layout application such as Adobe InDesign.

Extra credit

You can get great results converting a color image to black and white (with or without a tint) in Photoshop or Camera Raw.

In Photoshop:

1   Choose File > Open, and navigate to the bike.jpg file in the Lesson02 folder. Click Open.

2   If the file opens in Camera Raw, click Open Image to open it in Photoshop.

3   In the Adjustments panel, click the Black & White button to add a Black & White adjustment layer.

4   Adjust the color sliders to change the saturation of color channels. You can also experiment with options from the preset menu, such as Darker or Infrared. Or, select the tool in the upper left corner of the Adjustments panel, and then drag it across the image to adjust the colors associated with that area. (We darkened the bike itself and made the background areas lighter.)

5   If you want to add a tint to the photo, select Tint. Then, click the color swatch and select a tint color (we used R=227, G=209, and B=198).

In Camera Raw:

1   In Bridge, select the bike.jpg file, and choose File > Open In Camera Raw.

2   In Camera Raw, click the HSL/Grayscale tab.

3   Select Convert To Grayscale, and then adjust the color sliders in the Hue, Saturation, and Luminance panes to change the intensity of the shades.

Review questions

1 What does *resolution* mean?

2 What does the Crop tool do?

3 How can you adjust the tone and color of an image in Camera Raw?

4 What tools can you use to remove blemishes in an image?

5 What effect does the Unsharp Mask filter have on an image?

Review answers

1 The term *resolution* refers to the number of pixels that describe an image and establish its detail. *Image resolution* and *monitor resolution* are measured in pixels per inch (ppi). *Printer,* or *output, resolution* is measured in ink dots per inch (dpi).

2 You can use the Crop tool to trim, scale, or straighten an image.

3 Use the White Balance tool to adjust the color temperature. Then fine-tune the color and tone using sliders in the Basic panel.

4 The Healing Brush, Spot Healing Brush, Patch tool, and Clone Stamp tools, as well as content-aware fill, let you replace unwanted portions of an image with other areas of the image. The Clone Stamp tool copies the source area exactly; the Healing Brush and Spot Healing Brush tools blend the area with the surrounding pixels. The Spot Healing Brush tool doesn't require a source area at all; it "heals" areas to match the surrounding pixels. The Patch tool in Content-Aware mode, and content-aware fill replace a selection with content that matches the surrounding area.

5 The Unsharp Mask filter adjusts the contrast of the edge detail and creates the illusion of a more focused image.

3 WORKING WITH SELECTIONS

Lesson overview

In this lesson, you'll learn how to do the following:

- Make specific areas of an image active using selection tools.

- Reposition a selection marquee.

- Move and duplicate the contents of a selection.

- Use keyboard-mouse combinations that save time and hand motions.

- Deselect a selection.

- Constrain the movement of a selected area.

- Adjust the position of a selected area using the arrow keys.

- Add to and subtract from a selection.

- Rotate a selection.

- Use multiple selection tools to make a complex selection.

- Erase pixels within a selection.

 This lesson will take about an hour to complete. Copy the Lesson03 folder onto your hard drive if you haven't already done so. As you work on this lesson, you'll preserve the start files. If you need to restore the start files, copy them from the *Adobe Photoshop CS6 Classroom in a Book* DVD.

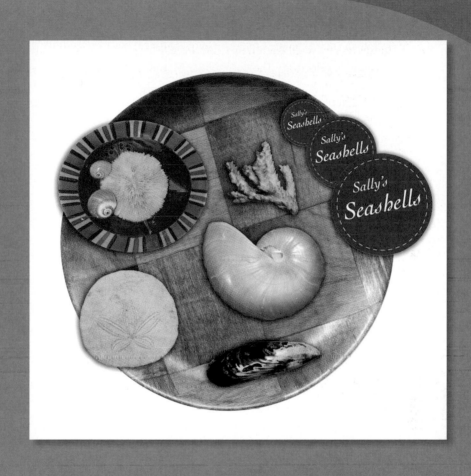

Learning how to select areas of an image is of primary importance—you must first select what you want to affect. Once you've made a selection, only the area within the selection can be edited.

About selecting and selection tools

● **Note:** You'll learn how to select vector areas using the pen tools in Lesson 8, "Vector Drawing Techniques."

Making changes to an area within an image in Photoshop is a two-step process. You first select the part of an image you want to change with one of the selection tools. Then, you use another tool, filter, or other feature to make changes, such as moving the selected pixels to another location or applying a filter to the selected area. You can make selections based on size, shape, and color. The selection process limits changes to within the selected area. Other areas are unaffected.

The best selection tool for a specific area often depends on the characteristics of that area, such as shape or color. There are four types of selections:

Geometric selections The Rectangular Marquee tool (▢) selects a rectangular area in an image. The Elliptical Marquee tool (○), which is hidden behind the Rectangular Marquee tool, selects elliptical areas. The Single Row Marquee tool (▭) and Single Column Marquee tool (▯) select either a 1-pixel-high row or a 1-pixel-wide column, respectively.

Freehand selections The Lasso tool (◯) traces a freehand selection around an area. The Polygonal Lasso tool (▱) sets anchor points in straight-line segments around an area. The Magnetic Lasso tool (▱) works something like a combination of the other two lasso tools, and gives the best results when good contrast exists between the area you want to select and its surroundings.

Edge-based selections The Quick Selection tool (✍) quickly "paints" a selection by automatically finding and following defined edges in the image.

Color-based selections The Magic Wand tool (✦) selects parts of an image based on the similarity in color of adjacent pixels. It is useful for selecting odd-shaped areas that share a specific range of colors.

Getting started

First, you'll look at the image you will create as you explore the selection tools in Adobe Photoshop.

1 Start Photoshop, and then immediately hold down Ctrl+Alt+Shift (Windows) or Command+Option+Shift (Mac OS) to restore the default preferences. (See "Restoring default preferences" on page 4.)

2 When prompted, click Yes to confirm that you want to delete the Adobe Photoshop Settings file.

3 Choose File > Browse In Bridge to open Adobe Bridge.

4 In the Favorites panel, click the Lessons folder. Then, double-click the Lesson03 folder in the Content panel to see its contents.

5 Study the 03End.psd file. Move the thumbnail slider to the right if you want to see the image in more detail.

The project is a collage of objects, including a piece of coral, a sand dollar, a mussel, a nautilus, a bowl of small shells, a wooden plate, and the "Sally's Seashells" logo. The challenge in this lesson is to arrange these elements, which were scanned together on the single page you see in the 03Start.psd file. The ideal composition is up to you, so this lesson won't describe precise locations. There is no right or wrong position for any of the objects.

6 Double-click the 03Start.psd thumbnail to open the image file in Photoshop.

7 Choose File > Save As, rename the file **03Working.psd**, and click Save. By saving another version of the start file, you don't have to worry about overwriting the original.

Using the Quick Selection tool

The Quick Selection tool provides one of the easiest ways to make a selection. You simply paint an area of an image, and the tool automatically finds the edges. You can add or subtract areas of the selection until you have exactly the area you want.

The image of the sand dollar in the 03Working.psd file has clearly defined edges, making it an ideal candidate for the Quick Selection tool. You'll select just the sand dollar, not the shadow or background behind it.

1 Select the Zoom tool in the Tools panel, and then zoom in so that you can see the sand dollar well.

2 Select the Quick Selection tool (✐) in the Tools panel.

3 Click on an off-white area near the outside edge of the sand dollar. The Quick Selection tool finds the full edge automatically, selecting the entire sand dollar.

Leave the selection active so that you can use it in the next exercise.

Moving a selected area

Once you've made a selection, any changes you make apply exclusively to the pixels within the selection. The rest of the image is not affected by those changes.

To move the selected area to another part of the composition, you use the Move tool. This image has only one layer, so the pixels you move will replace the pixels beneath them. This change is not permanent until you deselect the moved pixels, so you can try different locations for the selection you're moving before you make a commitment.

1 If the sand dollar is not still selected, repeat the previous exercise to select it.

2 Zoom out so you can see both the wooden plate and the sand dollar.

3 Select the Move tool (▸⊹). Notice that the sand dollar remains selected.

4 Drag the selected area (the sand dollar) toward the left of the collage so that the sand dollar overlaps the lower left edge of the wooden plate.

5 Choose Select > Deselect, and then choose File > Save.

In Photoshop, it's not easy to lose a selection. Unless a selection tool is active, clicking elsewhere in the image will not deselect the active area. To deliberately deselect a selection, you can choose Select > Deselect, press Ctrl+D (Windows) or Command+D (Mac OS), or click outside the selection with any selection tool to start a different selection.

Julieanne Kost is an official Adobe Photoshop evangelist.

Tool tips from the Photoshop evangelist

Move tool tip

If you're moving objects in a multilayer file with the Move tool and you suddenly need to select one of the layers, try this: With the Move tool selected, move the pointer over any area of an image and right-click (Windows) or Control-click (Mac OS). The layers that are under the pointer appear in the context menu. Choose the one you'd like to make active.

Manipulating selections

You can move selections, reposition them as you create them, and even duplicate them. In this section, you'll learn several ways to manipulate selections. Most of these methods work with any selection, but you'll use them here with the Elliptical Marquee tool, which lets you select ovals or perfect circles.

One of the best things about this section is the introduction of keyboard shortcuts that can save you time and arm motions.

Repositioning a selection marquee while creating it

Selecting ovals and circles can be tricky. It's not always obvious where you should start dragging, so sometimes the selection will be off-center, or the ratio of width to height won't match what you need. In this exercise, you'll learn techniques for managing those problems, including two important keyboard-mouse combinations that can make your Photoshop work much easier.

As you perform this exercise, be very careful to follow the directions about keeping the mouse button or specific keys pressed. If you accidentally release the mouse button at the wrong time, simply start the exercise again from step 1.

1 Select the Zoom tool (🔍), and click the bowl of shells on the right side of the image window to zoom in to at least 100% view (use 200% view if the entire bowl of shells will still fit in the image window on your screen).

2 Select the Elliptical Marquee tool (◯), hidden under the Rectangular Marquee tool (▢).

3 Move the pointer over the bowl of shells, and drag diagonally across the oval bowl to create a selection, but *do not release the mouse button*. It's OK if your selection does not match the bowl shape yet.

If you accidentally release the mouse button, draw the selection again. In most cases—including this one—the new selection replaces the previous one.

4 Still holding down the mouse button, press the spacebar, and continue to drag the selection. Instead of resizing the selection, now you're moving it. Position it so that it more closely aligns with the bowl.

5 Carefully release the spacebar (but not the mouse button) and continue to drag, trying to make the size and shape of the selection match the oval bowl of shells as closely as possible. If necessary, hold down the spacebar again and drag to move the selection marquee into position around the bowl of shells.

Begin dragging a selection.   Press the spacebar to move it.   Complete the selection.

6 When the selection border is positioned appropriately, release the mouse button.

7 Choose View > Zoom Out or use the slider in the Navigator panel to reduce the zoom view so that you can see all of the objects in the image window.

Leave the Elliptical Marquee tool and the selection active for the next exercise.

Moving selected pixels with a keyboard shortcut

Now you'll use a keyboard shortcut to move the selected pixels onto the wooden plate. The shortcut temporarily switches the active tool to the Move tool, so you don't need to select it from the Tools panel.

1 If the bowl of shells is not still selected, repeat the previous exercise to select it.

2 With the Elliptical Marquee tool (⊙) selected in the Tools panel, press Ctrl (Windows) or Command (Mac OS), and move the pointer within the selection. The pointer icon now includes a pair of scissors (▶ₓ) to indicate that the selection will be cut from its current location.

3 Drag the bowl of shells onto the wooden plate so that it overlaps the upper left edge of the wooden plate. (You'll use another technique to nudge the oval bowl into the exact position in a minute.)

4 Release the mouse button, but don't deselect the bowl of shells.

● **Note:** You can release the Ctrl or Command key after you start dragging, and the Move tool remains active. Photoshop reverts to the previously selected tool when you deselect, whether you click outside the selection or use the Deselect command.

Moving with the arrow keys

You can make minor adjustments to the position of selected pixels by using the arrow keys. You can nudge the selection in increments of either one pixel or ten pixels.

When a selection tool is active in the Tools panel, the arrow keys nudge the selection border, but not the contents. When the Move tool is active, the arrow keys move the selection border and its contents.

You'll use the arrow keys to nudge the bowl of shells. Before you begin, make sure that the bowl of shells is still selected in the image window.

1 Press the Up Arrow key (⬆) on your keyboard a few times to move the oval upward.

Notice that each time you press the arrow key, the bowl of shells moves one pixel. Experiment by pressing the other arrow keys to see how they affect the selection.

2 Hold down the Shift key as you press an arrow key.

When you hold down the Shift key, the selection moves ten pixels every time you press an arrow key.

Sometimes the border around a selected area can distract you as you make adjustments. You can hide the edges of a selection temporarily without actually deselecting, and then display the selection border once you've completed the adjustments.

3 Choose View > Show > Selection Edges or View > Extras.

Either command hides the selection border around the bowl of shells.

4 Use the arrow keys to nudge the bowl of shells until it's positioned where you want it. Then choose View > Show > Selection Edges to reveal the selection border again.

Hidden selection edges

Visible selection edges

5 Choose Select > Deselect, or press Ctrl+D (Windows) or Command+D (Mac OS).

6 Choose File > Save to save your work so far.

Selecting from a center point

In some cases, it's easier to make elliptical or rectangular selections by drawing a selection from the center point. You'll use this technique to select the logo graphic.

1 Select the Zoom tool (🔍), and zoom in on the logo to a magnification of about 300%. Make sure that you can see the entire Sally's Seashells graphic in your image window.

2 Select the Elliptical Marquee tool (⊙) in the Tools panel.

3 Move the pointer to the approximate center of the Sally's Seashells graphic.

4 Click and begin dragging. Then, without releasing the mouse button, press Alt (Windows) or Option (Mac OS) as you continue dragging the selection to the outer edge of the Sally's Seashells graphic.

The selection is centered over its starting point.

5 When you have the entire Sally's Seashells graphic selected, release the mouse button first, and then release Alt or Option (and the Shift key if you used it). Do not deselect, because you'll use this selection in the next exercise.

▶ **Tip:** To select a perfect circle, press Shift as you drag. Hold down Shift while dragging the Rectangular Marquee tool to select a perfect square.

 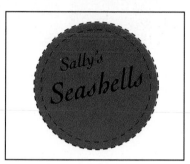

6 If necessary, reposition the selection border using one of the methods you learned earlier. If you accidentally released the Alt or Option key before you released the mouse button, try selecting the Sally's Seashells graphic again.

Moving and changing the pixels in a selection

Now you'll move the Sally's Seashells graphic to the upper right corner of the wooden plate. Then, you'll change its color for a dramatic effect.

Before you begin, make sure that the Sally's Seashells graphic is still selected. If it's not, reselect it by completing the previous exercise.

1 Choose View > Fit On Screen so that the entire image fits within the image window.

2 Select the Move tool (▶⊕) in the Tools panel.

3 Position the pointer within the Sally's Seashells graphic selection. The pointer becomes an arrow with a pair of scissors (▶✂), which indicates that dragging the selection will cut it from its current location and move it to the new location.

4 Drag the Sally's Seashells graphic onto the upper right corner of the plate. If you want to adjust the position after you stop dragging, simply start dragging again. The Sally's Seashells graphic remains selected throughout the process.

5 Choose Image > Adjustments > Invert.

The colors making up the Sally's Seashells graphic are inverted so that now it's effectively a color negative of itself.

6 Leaving the Sally's Seashells graphic selected, choose File > Save to save your work.

Moving and duplicating a selection simultaneously

You can move and duplicate a selection at the same time. You'll make a copy of the logo graphic. If the logo graphic image is no longer selected, reselect it now, using the techniques you learned earlier.

1 With the Move tool (▸+) selected, press Alt (Windows) or Option (Mac OS) as you position the pointer inside the Sally's Seashells graphic selection. The pointer becomes a double arrow, which indicates that a duplicate will be made when you move the selection.

2 Continue holding down the Alt or Option key as you drag a duplicate of the graphic down and to the right. The two copies of the graphic can overlap. Release the mouse button and the Alt or Option key, but don't deselect the duplicate graphic.

3 Choose Edit > Transform > Scale. A bounding box appears around the selection.

4 Press Shift as you drag one of the corner points to enlarge the graphic so that it becomes about 50% larger than the original. Then press Enter or Return to commit the change and remove the transformation bounding box.

As you resize the object, the selection marquee resizes, too. The duplicate graphic remains selected. Pressing the Shift key as you resize the selection constrains the proportions so that the enlarged object isn't distorted.

5 Hold down Alt+Shift (Windows) or Option+Shift (Mac OS), and drag a new copy of the second Sally's Seashells graphic down and to the right.

Pressing the Shift key as you move a selection constrains the movement horizontally or vertically in 45-degree increments.

6 Repeat steps 3 and 4 for the third Sally's Seashells graphic, making it about twice the size of the first one.

7 When you're satisfied with the size and position of the third Sally's Seashells graphic, press Enter or Return to confirm the scale, choose Select > Deselect, and then choose File > Save.

▶ **Tip:** Choose Edit > Transform > Again to duplicate the logo and enlarge it by twice as much as the last transformation.

For information on working with the center point in a transformation, see "Set or move the reference point for a transformation" in Photoshop Help.

Copying selections

You can use the Move tool to copy selections as you drag them within or between images, or you can copy and move selections using the Copy, Copy Merged, Cut, and Paste commands. Dragging with the Move tool saves memory because the clipboard is not used as it is with the commands.

Photoshop has several copy and paste commands:

- Copy copies the selected area on the active layer.
- Copy Merged creates a merged copy of all the visible layers in the selected area.
- Paste pastes a cut or copied selection into another part of the image or into another image as a new layer.
- Paste Into pastes a cut or copied selection inside another selection in the same or a different image. The source selection is pasted onto a new layer, and the destination selection border is converted into a layer mask.

Keep in mind that when a selection is pasted between images with different resolutions, the pasted data retains its pixel dimensions. This can make the pasted portion appear out of proportion to the new image. Use the Image Size command to make the source and destination images the same resolution before copying and pasting.

Using the Magic Wand tool

The Magic Wand tool selects all the pixels of a particular color or color range. It's most useful for selecting an area of similar colors surrounded by areas of very different colors. As with many of the selection tools, after you make the initial selection, you can add or subtract areas of the selection.

The Tolerance option sets the sensitivity of the Magic Wand tool. This value limits or extends the range of pixel similarity. The default tolerance value of 32 selects the color you click plus 32 lighter and 32 darker tones of that color. You may need to adjust the tolerance level up or down depending on the color ranges and variations in the image.

If a multicolored area that you want to select is set against a background of a different color, it can be much easier to select the background than the area itself. In this procedure, you'll use the Rectangular Marquee tool to select a larger area, and then use the Magic Wand tool to subtract the background from the selection.

1 Select the Rectangular Marquee tool ([⬚]), hidden behind the Elliptical Marquee tool (○).

2 Drag a selection around the piece of coral. Make sure that your selection is large enough so that a margin of white appears between the coral and the edges of the marquee.

At this point, the coral and the white background area are selected. You'll subtract the white area from the selection so that only the coral remains in the selection.

3 Select the Magic Wand tool (🪄), hidden under the Quick Selection tool (✐).

4 In the options bar, confirm that the Tolerance value is **32**. This value determines the range of colors the wand selects.

5 Select the Subtract From Selection button (🗇) in the options bar. A minus sign appears next to the wand in the pointer icon. Anything you select now will be subtracted from the initial selection.

6   Click in the white background area within the selection marquee.

The Magic Wand tool selects the entire background, subtracting it from the selection. Now all the white pixels are deselected, leaving the coral perfectly selected.

7 Select the Move tool (▶⊹), and drag the coral to the wooden plate, a little to the right and above the center of the plate.

8 Choose Select > Deselect, and then save your work.

Selecting with the lasso tools

Photoshop includes three lasso tools: the Lasso tool, the Polygonal Lasso tool, and the Magnetic Lasso tool. You can use the Lasso tool to make selections that require both freehand and straight lines, using keyboard shortcuts to move back and forth between the Lasso tool and the Polygonal Lasso tool. You'll use the Lasso tool to select the mussel. It takes a bit of practice to alternate between straight-line and freehand selections—if you make a mistake while you're selecting the mussel, simply deselect and start again.

1 Select the Zoom tool (🔍), and click the mussel until the view enlarges to 100%. Make sure you can see the entire mussel in the window.

2 Select the Lasso tool (👌). Starting at the lower left section of the mussel, drag around the rounded end of the mussel, tracing the shape as accurately as possible. *Do not release the mouse button.*

3 Press the Alt (Windows) or Option (Mac OS) key, and then release the mouse button so that the lasso pointer changes to the polygonal lasso shape (🔾). *Do not release the Alt or Option key.*

4 Begin clicking along the end of the mussel to place anchor points, following the contours of the mussel. Be sure to hold down the Alt or Option key throughout this process.

Drag with the Lasso tool.

Click with the Polygonal Lasso tool.

The selection border automatically stretches like a rubber band between anchor points.

5 When you reach the tip of the mussel, hold down the mouse button as you release the Alt or Option key. The pointer again appears as the lasso icon.

6 Carefully drag around the tip of the mussel, holding down the mouse button.

7 When you finish tracing the tip and reach the lower side of the mussel, first press Alt or Option again, and then release the mouse button. Click along the lower side of the mussel with the Polygonal Lasso tool as you did on the top. Continue to trace the mussel until you arrive back at the starting point of your selection near the left end of the image.

8 Click at the start of the selection, and then release the Alt or Option key. The mussel is now entirely selected. Leave the mussel selected for the next exercise.

Rotating a selection

So far, you've moved, resized, duplicated, and inverted the color of selected areas. In this exercise, you'll see how easy it is to rotate a selected object.

Before you begin, make sure that the mussel is still selected.

1 Choose View > Fit On Screen to resize the image window to fit on your screen.

2 Press Ctrl (Windows) or Command (Mac OS) as you drag the mussel to the lower section of the wooden plate. The pointer changes to the Move tool icon.

3 Choose Edit > Transform > Rotate. The mussel and selection marquee are enclosed in a bounding box.

4 Move the pointer outside the bounding box so that it becomes a curved, double-headed arrow (↷). Drag to rotate the mussel to a −15-degree angle. You can verify the angle in the Rotate box in the options bar. Press Enter or Return to commit the transformation changes.

5 If necessary, select the Move tool (▸⊹) and drag to reposition the mussel. When you're satisfied, choose Select > Deselect.

6 Choose File > Save.

Selecting with the Magnetic Lasso tool

You can use the Magnetic Lasso tool to make freehand selections of areas with high-contrast edges. When you draw with the Magnetic Lasso tool, the selection border automatically snaps to the edge between areas of contrast. You can also control the selection path by occasionally clicking the mouse to place anchor points in the selection border.

You'll use the Magnetic Lasso tool to select the nautilus so that you can move it to the center of the plate.

1 Select the Zoom tool ($\mathcal{Q}$), and click the nautilus to zoom in to at least 100%.

2 Select the Magnetic Lasso tool (), hidden under the Lasso tool ($\mathcal{P}$).

3 Click once along the left edge of the nautilus, and then move the Magnetic Lasso tool along the edge to trace its outline.

► **Tip:** In low-contrast areas, you may want to click to place your own fastening points. You can add as many as you need. To remove the most recent fastening point, press Delete, and then move the mouse back to the remaining fastening point and continue selecting.

Even though you're not holding down the mouse button, the tool snaps to the edge of the nautilus and automatically adds fastening points.

4 When you reach the left side of the nautilus again, double-click to return the Magnetic Lasso tool to the starting point, closing the selection. Or you can move the Magnetic Lasso tool over the starting point and click once.

5 Double-click the Hand tool ($\mathcal{W}$) to fit the image in the image window.

6 Select the Move tool ($\blacktriangleright_{+}$), and drag the nautilus onto the plate.

7 Choose Select > Deselect, and then choose File > Save.

Separating portions of an image into different files

To quickly create multiple images from one scan, use the Crop And Straighten Photos command. Images with a clearly delineated outline and a uniform background—such as the 03Start.psd file—work best. To try it, open the 03Start.psd file in the Lesson03 folder, and choose File > Automate > Crop And Straighten Photos. Photoshop automatically crops each image in the start file and creates individual Photoshop files for each. You can close each file without saving.

Original image

Result

Cropping an image and erasing within a selection

Now that your composition is in place, you'll crop the image to a final size and clean up some of the background scraps left behind when you moved selections. You can use either the Crop tool or the Crop command to crop an image.

1   Select the Crop tool (⊠), or press C to switch from the current tool to the Crop tool. Photoshop creates a crop boundary around the entire image.

2   In the options bar, choose Unconstrained, and then select Delete Cropped Pixels. With Unconstrained selected, you can crop the image with any proportions.

3   Drag the crop handles so that the plate is in the highlighted area, deleting the backgrounds and drop shadows that were left behind from the items that were arranged outside the plate.

4   When you're satisfied with the position of the crop area, click the Commit Current Crop Operation button (✔) in the options bar.

The cropped image may include some scraps of the background from which you selected and removed shapes. You'll fix that next.

5   If a scrap of background color or leftover drop shadow protrudes into the composition, use the Rectangular Marquee tool (⬚) or the Lasso tool (𝒫) to select it. Be careful not to include any part of the image that you want to keep.

6   Select the Eraser tool (🖊) in the Tools panel, and then make sure that the foreground and background color swatches in the Tools panel are set to the defaults: black in the foreground and white in the background.

7   In the options bar, open the Brushes pop-up panel, and specify an **80**-pixel brush with **100%** hardness.

8 Drag the Eraser tool across the area you want to remove. You can erase quickly, because the Eraser tool affects only the selected area.

9 Repeat steps 5–8 to remove any other unwanted scraps of background.

10 Choose File > Save to save your work.

You've used several different selection tools to move all the seashells into place. The collage is complete!

Softening the edges of a selection

To smooth the hard edges of a selection, you can apply anti-aliasing or feathering, or use the Refine Edge option.

Anti-aliasing smooths the jagged edges of a selection by softening the color transition between edge pixels and background pixels. Since only the edge pixels change, no detail is lost. Anti-aliasing is useful when cutting, copying, and pasting selections to create composite images.

Anti-aliasing is available for the Lasso, Polygonal Lasso, Magnetic Lasso, Elliptical Marquee, and Magic Wand tools. (Select the tool to display its options in the options bar.) To apply anti-aliasing, you must select the option before making the selection. Once a selection is made, you cannot add anti-aliasing to it.

Feathering blurs edges by building a transition boundary between the selection and its surrounding pixels. This blurring can cause some loss of detail at the edge of the selection.

You can define feathering for the marquee and lasso tools as you use them, or you can add feathering to an existing selection. Feathering effects become apparent when you move, cut, or copy the selection.

Once you have a selection, you can use the Refine Edge option to smooth the outline, feather it, or contract or expand it. Click Refine Edge in the options bar to open its dialog box.

- To use anti-aliasing, select a lasso tool, or the Elliptical Marquee or Magic Wand tool, and select Anti-alias in the options bar.

- To define a feathered edge for a selection tool, select any of the lasso or marquee tools. Enter a Feather value in the options bar. This value defines the width of the feathered edge and can range from 1 to 250 pixels.

- To define a feathered edge for an existing selection, choose Select > Modify > Feather. Enter a value for the Feather Radius, and click OK.

Review questions

1 Once you've made a selection, what area of the image can be edited?

2 How do you add to and subtract from a selection?

3 How can you move a selection while you're drawing it?

4 When drawing a selection with the Lasso tool, how should you finish drawing the selection to ensure it's the shape you want?

5 What does the Quick Selection tool do?

6 How does the Magic Wand tool determine which areas of an image to select? What is tolerance, and how does it affect a selection?

Review answers

1 Only the area within an active selection can be edited.

2 To add to a selection, click the Add To Selection button in the options bar, and then click the area you want to add. To subtract from a selection, click the Subtract From Selection button in the options bar, and then click the area you want to subtract. You can also add to a selection by pressing Shift as you drag or click; to subtract, press Alt (Windows) or Option (Mac OS) as you drag or click.

3 To reposition a selection, without releasing the mouse button, hold down the spacebar and drag.

4 To make sure that the selection is the shape you want when you use the Lasso tool, end the selection by dragging across the starting point of the selection. If you start and stop the selection at different points, Photoshop draws a straight line between the start point of the selection and the end point of the selection.

5 The Quick Selection tool expands outward from where you click to automatically find and follow defined edges in the image.

6 The Magic Wand tool selects adjacent pixels based on their similarity in color. The Tolerance value determines how many color tones the Magic Wand tool will select. The higher the tolerance setting, the more tones are selected.

4 LAYER BASICS

Lesson overview

In this lesson, you'll learn how to do the following:

- Organize artwork on layers.

- Create, view, hide, and select layers.

- Rearrange layers to change the stacking order of artwork.

- Apply blending modes to layers.

- Resize and rotate layers.

- Apply a gradient to a layer.

- Apply a filter to a layer.

- Add text and layer effects to a layer.

- Add an adjustment layer.

- Save a copy of the file with the layers flattened.

This lesson will take less than an hour to complete. Copy the Lesson04 folder onto your hard drive if you haven't already done so. As you work on this lesson, you'll preserve the start files. If you need to restore the start files, copy them from the *Adobe Photoshop CS6 Classroom in a Book* DVD.

Adobe Photoshop lets you isolate different parts of an image on layers. Each layer can then be edited as discrete artwork, allowing tremendous flexibility in composing and revising an image.

About layers

Every Photoshop file contains one or more *layers*. New files are generally created with a *background layer,* which contains a color or an image that shows through the transparent areas of subsequent layers. All new layers in an image are transparent until you add text or artwork (pixel values).

Working with layers is analogous to placing portions of a drawing on clear sheets of film, such as those viewed with an overhead projector: Individual sheets may be edited, repositioned, and deleted without affecting the other sheets. When the sheets are stacked, the entire composition is visible.

Getting started

You'll start the lesson by viewing an image of the final composition.

1   Start Photoshop, and then immediately hold down Ctrl+Alt+Shift (Windows) or Command+Option+Shift (Mac OS) to restore the default preferences. (See "Restoring default preferences" on page 4.)

2   When prompted, click Yes to delete the Adobe Photoshop Settings file.

3   Click the Mini Bridge tab to open the Mini Bridge panel. If Bridge isn't running in the background, click Launch Bridge.

4   In the Mini Bridge panel, choose Favorites from the pop-up menu on the left.

5   In the Favorites panel, double-click the Lessons folder, and then double-click the Lesson04 folder.

6   In the Content panel, select the 04End.psd file. Press the spacebar for a full-screen view.

This layered composite represents a postcard. You will create it now, and, in doing so, learn how to create, edit, and manage layers.

7   Press the spacebar again to return to the Mini Bridge panel, and then double-click the 04Start.psd file to open it in Photoshop.

8   Choose File > Save As, rename the file **04Working.psd**, and click Save. Click OK if you see the Photoshop Format Options dialog box.

Saving another version of the start file frees you to make changes without worrying about overwriting the original.

Using the Layers panel

The Layers panel lists all the layers in an image, displaying the layer names and thumbnails of the content on each layer. You can use the Layers panel to hide, view, reposition, delete, rename, and merge layers. The layer thumbnails are automatically updated as you edit the layers.

1 If the Layers panel is not visible in the work area, choose Window > Layers.

The Layers panel lists five layers for the 04Working.psd file (from top to bottom): Postage, HAWAII, Flower, Pineapple, and Background.

2 Select the Background layer to make it active (if it's not already selected). Notice the layer thumbnail and the icons on the Background layer level:

- The lock icon (🔒) indicates that the layer is protected.

- The eye icon (👁) indicates that the layer is visible in the image window. If you click the eye, the image window no longer displays that layer.

The first task for this project is to add a photo of the beach to the postcard. First, you'll open the beach image in Photoshop.

▶ **Tip:** Use the context menu to hide or resize the layer thumbnail. Right-click (Windows) or Control-click (Mac OS) a thumbnail in the Layers panel to open the context menu, and then choose a thumbnail size.

3 In the Mini Bridge panel, double-click the Beach.psd file in the Lesson04 folder to open it in Photoshop.

The Layers panel changes to display the layer information for the active Beach.psd file. Notice that only one layer appears in the Beach.psd image: Layer 1, not Background. (For more information, see the sidebar, "About the background layer.")

About the background layer

When you create a new image with a white or colored background, the bottom layer in the Layers panel is named Background. An image can have only one background. You cannot change the stacking order of a background layer, its blending mode, or its opacity. You can, however, convert a background layer to a regular layer.

When you create a new image with transparent content, the image doesn't have a background layer. The bottom layer isn't constrained like the background layer; you can move it anywhere in the Layers panel, and change its opacity and blending mode.

To convert a background layer into a regular layer:

1 Double-click the name Background in the Layers panel, or choose Layer > New > Layer From Background.

2 Rename the layer, and set any other layer options.

3 Click OK.

To convert a regular layer into a background layer:

1 Select a layer in the Layers panel.

2 Choose Layer > New > Background From Layer.

Renaming and copying a layer

To add content to an image and simultaneously create a new layer for it, drag an object or layer from one file into the image window of another file. Whether you drag from the image window of the original file or from its Layers panel, only the active layer is reproduced in the destination file.

You'll drag the Beach.psd image onto the 04Working.psd file. Before you begin, make sure that both the 04Working.psd and Beach.psd files are open, and that the Beach.psd file is selected.

First, you'll give Layer 1 a more descriptive name.

1   In the Layers panel, double-click the name Layer 1, type **Beach**, and then press Enter or Return. Keep the layer selected.

2   Choose Window > Arrange > 2-Up Vertical. Photoshop displays both of the open image files. Select the Beach.psd image so that it is the active file.

3   Select the Move tool (⊕), and use it to drag the Beach.psd image onto the 04Working.psd image window.

▶ **Tip:** If you hold down Shift as you drag an image from one file into another, the dragged image automatically centers itself in the target image window.

The Beach layer now appears in the 04Working.psd file image window and its Layers panel, between the Background and Pineapple layers. Photoshop always adds new layers directly above the selected layer; you selected the Background layer earlier.

4 Close the Beach.psd file without saving changes to it.

5 Double-click the Mini Bridge tab to close the panel.

Viewing individual layers

The 04Working.psd file now contains six layers. Some of the layers are visible and some are hidden. The eye icon (👁) next to a layer thumbnail in the Layers panel indicates that the layer is visible.

1 Click the eye icon (👁) next to the Pineapple layer to hide the image of the pineapple.

You can hide or show a layer by clicking this icon or clicking in its column—also called the Show/Hide Visibility column.

2 Click again in the Show/Hide Visibility column to display the pineapple.

Adding a border to a layer

Now you'll add a white border around the Beach layer to create the impression that it's a photograph.

1 Select the Beach layer. (To select the layer, click the layer name in the Layers panel.)

The layer is highlighted, indicating that it is active. Changes you make in the image window affect the active layer.

2 To make the opaque areas on this layer more obvious, hide all layers except the Beach layer: Press Alt (Windows) or Option (Mac OS) as you click the eye icon (◉) next to the Beach layer.

The white background and other objects in the image disappear, leaving only the beach image against a checkerboard background. The checkerboard indicates transparent areas of the active layer.

3 Choose Layer > Layer Style > Stroke.

The Layer Style dialog box opens. Now you'll select the options for the white stroke around the beach image.

4 Specify the following settings:

- Size: **5 px**

- Position: Inside

- Blend Mode: Normal

- Opacity: **100**%

- Color: White (Click the Color box, and select white in the Color Picker.)

5 Click OK. A white border appears around the beach photo.

Rearranging layers

The order in which the layers of an image are organized is called the *stacking order*. The stacking order determines how the image is viewed—you can change the order to make certain parts of the image appear in front of or behind other layers.

You'll rearrange the layers so that the beach image is in front of another image that is currently hidden in the file.

1   Make the Postage, HAWAII, Flower, Pineapple and Background layers visible by clicking the Show/Hide Visibility column next to their layer names.

The beach image is almost entirely blocked by images on other layers.

2   In the Layers panel, drag the Beach layer up so that it is positioned between the Pineapple and Flower layers—when you've positioned it correctly, you'll see a thick line between the layers in the panel—and then release the mouse button.

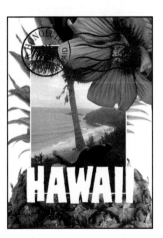

The Beach layer moves up one level in the stacking order, and the beach image appears on top of the pineapple and background images, but under the flower and "HAWAII."

▶ **Tip:** You can also control the stacking order of layered images by selecting them in the Layers panel and choosing Layer > Arrange, and then choosing Bring To Front, Bring Forward, Send To Back, or Send Backward.

Changing the opacity of a layer

You can reduce the opacity of any layer to let other layers show through it. In this case, the postmark is too dark on the flower. You'll edit the opacity of the Postage layer to let the flower and other images show through.

1   Select the Postage layer, and then click the arrow next to the Opacity box to display the Opacity slider. Drag the slider to **25%**. You can also type the value in the Opacity box or scrub the Opacity label.

The Postage layer becomes partially transparent, so you can see the other layers underneath. Notice that the change in opacity affects only the image area of the Postage layer. The Pineapple, Beach, Flower and HAWAII layers remain opaque.

2   Choose File > Save to save your work.

Duplicating a layer and changing the blending mode

You can apply different blending modes to a layer. *Blending modes* affect how the color pixels on one layer blend with pixels in the layers underneath. First you'll use blending modes to increase the intensity of the image on the Pineapple layer so that it doesn't look so dull. Then you'll change the blending mode on the Postage layer. (Currently, the blending mode for both layers is Normal.)

1   Click the eye icons next to the HAWAII, Flower, and Beach layers to hide them.

2   Right-click or Control-click the Pineapple layer, and choose Duplicate Layer from the context menu. (Make sure you click the layer name, not its thumbnail, or you'll see the wrong context menu.) Click OK in the Duplicate Layer dialog box.

A layer called "Pineapple copy" appears above the Pineapple layer in the Layers panel.

Julieanne Kost is an official Adobe Photoshop evangelist.

Tool tips from the Photoshop evangelist

Blending effects

Blending layers in different order or a different grouping changes the effect. You can apply a blending mode to an entire layer group and get a very different result than if you apply the same blending mode to each of the layers individually. When a blending mode is applied to a group, Photoshop treats the group as a single merged object and then applies the blending mode. Experiment with blending modes to get the effect you want.

3 With the Pineapple copy layer selected, choose Overlay from the Blending Modes menu in the Layers panel.

The Overlay blending mode blends the Pineapple copy layer with the Pineapple layer beneath it to create a vibrant, more colorful pineapple with deeper shadows and brighter highlights.

▶ **Tip:** For more about blending modes, including definitions and visual examples, see Photoshop Help.

4 Select the Postage layer, and choose Multiply from the Blending Modes menu. The Multiply blending mode multiplies the colors in the underlying layers with the color in the top layer. In this case, the postmark becomes a little stronger.

5 Choose File > Save to save your work.

Resizing and rotating layers

You can resize and transform layers.

1 Click the Visibility column on the Beach layer to make it visible.

2 Select the Beach layer in the Layers panel, and then choose Edit > Free Transform. A Transform bounding box appears around the beach image. The bounding box has handles on each corner and each side.

First, you'll resize and angle the layer.

3 Press Shift as you drag a corner handle inward to scale the beach photo down by about 50%. (Watch the Width and Height percentages in the options bar.)

4 With the bounding box still active, position the pointer just outside one of the corner handles until it becomes a curved double arrow. Drag clockwise to rotate the beach image approximately 15 degrees. You can also enter **15** in the Set Rotation box in the options bar.

5 Click the Commit Transform button (✔) in the options bar.

6 Make the Flower layer visible. Then, select the Move tool (▸✛), and drag the beach photo so that its corner is tucked neatly beneath the flower, as in the illustration.

7 Choose File > Save.

Using a filter to create artwork

Next, you'll create a new layer with no artwork on it. (Adding empty layers to a file is comparable to adding blank sheets of acetate to a stack of images.) You'll use this layer to add realistic-looking clouds to the sky with a Photoshop filter.

1   In the Layers panel, select the Background layer to make it active, and then click the New Layer button (▣) at the bottom of the Layers panel.

● **Note:** You can also create a new layer by choosing Layer > New > Layer, or by choosing New Layer from the Layers panel menu.

A new layer, named Layer 1, appears between the Background and Pineapple layers. The layer has no content, so it has no effect on the image.

2   Double-click the name Layer 1, type **Clouds**, and press Enter or Return to rename the layer.

3   In the Tools panel, click the Foreground Color swatch, select a sky blue color from the Color Picker, and click OK. We selected a color with the following values: R=48, G=138, and B=174. The Background Color remains white.

4   With the Clouds layer still active, choose Filter > Render > Clouds. Realistic-looking clouds appear behind the image.

5   Choose File > Save.

Dragging to add a new layer

You can add a layer to an image by dragging an image file from the desktop, Bridge, or Explorer (Windows) or the Finder (Mac OS). You'll add another flower to the postcard now.

1 If Photoshop fills your monitor, reduce the size of the Photoshop window:

   • In Windows, click the Maximize/Restore button (▣) in the upper right corner, and then drag the lower right corner of the Photoshop window to make it smaller.

   • In Mac OS, click the green Maximize/Restore button (●) in the upper left corner of the image window.

2 In Photoshop, select the Pineapple copy layer in the Layers panel to make it the active layer.

3 In Explorer (Windows) or the Finder (Mac OS), navigate to the Lessons folder you copied from the *Adobe Photoshop CS6 Classroom in a Book* DVD. Then navigate to the Lesson04 folder.

4 Select Flower2.psd, and drag it from Explorer or the Finder onto your image.

The Flower2 layer appears in the Layers panel, directly above the Pineapple copy layer. Photoshop places the image as a Smart Object, which is a layer you can edit without making permanent changes. You'll work with Smart Objects in Lessons 5 and 8.

5 Position the Flower2 layer in the lower left corner of the postcard, so that about half of the flower is visible.

6 Click the Commit Transform button (✔) in the options bar to accept the layer.

Adding text

Now you're ready to create some type using the Horizontal Type tool, which places the text on its own type layer. You'll then edit the text and apply a special effect.

1 Make the HAWAII layer visible. You'll add text just below this layer, and apply special effects to both layers.

2 Choose Select > Deselect Layers, so that no layers are selected.

3 Click the Foreground Color swatch in the Tools panel, and then select a shade of grassy green in the Color Picker. Click OK to close the Color Picker.

4 In the Tools panel, select the Horizontal Type tool (T). Then, choose Window > Character to open the Character panel. Do the following in the Character panel:

- Select a serif font (we used Birch Std).

- Select a font style (we used Regular).

- Select a large font size (we used 36 points).

- Select Crisp from the Anti-aliasing menu (ªₐ).

- Select a large tracking value (🅼) (we used 250).

- Click the All Caps button (TT).

- Click the Faux Bold button (T).

5 Click just below the "H" in the word "HAWAII," and type **Island Paradise**. Then click the Commit Any Current Edits button (✔) in the options bar.

● **Note:** If you make a mistake when you click to set the type, simply click away from the type and repeat step 5.

The Layers panel now includes a layer named Island Paradise with a "T" thumbnail, indicating that it is a type layer. This layer is at the top of the layer stack.

The text appears where you clicked, which probably isn't exactly where you want it to be positioned.

6 Select the Move tool (▶✛), and drag the "Island Paradise" text so that it is centered below "HAWAII."

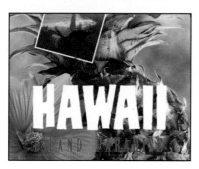

Applying a gradient to a layer

You can apply a color gradient to all or part of a layer. In this example, you'll apply a gradient to the HAWAII type to make it more colorful. First you'll select the letters, and then you'll apply the gradient.

1 Select the HAWAII layer in the Layers panel to make it active.

2 Right-click or Control-click the thumbnail in the HAWAII layer, and choose Select Pixels. Everything on the HAWAII layer (the white lettering) is selected.

Now that you've selected the area to fill, you'll apply a gradient.

3 In the Tools panel, select the Gradient tool (▣).

4 Click the Foreground Color swatch in the Tools panel, select a bright color of orange in the Color Picker, and click OK. The Background Color should still be white.

5 In the options bar, make sure that Linear Gradient (▣) is selected.

6 In the options bar, click the arrow next to the Gradient Editor box to open the gradient picker. Select the Foreground To Background swatch (it's the first one), and then click anywhere outside the gradient picker to close it.

7 With the selection still active, drag the Gradient tool from the bottom to the top of the letters. If you want to be sure you drag straight up, press the Shift key as you drag.

▶ **Tip:** To list the gradient options by name rather than by sample, click the gradient picker menu button, and choose either Small List or Large List. Or, hover the pointer over a thumbnail until a tool tip appears, showing the gradient name.

The gradient extends across the type, starting with orange at the bottom and gradually blending to white at the top.

8 Choose Select > Deselect to deselect the HAWAII type.

9 Save the work you've done so far.

Applying a layer style

You can enhance a layer by adding a shadow, stroke, satin sheen, or other special effect from a collection of automated and editable layer styles. These styles are easy to apply and link directly to the layer you specify.

Like layers, layer styles can be hidden by clicking eye icons (👁) in the Layers panel. Layer styles are nondestructive, so you can edit or remove them at any time. You can apply a copy of a layer style to a different layer by dragging the effect onto the destination layer.

Earlier, you used a layer style to add a stroke to the beach photo. Now, you'll add drop shadows to the text to make it stand out.

1 Select the Island Paradise layer, and then choose Layer > Layer Style > Drop Shadow.

2 In the Layer Style dialog box, make sure that the Preview option is selected, and then, if necessary, move the dialog box so that you can see the Island Paradise text in the image window.

▶ **Tip:** You can also open the Layer Style dialog box by clicking the Add A Layer Style button at the bottom of the Layers panel and then choosing a layer style, such as Bevel And Emboss, from the pop-up menu.

3 In the Structure area, select Use Global Light, and then specify the following settings:

- Blend Mode: Multiply
- Opacity: **75**%
- Angle: **78** degrees
- Distance: **5** px
- Spread: **30**%
- Size: **10** px

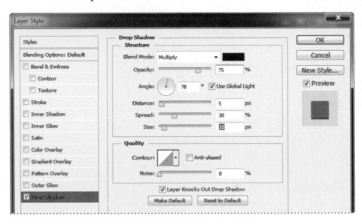

Photoshop adds a drop shadow to the "Island Paradise" text in the image.

4 Click OK to accept the settings and close the Layer Style dialog box.

Photoshop nests the layer style in the Island Paradise layer. First it lists Effects, and then the layer styles applied to the layer. An eye icon (⬤) appears next to the effect category and next to each effect. To turn off an effect, click the eye icon. Click the visibility column again to restore the effect. To hide all layer styles, click the eye icon next to Effects. To collapse the list of effects, click the arrow next to the layer.

5 Make sure that eye icons appear for both items nested in the Island Paradise layer.

6 Press Alt (Windows) or Option (Mac OS) and drag the Effects line or the fx symbol (*fx*) onto the HAWAII layer. The Drop Shadow layer style is applied to the HAWAII layer, using the same settings you applied to the Island Paradise layer.

Now you'll add a green stroke around the word HAWAII.

7 Select the HAWAII layer in the Layers panel, click the Add A Layer Style button (*fx*) at the bottom of the panel, and choose Stroke from the pop-up menu.

8 In the Structure area of the Layer Styles dialog box, specify the following settings:

- Size: **4** px
- Position: Outside
- Blend Mode: Normal
- Opacity: **100**%
- Color: Green (Select a shade that goes well with the one you used for the "Island Paradise" text.)

9 Click OK to apply the stroke.

Now you'll add a drop shadow and a satin sheen to the flower.

10 Select the Flower layer, and choose Layer > Layer Style > Drop Shadow. Then change the following settings in the Structure area:

* Opacity: **60**%

* Distance: **13** px

* Spread: **9**%.

* Make sure Use Global Light is selected, and that the Blend Mode is Multiply. Do not click OK.

11 With the Layer Style dialog box still open, select Satin on the left. Then make sure Invert is selected, and apply the following settings:

* Color (next to Blend Mode): Fuchsia (choose a color that complements the flower color)

- Opacity: **20%**
- Distance: **22** px

12 Click OK to apply both layer styles.

Adding an adjustment layer

Adjustment layers can be added to an image to apply color and tonal adjustments without permanently changing the pixel values in the image. For example, if you add a Color Balance adjustment layer to an image, you can experiment with different colors repeatedly, because the change occurs only on the adjustment layer. If you decide to return to the original pixel values, you can hide or delete the adjustment layer.

You've used adjustment layers in other lessons. Here, you'll add a Hue/Saturation adjustment layer to change the color of the purple flower. An adjustment layer affects all layers below it in the image's stacking order unless a selection is active when you create it or you create a clipping mask.

1 Select the Flower2 layer in the Layers panel.

2 Click the Hue/Saturation icon in the Adjustments panel to add a Hue/Saturation adjustment layer.

3 In the Properties panel, apply the following settings

- Hue: **43**

- Saturation: **19**

- Lightness: **0**

The changes affect the Flower2, Pineapple Copy, Pineapple, Clouds, and Background layers. The effect is interesting, but you only want to change the Flower2 layer.

4 Right-click (Windows) or Ctrl-click (Mac OS) the Hue/Saturation adjustment layer, and choose Create Clipping Mask.

An arrow appears in the Layers panel indicating that the adjustment layer applies only to the Flower2 layer. You'll learn more about clipping masks in Lessons 6 and 7.

Updating layer effects

Layer effects are automatically updated when you make changes to a layer. You can edit the text and watch how the layer effect tracks the change. First, you'll use the new search feature in the Layers panel to isolate the text layer.

1 In the Layers panel, choose Kind from the Pick A Filter Type menu.

The filter type determines the search options available to you.

2 Select the Filter For Type Layers button from the filter options at the top of the Layers panel.

Only the Island Paradise layer is listed in the Layers panel. The search feature lets you find specific layers quickly, but has no effect on which layers are visible or their stacking order.

3 Select the Island Paradise layer in the Layers panel.

4 In the Tools panel, select the Horizontal Type tool (T).

5 In the options bar, set the font size to **32** points, and press Enter or Return.

▶ **Tip:** You can search for layers in the Layers panel by layer type, layer name, effect, mode, attribute, and color. When you work in a complex file with numerous layers, searching for the layer you need can save you time.

Although you didn't select the text by dragging the Type tool (as you would have to do in a word-processing program), "Island Paradise" now appears in 32-point type.

6 Using the Horizontal Type tool, click between "Island" and "Paradise," and type **of**.

As you edit the text, the layer styles are applied to the new text.

7 You don't actually need the word "of," so delete it.

8 Select the Move tool (⊕) and drag "Island Paradise" to center it beneath the word "HAWAII."

● **Note:** You don't have to click the Commit Any Current Edits button after making any text edits, because selecting the Move tool has the same effect.

9 Click the red Filtering On/Off button at the top of the Layers panel to toggle filtering off and see all the layers in the file.

10 Choose File > Save.

Adding a border

The Hawaii postcard is nearly done. The elements are almost all arranged correctly in the composition. You'll finish up by positioning the postmark and then adding a white postcard border.

1 Select the Postage layer, and then use the Move tool (⊕) to drag it to the middle right of the image, as in the illustration.

2 Select the Island Paradise layer in the Layers panel, and then click the Create A New Layer button () at the bottom of the panel.

3 Choose Select > All.

4 Choose Select > Modify > Border. In the Border Selection dialog box, type **10** pixels for the Width, and click OK.

A 10-pixel border is selected around the entire image. Now, you'll fill it with white.

5 Select white for the Foreground Color, and then choose Edit > Fill.

6 In the Fill dialog box, choose Foreground Color from the Use menu, and click OK.

7 Choose Select > Deselect.

8 Double-click the Layer 1 name in the Layers panel, and rename the layer **Border.**

Flattening and saving files

When you finish editing all the layers in your image, you can merge or *flatten* layers to reduce the file size. Flattening combines all the layers into a single background layer. However, you cannot edit layers once you've flattened them, so you shouldn't flatten an image until you are certain that you're satisfied with all your design decisions. Rather than flattening your original PSD files, it's a good idea to save a copy of the file with its layers intact, in case you need to edit a layer later.

● **Note:** If the sizes do not appear in the status bar, click the status bar pop-up menu arrow and choose Show > Document Sizes.

To appreciate what flattening does, notice the two numbers for the file size in the status bar at the bottom of the image window. The first number represents what the file size would be if you flattened the image. The second number represents the file size without flattening. This lesson file, if flattened, would be about 2.29 MB, but the current file is actually much larger—about 27 MB. So flattening is well worth it in this case.

1 Select any tool but the Type tool (T), to be sure that you're not in text-editing mode. Then choose File > Save (if it is available) to be sure that all your changes have been saved in the file.

2 Choose Image > Duplicate.

3 In the Duplicate Image dialog box, name the file **04Flat.psd**, and click OK.

4 Leave the 04Flat.psd file open, but close the 04Working.psd file.

5 Choose Flatten Image from the Layers panel menu.

Only one layer, named Background, remains in the Layers panel.

▶ **Tip:** If you want to flatten only some of the layers in a file, click the eye icons to hide the layers you don't want to flatten, and then choose Merge Visible from the Layers panel menu.

6 Choose File > Save. Even though you chose Save rather than Save As, the Save As dialog box appears.

7 Make sure the location is the Lessons/Lesson04 folder, and then click Save to accept the default settings and save the flattened file.

You have saved two versions of the file: a one-layer, flattened copy as well as the original file, in which all the layers remain intact.

About layer comps

Layer comps provide one-click flexibility in switching between different views of a multilayered image file. A layer comp is simply a definition of the settings in the Layers panel. Once you've defined a layer comp, you can change as many settings as you please in the Layers panel and then create another layer comp to preserve that configuration of layer properties. Then, by switching from one layer comp to another, you can quickly review the two designs. The beauty of layer comps becomes apparent when you want to demonstrate a number of possible design arrangements. When you've created a few layer comps, you can review the design variations without having to tediously select and deselect eye icons or change settings in the Layers panel.

Say, for example, that you are designing a brochure, and you're producing a version in English as well as in French. You might have the French text on one layer, and the English text on another in the same image file. To create two different layer comps, you would simply turn on visibility for the French layer and turn off visibility for the English layer, and then click the Create New Layer Comp button on the Layer Comps panel. Then you'd do the inverse—turn on visibility for the English layer and turn off visibility for the French layer, and click the Create New Layer Comp button—to create an English layer comp.

To view the different layer comps, click the Apply Layer Comp box for each comp in the Layer Comps panel in turn. With a little imagination, you can appreciate how much time this saves for more complex variations. Layer comps can be an especially valuable feature when the design is in flux or when you need to create multiple versions of the same image file.

You've created a colorful, attractive postcard. This lesson only begins to explore the vast possibilities and the flexibility you gain when you master the art of using Photoshop layers. You'll get more experience and try out different techniques for layers in almost every chapter as you move forward in this book.

Extra credit

Take the blinking and bad poses out of an otherwise great family portrait with the Auto-Align Layers feature.

1 Open FamilyPhoto.psd in your Lesson04 folder.

2 In the Layers panel, turn Layer 2 on and off to see the two similar photos. When both layers are visible, Layer 2 shows the tall man in the center blinking, and the two girls in the front looking away.

You'll align the two photos, and then use the Eraser tool to brush out the parts of the photo on Layer 2 that you want to improve.

3 Make both layers visible, and Shift-click to select them. Choose Edit > Auto-Align Layers; click OK to accept the default Auto position. Toggle the eye icon next to Layer 2 off and on to see that the layers are perfectly aligned.

Now for the fun part! You'll brush out the photo where you want to improve it.

4 Select the Eraser tool in the Tools panel, and pick a soft, 45-pixel brush in the options bar. Select Layer 2, and start brushing in the center of the blinking man's head to reveal the smiling face below.

5 Use the Eraser tool on the two girls looking away,
revealing the image below, where they look into the camera.

You've created a natural family snapshot.

Review questions

1 What is the advantage of using layers?

2 When you create a new layer, where does it appear in the Layers panel stack?

3 How can you make artwork on one layer appear in front of artwork on another layer?

4 How can you apply a layer style?

5 When you've completed your artwork, what can you do to minimize the file size without changing the quality or dimensions?

Review answers

1 Layers let you move and edit different parts of an image as discrete objects. You can also hide individual layers as you work on other layers.

2 A new layer always appears immediately above the active layer.

3 You can make artwork on one layer appear in front of artwork on another layer by dragging layers up or down the stacking order in the Layers panel, or by using the Layer > Arrange subcommands—Bring To Front, Bring Forward, Send To Back, and Send Backward. However, you can't change the layer position of a background layer.

4 To apply a layer style, select the layer, and then click the Add A Layer Style button in the Layers panel, or choose Layer > Layer Style > [style].

5 To minimize file size, you can flatten the image, which merges all the layers onto a single background. It's a good idea to duplicate image files with layers intact before you flatten them, in case you have to make changes to a layer later.

5 CORRECTING AND ENHANCING DIGITAL PHOTOGRAPHS

Lesson overview

In this lesson, you'll learn how to do the following:

- Process a proprietary camera raw image and save your adjustments.

- Make typical corrections to a digital photograph, including removing red eye and noise and bringing out shadow and highlights detail.

- Apply optical lens correction to an image.

- Align and blend two images to extend the depth of field.

- Adopt best practices for organizing, managing, and saving your images.

- Merge images of different exposures to create a high dynamic range (HDR) image.

 This lesson will take about 1½ hours to complete. Copy the Lesson05 folder onto your hard drive if you haven't already done so. As you work on this lesson, you'll preserve the start files. If you need to restore the start files, copy them again from the *Adobe Photoshop CS6 Classroom in a Book* DVD.

Whether you have a collection of digital images amassed for clients or projects, or a personal collection that you want to refine, archive, and preserve for posterity, Photoshop has an array of tools for importing, editing, and archiving digital photographs.

Getting started

In this lesson, you'll edit several digital images using Photoshop and Adobe Camera Raw, which comes with Photoshop. You'll use a variety of techniques to touch up and improve the appearance of digital photographs. You'll start by viewing the before and after images in Adobe Bridge.

1 Start Photoshop, and then immediately hold down Ctrl+Alt+Shift (Windows) or Command+Option+Shift (Mac OS) to restore the default preferences. (See "Restoring default preferences" on page 4.)

2 When prompted, click Yes to delete the Adobe Photoshop Settings file.

3 Choose File > Browse In Bridge to open Adobe Bridge.

4 In the Favorites panel in Bridge, click the Lessons folder. Then, in the Content panel, double-click the Lesson05 folder to open it.

5 Adjust the thumbnail slider, if necessary, so that you can see the thumbnail previews clearly. Then look at the 05A_Start.crw and 05A_End.psd files.

05A_Start.crw   05A_End.psd

The original photograph of a Spanish-style church is a camera raw file, so it doesn't have the usual .psd file extension you've worked with so far in this book. It was shot with a Canon Digital Rebel camera and has the Canon proprietary .crw file extension instead. You'll process this proprietary camera raw image to make it brighter, sharper, and clearer, and then save it as a JPEG file for the web and as a PSD file so that you could work on it further in Photoshop.

6 Compare the 05B_Start.psd and 05B_End.psd thumbnail previews.

05B_Start.psd

05B_End.psd

You'll perform color corrections and image enhancements in Photoshop to achieve the end result.

7 Look at the 05C_Start.psd and 05C_End.psd thumbnail previews.

05C_Start.psd

05C_End.psd

You'll make several corrections to this portrait of a girl on the beach, including bringing out shadow and highlight detail, removing red eye, and sharpening the image.

8 Look at the 05D_Start.psd and 05D_End.psd thumbnail previews.

05D_Start.psd   05D_End.psd

The original image is distorted, with the columns appearing to be bowed. You'll correct the lens barrel distortion.

9 Look at the 05E_Start.psd and 05E_End.psd thumbnail previews.

05E_Start.psd   05E_End.psd

The first image has two layers. Depending on which layer is visible, either the glass in the foreground or the beach in the background is in focus. You'll extend the depth of field to make both clear. You'll also add posts and apply an iris blur to the glass.

About camera raw files

A *camera raw* file contains unprocessed picture data from a digital camera's image sensor. Many digital cameras can save images in camera raw format. The advantage of camera raw files is that they let the photographer—rather than the camera—interpret the image data and make adjustments and conversions. (In contrast, shooting JPEG images with your camera locks you into your camera's processing.) Because the camera doesn't do any image processing when you shoot a camera raw photo, you can use Adobe Camera Raw to set the white balance, tonal range, contrast, color saturation, and sharpening. Think of camera raw files as photo negatives. You can go back and reprocess the file any time you like to achieve the results you want.

To create camera raw files, set your digital camera to save files in its own, possibly proprietary, raw file format. When you download the file from your camera, it has a file extension such as .nef (from Nikon) or .crw (from Canon). In Bridge or Photoshop, you can process camera raw files from a myriad of supported digital cameras from Canon, Kodak, Leica, Nikon, and other makers—and even process multiple images simultaneously. You can then export the proprietary camera raw files to DNG, JPEG, TIFF, or PSD file format.

● **Note:** The Photoshop Raw format (.raw extension) is a file format for transferring images between applications and computer platforms. Don't confuse Photoshop Raw with camera raw file formats.

You can process camera raw files obtained from supported cameras, but you can also open TIFF and JPEG images in Camera Raw, which includes some editing features that aren't in Photoshop. However, you won't have the same flexibility with white balance and other settings if you're using a TIFF or JPEG image. Although Camera Raw can open and edit a camera raw image file, it cannot save an image in camera raw format.

You used Camera Raw to edit the color and lighting in an image in Lesson 2. In this exercise, you'll take advantage of more of its features.

Processing files in Camera Raw

When you make adjustments to an image in Camera Raw, such as straightening or cropping the image, Photoshop and Bridge preserve the original file data. This way, you can edit the image as you desire, export the edited image, and keep the original intact for future use or other adjustments.

Opening images in Camera Raw

You can open Camera Raw from either Bridge or Photoshop, and you can apply the same edits to multiple files simultaneously. This is especially useful if you're working with images that were all shot in the same environment, and which therefore need the same lighting and other adjustments.

Camera Raw provides extensive controls for adjusting white balance, exposure, contrast, sharpness, tone curves, and much more. In this exercise, you'll edit one image and then apply the settings to similar images.

1   In Bridge, open the Lessons/Lesson05/Mission folder, which contains three shots of the Spanish church you previewed earlier.

2   Shift-click to select all of the images—Mission01.crw, Mission02.crw, and Mission03.crw—and then choose File > Open In Camera Raw.

A. Filmstrip
B. Toggle Filmstrip
C. Toolbar
D. Toggle Full-Screen Mode
E. RGB values
F. Image adjustment tabs
G. Histogram
H. Camera Raw Settings menu
I. Zoom levels
J. Click to display workflow options
K. Multi-image navigation controls
L. Adjustment sliders

The Camera Raw dialog box displays a large preview of the first image, and a filmstrip down the left side displays all open images. The histogram in the upper right corner shows the tonal range of the selected image; the workflow options link below the preview window displays the selected image's color space, bit depth, size, and resolution. Tools along the top of the dialog box let you zoom, pan, straighten, and make other adjustments to the image. Tabbed panels on the right side of the dialog box give you more nuanced options for adjusting the image: You can correct the white balance, adjust the tone, sharpen the image, remove noise, adjust color, and make other changes. You can also save settings as a preset, and then apply them later.

For the best results using Camera Raw, plan your workflow to move from left to right and top to bottom. That is, you'll often want to use the tools across the top first, and then move through the panels in order, making changes as necessary.

You will explore these controls now as you edit the first image file.

3 Click each thumbnail in the filmstrip to preview all the images before you begin. Or, you can click the Forward button under the main preview window to cycle through them. When you've seen all three, select the Mission01.crw image again.

4 Make sure that Preview is selected at the top of the dialog box, so that you can see the effect of the adjustments you're about to make.

Adjusting white balance

An image's white balance reflects the lighting conditions under which it was captured. A digital camera records the white balance at the time of exposure; this is the value that initially appears in the Camera Raw dialog box image preview.

White balance comprises two components. The first is *temperature*, which is measured in kelvins and determines the level of "coolness" or "warmness" of the image—that is, its cool blue-green tones or warm yellow-red tones. The second component is *tint*, which compensates for magenta or green color casts in the image.

Depending on the settings you're using on your camera and the environment in which you're shooting (for example, if there's glare or uneven lighting), you may want to adjust the white balance for the image. If you plan to modify the white balance, make that the first thing you do, as it will affect all other changes in the image.

1 If the Basic panel isn't already displayed on the right side of the dialog box, click the Basic button (◉) to open it.

By default, As Shot is selected in the White Balance menu. Camera Raw applies the white balance settings that were in your camera at the time of exposure. Camera Raw includes several White Balance presets, which you can use as a starting point to see different lighting effects.

2 Choose Cloudy from the White Balance menu.

Camera Raw adjusts the temperature and tint for a cloudy day. Sometimes a preset does the trick. In this case, though, there's still a blue cast to the image. You'll adjust the white balance manually.

3 Select the White Balance tool (🖊) at the top of the Camera Raw dialog box.

To set an accurate white balance, select an object that should be white or gray. Camera Raw uses that information to determine the color of the light in which the scene was shot, and then adjusts for scene lighting automatically.

4 Click the white clouds in the image. The lighting of the image changes.

5 Click a different area of the clouds. The lighting shifts.

You can use the White Balance tool to find the best lighting for the scene quickly and easily. Clicking different areas changes the lighting without making any permanent changes to the file, so you can experiment freely.

6 Click the clouds directly to the left of the steeple. This selection removes most of the color casts and results in realistic lighting.

7 Move the Tint slider to **-22** to intensify the greens.

▶ **Tip:** To undo the settings, press Ctrl+Z (Windows) or Command+Z (Mac OS). To compare the changes you've made in the current panel with the original image, deselect Preview. Select Preview again to see the modified image.

Making tonal adjustments in Camera Raw

Other sliders in the Basic panel affect exposure, brightness, contrast, and saturation in the image. Except for Contrast, moving a slider to the right lightens the affected areas of the image, and moving it to the left darkens those areas. Exposure essentially defines the *white point*, or the lightest point of the image, so that Camera Raw adjusts everything else accordingly. Conversely, the Blacks slider sets the *black point*, or the darkest point in the image. The Highlights and Shadows sliders increase detail in the highlights and the shadows, respectively.

The Contrast slider adjusts the contrast. For more nuanced contrast adjustments, you can use the Clarity slider, which adds depth to an image by increasing local contrast, especially on the midtones.

The Saturation slider adjusts the saturation of all colors in the image equally. The Vibrance slider, on the other hand, has a greater effect on undersaturated colors, so you can bring life to a background without oversaturating skin tones, for example.

You can use the Auto option to let Camera Raw attempt to correct the image tone, or you can select your own settings.

▶ **Tip:** For the best effect, increase the Clarity slider until you see halos near the edge details, and then reduce the setting slightly.

1 Click Auto in the Basic panel.

Camera Raw increases the exposure and changes several other settings. You could use this as a starting point. However, in this exercise, you'll return to the default settings and adjust them yourself.

2 Click Default in the Basic panel.

3 Change the sliders as follows:

- Leave Exposure at 0.00.
- Increase Contrast to **18**.
- Leave Highlights at 0.00.
- Increase Shadows to **+63**.
- Decrease Whites to **-2**.
- Decrease Blacks to **-18**.
- Increase Clarity to **+3**.
- Increase Vibrance to **+4**.
- Decrease Saturation to **-3**.

These settings help pump up the midtones of the image, so that it looks bolder and more dimensional without being oversaturated.

About the Camera Raw histogram

The histogram in the upper right corner of the Camera Raw dialog box simultaneously shows the red, green, and blue channels of the selected image, and updates interactively as you adjust any settings. Also, as you move any tool over the preview image, the RGB values for the area under the cursor appear below the histogram.

Applying sharpening

Photoshop offers several sharpening filters, but when you need to sharpen an entire image, Camera Raw provides the best control. The sharpening controls are in the Detail panel. To see the effect of sharpening in the preview panel, you must view the image at 100% or greater.

1　Double-click the Zoom tool (🔍) on the left side of the toolbar to zoom in to 100%. Then select the Hand tool (✋), and pan the image to see the cross at the top of the mission tower.

2　Click the Detail tab (◢) to open the Detail panel.

The Amount slider determines how much sharpening Camera Raw applies. Typically, you'll want to exaggerate the amount of sharpening first, and then adjust it after you've set the other sliders.

3　Move the Amount slider to **100**.

The Radius slider determines the pixel area Camera Raw analyzes as it sharpens the image. For most images, you'll get the best results if you keep the radius low, even below one pixel, as a larger radius can begin to cause an unnatural look, almost like a watercolor.

4　Move the Radius slider to **0.9**.

The Detail slider determines how much detail you'll see. Even when this slider is set to 0, Camera Raw performs some sharpening. Typically, you'll want to keep the Detail setting relatively low.

▶ **Tip:** If you want to make an adjustment to only a specific part of an image, use the Adjustment Brush tool or the Graduated Filter tool. With the Adjustment Brush tool, you can apply Exposure, Highlights, Clarity, and other adjustments by "painting" them onto the photo. With the Graduated Filter tool, you can apply the same types of adjustments gradually across a region of a photo.

5 Move the Detail slider to **25**, if it isn't already there.

The Masking slider determines which parts of the image Camera Raw sharpens. When the Masking value is high, Camera Raw sharpens only those parts of the image that have strong edges.

▶ **Tip:** Press Alt (Windows) or Option (Mac OS) as you move the Masking slider to see what Camera Raw will sharpen.

6 Move the Masking slider to **61**.

After you've adjusted the Radius, Detail, and Masking sliders, you can lower the Amount slider to finalize the sharpening.

7 Decrease the Amount slider to **70**.

● **Note:** If you zoom out, the image won't appear to be sharpened. You can preview sharpening effects only at zoom levels of 100% or greater.

Sharpening the image gives stronger definition to the details and edges. The Masking slider lets you target the sharpening effect to the lines in the image, so that artifacts don't appear in unfocused or background areas.

When you make adjustments in Camera Raw, the original file data is preserved. Your adjustment settings for the image are stored either in the Camera Raw database file or in "sidecar" XMP files that accompany the original image file in the same folder. These XMP files retain the adjustments you made in Camera Raw when you move the image file to a storage medium or another computer.

Synchronizing settings across images

All three of the mission images were shot at the same time under the same lighting conditions. Now that you've made the first one look stunning, you can automatically apply the same settings to the other two images. You do this using the Synchronize command.

1 In the upper left corner of the Camera Raw dialog box, click Select All to select all of the images in the filmstrip.

2 Click the Synchronize button.

The Synchronize dialog box appears, listing all the settings you can apply to the images. By default, all options except Crop, Spot Removal, and Local Adjustments are selected. You can accept the default for this project, even though you didn't change all the settings.

3 Click OK in the Synchronize dialog box.

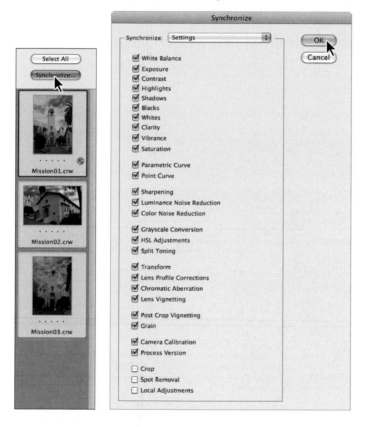

When you synchronize the settings across all of the selected images, the thumbnails update to reflect the changes you made. To preview the images, click each thumbnail in the filmstrip.

Saving Camera Raw changes

You can save your changes in different ways for different purposes. First, you'll save the images with adjustments as low-resolution JPEG files that you can share on the web. Then, you'll save one image, Mission01, as a Photoshop file that you can open as a Smart Object in Photoshop. When you open an image as a Smart Object in Photoshop, you can return to Camera Raw at any time to make further adjustments.

1 Click Select All in the Camera Raw dialog box to select all three images.

2 Click Save Images in the lower left corner.

3 In the Save Options dialog box, do the following:

   • Choose Save In Same Location from the Destination menu.

   • In the File Naming area, leave "Document Name" in the first box.

   • Choose JPEG from the Format menu.

These settings will save your corrected images as smaller, downsampled JPEG files, which you can share with colleagues on the web. Your files will be named Mission01.jpg, Mission02.jpg, and Mission03.jpg.

4 Click Save.

● **Note:** Before sharing these images on the web, you would probably want to open them in Photoshop and resize them to 640 x 480 pixels. They are currently much larger, and most viewers would need to scroll to see the full-size images.

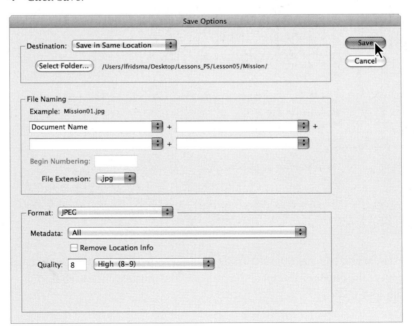

Bridge returns you to the Camera Raw dialog box, and indicates how many images have been processed until all the images have been saved. The CRW thumbnails still appear in the Camera Raw dialog box. In Bridge, however, you now also have JPEG versions as well as the original CRW image files, which you can continue to edit or leave for another time.

Now, you'll open a copy of the Mission01 image in Photoshop.

5   Select the Mission01.crw image thumbnail in the filmstrip in the Camera Raw dialog box. Then press the Shift key, and click Open Object at the bottom of the dialog box.

The Open Object button opens the image as a Smart Object in Photoshop, and you can return to Camera Raw to continue making adjustments at any time. If you click Open Image, the image opens as a standard Photoshop image. Pressing the Shift key changes the Open Image button to the Open Object button.

6   In Photoshop, choose File > Save As. In the Save As dialog box, choose Photoshop for the Format, rename the file **Mission_Final.psd**, navigate to the Lesson05 folder, and click Save. Click OK if the Photoshop Format Options dialog box appears. Then close the file.

▶ **Tip:** To make the Open Object button the default, click the workflow options link (In blue) below the preview window, select Open In Photoshop As Smart Objects, and click OK.

About saving files in Camera Raw

Every camera model saves raw images in a unique format, but Adobe Camera Raw can process many raw file formats. Camera Raw processes the raw files with default image settings based on built-in camera profiles for supported cameras and the EXIF data.

You can save the proprietary files in DNG format (the format saved by Adobe Camera Raw), JPEG, TIFF, and PSD. All of these formats can be used to save RGB and CMYK continuous-tone, bitmapped images, and all of them except DNG are also available in the Photoshop Save and Save As dialog boxes.

- The **DNG (Adobe Digital Negative)** format contains raw image data from a digital camera and metadata that defines what the image data means. DNG is meant to be an industry-wide standard format for raw image data, helping photographers manage the variety of proprietary raw formats and providing a compatible archival format. (You can save this format only from the Camera Raw dialog box.)

- The **JPEG (Joint Photographic Experts Group**) file format is commonly used to display photographs and other continuous-tone RGB images on the web. Higher-resolution JPEG files may be used for other purposes, including high-quality printing. JPEG format retains all color information in an image, but compresses file size by selectively discarding data. The greater the compression, the lower the image quality.

- **TIFF (Tagged Image File Format)** is used to exchange files between applications and computer platforms. TIFF is a flexible format supported by virtually all paint, image-editing, and page layout applications. Also, virtually all desktop scanners can produce TIFF images.

- **PSD format** is the Photoshop native file format. Because of the tight integration between Adobe products, other Adobe applications such as Adobe Illustrator and Adobe InDesign can directly import PSD files and preserve many Photoshop features.

Once you open a file in Photoshop, you can save it in many different formats, including Large Document Format (PSB), Cineon, Photoshop Raw, or PNG. Not to be confused with camera raw file formats, the Photoshop Raw format (RAW) is a file format for transferring images between applications and computer platforms.

For more information about file formats in Camera Raw and Photoshop, see Photoshop Help.

Applying advanced color correction

You'll use Levels, the Healing Brush tool, and other Photoshop features to enhance the image of this model.

Adjusting levels

The tonal range of an image represents the amount of contrast, or detail, in the image and is determined by the image's distribution of pixels, ranging from the darkest pixels (black) to the lightest pixels (white). You'll use a Levels adjustment layer to fine-tune the tonal range in this image.

1   In Photoshop, choose File > Open. Navigate to the Lesson05 folder, and double-click the 05B_Start.psd file to open it.

2   Choose File > Save As. Name the file **Model_final.psd**, and click Save. Click OK if you see the Photoshop Format Options dialog box.

3   Click the Levels button in the Adjustments panel.

Photoshop adds a Levels adjustment layer to the Layers panel. The Levels controls and a histogram appear in the Adjustments panel. The histogram displays the range of dark and light values in the image. The left (black) triangle represents the shadows; the right (white) triangle represents the highlights; and the middle (gray) triangle represents the midtones, or gamma. Unless you're aiming for a special effect, the ideal histogram has its black point at the beginning of the data and its white point at the end of the data, and the middle portion has fairly uniform peaks and valleys, representing adequate pixel data in the midtones.

4 Click the Calculate A More Accurate Histogram button () on the left side of the histogram. Photoshop replaces the histogram.

There is a single line on the far left side of the histogram, representing the current black point, but the bulk of the data begins further to the right. You want to set the black point to match the beginning of that data.

5 Drag the left (black) triangle toward the right to the point where the histogram indicates the darkest colors begin.

As you drag, the first Input Levels value (beneath the histogram graph) changes, and so does the image itself.

6 Pull the middle (gray) triangle a little bit to the left to slightly lighten the midtones. We moved it to a value of 1.18.

Using the Healing Brush tools to remove blemishes

Now you're ready to give the model's face some focused attention. You'll use the Healing Brush and Spot Healing Brush tools to heal blemishes and freckles, remove red veins from the eyes, and clear hair from the face.

1 In the Layers panel, select the Background layer. Then, choose Duplicate Layer from the Layers panel menu. Name the layer **Corrections**, and click OK.

Working on a duplicate layer preserves the original pixels so you can make changes later.

2 Zoom in on the model's face so that you can see it clearly—to at least 100%.

3 Select the Spot Healing Brush tool (🖌).

4 In the options bar, select the following settings:

- Brush size: 7 px

- Mode: Normal

- Type: Content-Aware

5 With the Spot Healing Brush tool, brush out the hair across the face. Because you've selected Content-Aware in the options bar, the Spot Healing Brush tool replaces the hair with skin that is similar to that around it.

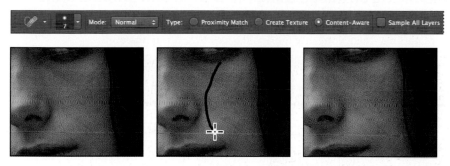

6 Paint over fine lines around the eyes and mouth. You can also brush away the red veins in the model's eyes, and freckles and spots on her face. Experiment with simply clicking, using very short strokes, and creating longer brush strokes. Remove obtrusive or distracting lines and blemishes, but leave enough that the face retains its character.

Now you'll use the Healing Brush tool to remove the darker makeup smudges under the model's eyes.

7   Select the Healing Brush tool (🖌), hidden under the Spot Healing Brush tool (🖌). Select a brush with a size of **19** pixels and a hardness of **50**%.

8   Alt-click (Windows) or Option-click (Mac OS) an area just below the dark areas beneath her eyes to create the sampling source.

9   Brush beneath her eyes to remove the dark makeup. You're changing the color now. You'll smooth out the texture later.

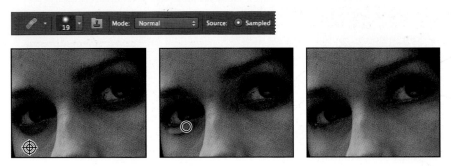

10 Choose File > Save to save your work so far.

Enhancing an image using the Dodge and Sponge tools

You'll use the Dodge tool to further lighten the color under the eyes so that it looks more natural. Then, you'll use the Sponge tool to saturate the eyes.

1   With the Corrections layer still active, select the Dodge tool (🔍).

2   In the options bar, change the brush size to **65** px and the Exposure to **30**%. Make sure Midtones is selected in the Range menu.

3   Brush the Dodge tool over the shadows under the eyes to lighten them.

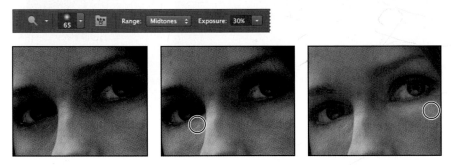

4 Select the Sponge tool (⬤), hidden under the Dodge tool. In the options bar, make sure Vibrance is selected, and then select the following settings:

- Brush size: **35** px
- Brush hardness: **0**%
- Mode: Saturate
- Flow: **50**%

5 Move the Sponge tool over the irises in the eyes to increase their saturation.

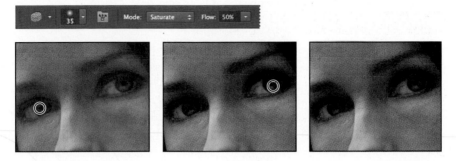

6 Select the Dodge tool again, and select Shadows from the Range menu in the options bar.

7 Use the Dodge tool to lighten the shadow area above the eyes and the areas around the irises to bring out the color.

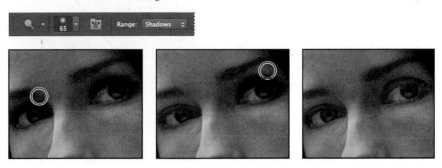

Adjusting skin tones

In Photoshop CS6 you can select a color range that targets skin tones so that it's easier to adjust the levels and color tone of skin without affecting the entire image. The skin tone color range selects other areas of the image with a similar color, but if you're making slight adjustments, this is usually acceptable.

1 Choose Select > Color Range.

2 In the Color Range dialog box, choose Skin Tones from the Select menu.

The preview shows that much of the image has been selected.

3 Select Detect Faces.

The preview in the selection changes. Now, the face, hair highlights and lighter areas of the background are selected, as well as some creases in the sleeve.

4 Decrease the Fuzziness slider to **28**. Then click OK.

The selection appears on the image itself as marching ants. You'll apply a Curves adjustment layer to the selection to lighten those areas of the image.

5 Click the Curves icon in the Adjustments panel.

Photoshop adds a Curves adjustment layer above the Corrections layer.

6 Click in the middle of the graph, and pull the curve slightly up. The selected areas lighten. The adjustment affects more of the image than the skin tones, but the effect blends well and is subtle.

A photographer for more than 25 years, Jay Graham began his career designing and building custom homes. Today, Graham has clients in the advertising, architectural, editorial, and travel industries.

See Jay Graham's portfolio on the web at jaygraham.com.

Pro photo workflow

Good habits make all the difference

A sensible workflow and good work habits will keep you enthused about digital photography, help your images shine—and save you from the night terrors of losing work you never backed up. Here's an outline of the basic workflow for digital images from a professional photographer with more than 25 years' experience. To help you get the most from the images you shoot, Jay Graham offers guidelines for setting up your camera, creating a basic color workflow, selecting file formats, organizing images, and showing off your work.

Graham uses Adobe Photoshop Lightroom® to organize thousands of images.

"The biggest complaint from people is they've lost their image. Where is it? What does it look like?" says Graham. "So naming is important."

Start out right by setting up your camera preferences

If your camera has the option, it's generally best to shoot in its camera raw file format, which captures all the image information you need. With one camera raw photo, says Graham, "You can go from daylight to an indoor tungsten image without degradation" when it's reproduced. If it makes more sense to shoot in JPEG for your project, use fine compression and high resolution.

Start with the best material

Get all the data when you capture—at fine compression and high resolution. You can't go back later.

Organize your files

Name and catalogue your images as soon after downloading them as possible. "If the camera names files, eventually it resets and produces multiple files with the same name," says Graham. Use Adobe Photoshop Lightroom to rename, rank, and add metadata to the photos you plan to keep; cull those you don't.

Graham names his files by date (and possibly subject). He would store a series of photos taken Dec. 12, 2011 at Stinson Beach in a folder named "20111212_Stinson_01"; within the folder, he names each image incrementally, and each image has a unique filename. "That way, it lines up on the hard drive real easily," he says. Follow Windows naming conventions to keep filenames usable on non-Macintosh platforms (32 characters maximum; only numbers, letters, underscores, and hyphens).

Convert raw images to Adobe Camera Raw

It may be best to convert all your camera raw Images to the DNG format. Unlike many cameras' proprietary raw formats, this open-source format can be read by any device.

Keep a master image

Save your master in PSD, TIFF, or DNG format, not in JPEG. Each time a JPEG is re-edited and saved, compression is reapplied and the image quality degrades.

Show off to clients and friends

When you prepare your work for delivery, choose the appropriate color file for the destination. Convert the image to that profile, rather than assigning the profile. sRGB is generally best for viewing electronically or for printing from most onllne prlntlng services. Adobe 1998 or Colormatch are the best profiles to use for RGB images destined for traditionally printed material such as brochures. Adobe 1998 or ProPhoto RGB are best for printing with inkjet printers. Use 72 dpi for electronic viewing and 180 dpi or higher for printing.

Back up your images

You've devoted a lot of time and effort to your images: don't lose them. Because the lifespan of CDs and DVDs is uncertain, it's best to back up to an external hard drive (or drives!), ideally set to back up automatically. "The question is not if your [internal] hard drive is going to crash," says Graham, reciting a common adage. "It's when."

Applying surface blur

You're almost done with the model. As a finishing touch, you'll apply the Surface Blur filter to give her a smooth appearance.

1 Select the Corrections layer, and choose Layer > Duplicate Layer. Name the layer **Surface Blur**, and click OK in the Duplicate Layer dialog box.

2 Move the Surface Blur layer between the Curves 1 and Levels 1 layers in the Layers panel.

3 With the Surface Blur layer selected, choose Filter > Blur > Surface Blur.

4 In the Surface Blur dialog box, leave the Radius at 5 pixels, and move the Threshold to **10** levels. Then click OK.

The Surface Blur filter has left the model looking a little glassy. You'll reduce its effect by reducing its opacity.

5 With the Surface Blur layer selected, change the Opacity to **30%** in the Layers panel.

She looks more realistic now, but you can target the surface blur more precisely using the Eraser tool.

6 Select the Eraser tool (). In the options bar, select a midsized brush between **10** and **50** pixels, with **10%** hardness. Set the opacity to **90%**.

7 Brush over the eyes, eyebrows, the defining lines of the nose, and the teeth. You're erasing part of the blurred layer to let the sharper layer below show through in these areas.

8 Zoom out so you can see the entire image.

9 Increase the brush size to 400 pixels, and then lightly sweep across the background, the shirt, and the hair to bring those areas back to their full sharpness. Now only the model's face has the surface blur.

10 Save your work, and close the image.

Correcting digital photographs in Photoshop

As you've seen, Photoshop provides many features to help you easily improve the quality of digital photographs. These include the ability to bring out details in the shadow and highlight areas of an image, gracefully remove red eye, reduce unwanted noise, and sharpen targeted areas of an image. To explore these capabilities, you will edit a different digital image now: a portrait of a girl on the beach.

Adjusting shadows and highlights

To bring out the detail in dark or light areas of an image, you can use the Shadows/Highlights command. Shadows/Highlights adjustments work best when the subject of the image is silhouetted against strong backlighting or is washed out because the camera flash was too close. You can also use the adjustments to pull details from the shadows in an image that is otherwise well-lit.

1 Choose File > Browse In Bridge. In the Favorites panel in Bridge, click the Lessons folder. In the Content panel, double-click the Lesson05 folder. Then double-click the 05C_Start.psd image to open it in Photoshop.

2 Choose File > Save As. Name the file **05C_Working.psd**, and click Save.

3 Choose Image > Adjustments > Shadows/Highlights. Photoshop automatically applies default settings to the image, lightening the background. You'll customize the settings to bring out more detail in both the shadows and the highlights, and to enhance the sunset.

4 In the Shadows/Highlights dialog box, select Show More Options to expand the dialog box. Then do the following:

- In the Shadows area, set Amount to **50**%, Tonal Width to **50**%, and Radius to **38** px.

- In the Highlights area, set Amount to **14**%, Tonal Width to **46**%, and Radius to **43** px.

- In the Adjustments area, drag the Color Correction slider to **+5**, set the Midtone Contrast slider to **+22**, and leave the Black Clip and White Clip settings at their defaults.

5 Click OK to accept your changes.

6 Choose File > Save to save your work so far.

Correcting red eye

Red eye occurs when the retina of a subject's eye is reflected by the camera flash. It commonly occurs in photographs of a subject in a darkened room, because the subject's irises are wide open. Red eye is easy to fix in Photoshop. In this exercise, you will remove the red eye from the girl's eyes in the portrait.

1   Select the Zoom tool (🔍), and then drag a marquee around the girl's eyes to zoom in to them. You may need to deselect Scrubby Zoom in the options bar to drag a marquee.

2   Select the Red Eye tool (⁺◉), hidden under the Healing Brush tool (✐).

3   In the options bar, leave Pupil Size set to 50%, but change Darken Amount to **74%**. The Darken Amount specifies how dark the pupil should be.

4   Click on the red area in the girl's left eye. The red reflection disappears.

5   Click on the red area in the girl's right eye to remove that reflection, as well.

6   Double-click the Zoom tool to zoom out to 100%.

7   Choose File > Save to save your work so far.

Reducing noise

Random, extraneous pixels that aren't part of the image detail are called *noise*. Noise can result from using a high ISO setting on a digital camera, from underexposure, or from shooting in darkness with a long shutter speed. Scanned images may contain noise that results from the scanning sensor, or from a grain pattern from the scanned film.

There are two types of image noise: *luminance noise*, which is grayscale data that makes an image look grainy or patchy; and *color noise*, which appears as colored artifacts in the image. The Reduce Noise filter can address both types of noise in individual color channels while preserving edge detail, and can also correct JPEG compression artifacts.

First, zoom in to the girl's face to get a good look at the noise in this image.

1   Using the Zoom tool (🔍), click in the center of the face and zoom in to about 300%.

The noise in this image is speckled and rough, with uneven graininess in the skin. Using the Reduce Noise filter, you can smooth out this area.

2   Choose Filter > Noise > Reduce Noise.

3   In the Reduce Noise dialog box, do the following:

   •   Increase Strength to **8**. (Strength controls the amount of luminance noise.)

   •   Decrease Preserve Details to **30**%.

   •   Increase Reduce Color Noise to **80**%.

   •   Move Sharpen Details to **30**%.

● **Note:** To correct noise in individual channels of the image, select Advanced and click the Per Channel tab to adjust the settings in each channel.

You don't need to select Remove JPEG Artifact, because this image is not a JPEG and has no JPEG artifacts.

4   Drag to position the face in the preview area. Click and hold the mouse button down in the preview area to see the "before" image, and release the mouse button to see the corrected result.

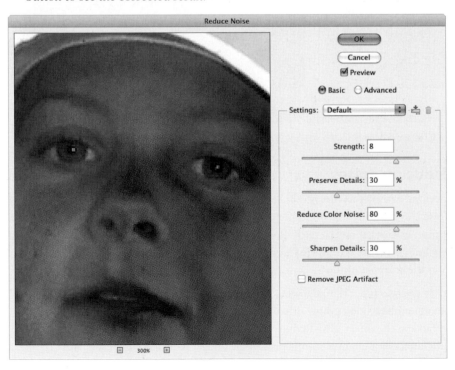

5 Click OK to apply your changes and to close the Reduce Noise dialog box, and then double-click the Zoom tool to return to 100%.

6 Choose File > Save to save your work, and then close the file.

Correcting image distortion

The Lens Correction filter fixes common camera lens flaws, such as barrel and pincushion distortion, chromatic aberration, and vignetting. *Barrel distortion* is a lens defect that causes straight lines to bow out toward the edges of the image. *Pincushion distortion* is the opposite effect, causing straight lines to bend inward. *Chromatic aberration* appears as a color fringe along the edges of image objects. *Vignetting* occurs when the edges of an image, especially the corners, are darker than the center.

Some lenses exhibit these defects depending on the focal length or the f-stop used. The Lens Correction filter can apply settings based on the camera, lens, and focal length that were used to make the image. The filter can also rotate an image or fix image perspective caused by tilting a camera vertically or horizontally. The filter's image grid makes it easier and more accurate to make these adjustments than using the Transform command.

In this exercise, you will adjust the lens distortion in an image of a Greek temple.

1 Choose File > Browse In Bridge. In Bridge, navigate to the Lesson05 folder. Double-click the 05D_Start.psd image to open it in Photoshop.

The columns in this image bend toward the camera and appear to be warped. This photo was shot at a range that was too close with a wide-angle lens.

2 Choose File > Save As. In the Save As dialog box, name the file **Columns_Final.psd**, and save it in the Lesson05 folder. Click OK if the Photoshop Format Options dialog box appears.

3 Choose Filter > Lens Correction. The Lens Correction dialog box opens.

4 Select Show Grid at the bottom of the dialog box, if it's not already selected. An alignment grid overlays the image, next to options for removing distortion, correcting chromatic aberration, removing vignettes, and transforming perspective.

The Lens Correction dialog box includes auto-correction options. You'll adjust one setting in the Auto Correction tab and then customize the settings.

5 In the Correction area of the Auto Correction tab, make sure Auto Scale Image is selected, and that Transparency is selected from the Edge menu.

6 Select the Custom tab.

7 In the Custom tab, drag the Remove Distortion slider to about **+52.00** to remove the barrel distortion in the image. Alternatively, you could select the Remove Distortion tool (▦) and drag in the image preview area until the columns are straight.

The adjustment causes the image borders to bow inward. However, because you selected Auto Scale Image, the Lens Correction filter automatically scales the image to adjust the borders.

▶ **Tip:** Watch the alignment grid as you make these changes so that you can see when the vertical columns are straightened in the image.

8 Click OK to apply your changes and close the Lens Correction dialog box.

The curving distortion caused by the wide-angle lens and low shooting angle are eliminated.

9 (Optional) To see the effect of your change in the main image window, press Ctrl+Z (Windows) or Command+Z (Mac OS) twice to undo and redo the filter.

10 Choose File > Save to save your changes, and then close the image.

Adding depth of field

When you're shooting a photo, you often have to choose to focus either the background or the foreground. If you want the entire image to be in focus, take two photos—one with the background in focus and one with the foreground in focus—and then merge the two in Photoshop.

Because you'll need to align the images exactly, it's helpful to use a tripod to keep the camera steady. Even with a handheld camera, though, you can get some amazing results. You'll add depth of field to an image of a wine glass in front of a beach.

1 In Photoshop, choose File > Open. Navigate to the Lessons/Lesson05 folder, and double-click the 05E_Start.psd file to open it.

2 Choose File > Save As. Name the file **Glass_Final.psd**, and save it in the Lesson05 folder. Click OK if the Photoshop Format Options dialog box appears.

3 In the Layers panel, hide the Beach layer, so that only the Glass layer is visible. The glass is in focus, but the background is blurred. Then, show the Beach layer and hide the Glass layer. Now the beach is in focus, but the glass is blurred.

You'll merge the layers, using the part of each layer that is in focus. First, you need to align the layers.

4 Show both layers again, and then Shift-click to select both of them.

5 Choose Edit > Auto-Align Layers.

Because these images were shot from the same angle, Auto will work just fine.

6 Select Auto, if it isn't already selected. Make sure neither Vignette Removal nor Geometric Distortion is selected. Then click OK to align the layers.

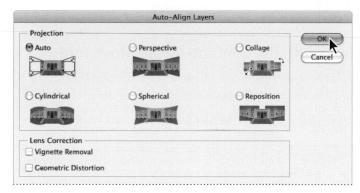

Now that the layers are perfectly aligned, you're ready to blend them.

7 Make sure both layers are still selected in the Layers panel. Then choose Edit > Auto-Blend Layers.

8 Select Stack Images and Seamless Tones And Colors, and then click OK.

Both the wine glass and the beach behind it are in focus. Now, you'll merge the layers to make it easier to make other adjustments.

9 Choose Layer > Merge Visible.

Extending objects with the Content-Aware Move tool

You'll use the new Content-Aware Move tool to add a few more posts to the beach, so that they echo the deck rails, creating a smoother rhythm for the composition.

1 Select the Content-Aware Move tool (✖), which is hidden beneath the Red Eye Removal tool (⁺☉).

2 In the options bar, choose Extend from the Mode menu and Strict from the Adaptation menu.

3 Draw a marquee around the two pier posts on the end of the row, including some of the sand where their shadows fall.

4 Drag the selection slightly down and to the right of the original posts to continue the row.

When you release the mouse, Photoshop adds two new posts and blends them in with the scene neatly.

5 Choose Select > Deselect.

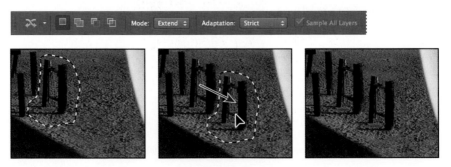

Adding interactive blur

Photoshop CS6 introduces interactive blurs, which let you customize the blur as you preview it on your image. You'll apply an iris blur to add a vignette around the glass.

1 Choose Filter > Blur > Iris Blur.

A blur ellipse is centered on your image. You can adjust the location and scope of the blur by moving the center pin, feather handles, and ellipse handles. Photoshop also opens the Blur Tools and Blur Effects panels.

2 Drag the center pin so that it's on the right side of the wine glass.

3 Click the ellipse and drag to enlarge the scope of the blur.

4 Press Alt (Windows) or Option (Mac OS) as you click and drag the feather handles to match those in the second image below.

A. Center Pin **B.** Ellipse **C.** Feather handle **D.** Focus Ring

5 Click and drag next to the focus ring to reduce the amount of blur to **6** px, creating a gradual but noticeable blur. You can also change the amount of blur by moving the Blur slider in the Iris Blur area of the Blur Tools panel.

6 Click OK in the options bar to apply the blur.

The image looks great. You're almost done. You'll just add a Vibrance adjustment layer to give the image a little extra punch.

7 Click the Vibrance button in the Adjustments panel.

8 Move the Vibrance slider to **+33**, and then move the Saturation slider to **-5**.

 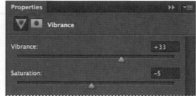

The Vibrance adjustment layer affects all the layers beneath it.

9 Choose File > Save to save your work. Then close the file.

You've enhanced five images, using different techniques to adjust lighting and tone, remove red eye, correct lens distortion, add depth of field, and more. You can use these techniques separately or together on your own images.

Extra credit

High dynamic range (HDR) images

When you look at the world, your eyes adapt to different brightness levels so that you can see the detail in shadows or highlights. Cameras and computer monitors, however, are more limited in the dynamic range (the ratio between dark and bright regions) they can reproduce. The ability to create high dynamic range (HDR) images in Photoshop lets you bring the brightness you can see in the real world into your images. HDR images are used mostly in movies, special effects, and other high-end photography. However, you can create an HDR image using multiple photographs, each captured at a different exposure, to bring the detail revealed in each shot into a single image.

You'll use the Merge To HDR Pro filter to combine three photos of a streetscape.

1   In Bridge, open the Lesson05/HDR_ExtraCredit folder, and view the StreetA.jpg, StreetB.jpg, and StreetC.jpg files. These images are of the same scene, shot at different exposures. Though we're using JPEG images, you could use raw images, too.

2   In Photoshop, choose File > Automate > Merge To HDR Pro.

3   In the Merge To HDR Pro dialog box, click Browse. Then navigate to the Lesson05/HDR_ ExtraCredit folder, and Shift-select the StreetA.jpg, StreetB.jpg, and StreetC.jpg files. Click OK or Open.

4   Make sure Attempt To Automatically Align Source Images is selected, and then click OK.

Photoshop opens each of the files briefly and merges them into a single image. That image appears in the Merge To HDR Pro dialog box, with default settings applied. The three images you merged are shown in the lower left corner of the dialog box.

(continues on next page)

Extra Credit (continued)

5   Adjust the following settings in the Merge To HDR Pro dialog box:

- In the Edge Glow area, move the Radius slider to **403** px and the Strength to **0.75**. These settings determine how a glow effect is applied.

- In the Tone And Detail area, change the Gamma to **1.15**, Exposure to **0.30**, and Detail to **300**%. Each of these settings affects the overall tone of the image.

- In the Advanced area, change the Shadow to **2**% and Highlight to **11**% to specify how much detail is revealed in shadows and highlights. Change the Vibrance to **65**% and the Saturation to **55**% to adjust the color intensity.

6   Click OK to accept the changes and close the Merge To HDR Pro dialog box. Photoshop merges the layers into a single layer as it applies the settings you chose.

7   Choose File > Save. Save the file as **ExtraCredit_final.psd.**

Review questions

1 What happens to camera raw images when you edit them in Camera Raw?

2 What is the advantage of the Adobe Digital Negative (DNG) file format?

3 How do you correct red eye in Photoshop?

4 Describe how to fix common camera lens flaws in Photoshop. What causes these defects?

Review answers

1 A camera raw file contains unprocessed picture data from a digital camera's image sensor. Camera raw files give photographers control over interpreting the image data, rather than letting the camera make the adjustments and conversions. When you edit the image in Camera Raw, it preserves the original raw file data. This way, you can edit the image as you desire, export it, and keep the original intact for future use or other adjustments.

2 The Adobe Digital Negative (DNG) file format contains the raw image data from a digital camera as well as metadata that defines what the image data means. DNG is an industry-wide standard for camera raw image data that helps photographers manage proprietary camera raw file formats and provides a compatible archival format.

3 Red eye occurs when the retinas of a subject's eyes are reflected by the camera flash. To correct red eye in Adobe Photoshop, zoom in to the subject's eyes, select the Red Eye tool, and then click the red eyes.

4 The Lens Correction filter fixes common camera lens flaws, such as barrel and pincushion distortion, in which straight lines bow out towards the edges of the image (barrel) or bend inward (pincushion); chromatic aberration, where a color fringe appears along the edges of image objects; and vignetting at the edges of an image, especially corners, that are darker than the center. Defects can occur from incorrectly setting the lens's focal length or f-stop, or by tilting the camera vertically or horizontally.

6 MASKS AND CHANNELS

Lesson overview

In this lesson, you'll learn how to do the following:

- Create a mask to remove a subject from a background.

- Refine a mask to include complex edges.

- Create a quick mask to make changes to a selected area.

- Edit a mask using the Properties panel.

- Manipulate an image using Puppet Warp.

- Save a selection as an alpha channel.

- View a mask using the Channels panel.

- Load a channel as a selection.

- Isolate a channel to make specific image changes.

This lesson will take about an hour to complete. Copy the Lesson06 folder onto your hard drive if you haven't already done so. As you work on this lesson, you'll preserve the start files. If you need to restore the start files, copy them from the *Adobe Photoshop CS6 Classroom in a Book* DVD.

Use masks to isolate and manipulate specific parts
of an image. The cutout portion of a mask can be
altered, but the area surrounding the cutout is protected from change. You can create a temporary mask
to use once, or you can save masks for repeated use.

Working with masks and channels

Photoshop masks isolate and protect parts of an image, just as masking tape protects window panes or trim from paint when a house is painted. When you create a mask based on a selection, the area you haven't selected is *masked,* or protected from editing. With masks, you can create and save time-consuming selections and then use them again. In addition, you can use masks for other complex editing tasks—for example, to apply color changes or filter effects to an image.

In Photoshop, you can make temporary masks, called *quick masks,* or you can create permanent masks and store them as special grayscale channels called *alpha channels.* Photoshop also uses channels to store an image's color information. Unlike layers, channels do not print. You use the Channels panel to view and work with alpha channels.

A key concept in masking is that black hides and white reveals. As in life, rarely is anything black and white. Shades of gray partially hide, depending on the gray levels (255 is the value for black, hiding artwork completely; 0 is the value for white, revealing artwork completely).

Getting started

First, you'll view the image that you'll create using masks and channels.

1 Start Photoshop, and then immediately hold down Ctrl+Alt+Shift (Windows) or Command+Option+Shift (Mac OS) to restore the default preferences. (See "Restoring default preferences" on page 4.)

2 When prompted, click Yes to delete the Adobe Photoshop Settings file.

3 Choose File > Browse In Bridge to open Adobe Bridge.

4 Click the Favorites tab on the left side of the Bridge window. Select the Lessons folder, and then double-click the Lesson06 folder in the Content panel.

5 Study the 06End.psd file. To enlarge the thumbnail so that you can see it more clearly, move the thumbnail slider at the bottom of the Bridge window to the right.

In this lesson, you'll create a magazine cover. The model for the cover was photographed in front of a different background. You'll use masking and the Refine Mask feature to place the model on the appropriate background.

6 Double-click the 06Start.psd file's thumbnail to open it in Photoshop. Click OK if you see an Embedded Profile Mismatch dialog box.

Creating a mask

You'll use the Quick Selection tool to create the initial mask in order to separate the model from the background.

1   Choose File > Save As, rename the file **06Working.psd**, and click Save. Click OK if the Photoshop Format Options dialog box appears.

Saving a working version of the file lets you return to the original if you need it.

2   Select the Quick Selection tool (✎). In the options bar, set up a brush with a size of **15** px and hardness of **100%**.

▶ **Tip:** For help making selections, refer to Lesson 3, "Working with Selections."

3   Select the man. It's fairly easy to select his shirt and face, but the hair is trickier. Don't worry if the selection isn't perfect. You'll refine the mask in the next exercise.

4   At the bottom of the Layers panel, click the Add Layer Mask button (▣) to create a layer mask.

The selection becomes a pixel mask, and it appears as part of Layer 0 in the Layers panel. Everything outside the selection is transparent, represented by a checkerboard pattern.

Refining a mask

The mask is pretty good, but the Quick Selection tool couldn't quite capture all of the model's hair. The mask is also a little choppy around the contours of the shirt and face. You'll smooth the mask, and then fine-tune the area around the hair.

1   Choose Window > Properties to open the Properties panel.

2   If it isn't already selected, click the mask on Layer 0 in the Layers panel.

3 In the Properties panel, click Mask Edge. The Refine Mask dialog box opens.

4 In the View Mode area of the dialog box, click the arrow next to the preview window. Choose On Black from the pop-up menu.

The mask appears against a black background, which makes it easier to see the edge of the white shirt and the face.

5 In the Adjust Edge area of the dialog box, move the sliders to create a smooth, unfeathered edge along the shirt and face. The optimal settings depend on the selection you created, but they'll probably be similar to ours. We moved the Smooth slider to 15, Contrast to 40%, and Shift Edge to -8%.

6 In the Output area of the dialog box, select Decontaminate Colors. Choose New Layer With Layer Mask from the Output To menu.

7 Select the Zoom tool in the Refine Mask dialog box, and then click the face to zoom in so you can see its edges more clearly.

8 Select the Refine Radius tool (🖌) in the Refine Mask dialog box. Use it to paint out any white background that remains around the lips and the nose. Press the left bracket ([) to decrease the brush size and the right bracket (]) to increase it.

9 When you're satisfied with the mask around the face, click OK.

A new layer, named Layer 0 copy, appears in the Layers panel. You'll use this layer to add the spikes to the mask of the hair.

10 With Layer 0 copy active, click Mask Edge in the Properties panel to open the Refine Mask dialog box again.

11 From the View pop-up menu, choose On White. The black hair shows up well against the white matte. If necessary, zoom out or use the Hand tool to reposition the image so that you can see all of the hair.

12 Select the Refine Radius tool in the Refine Mask dialog box. Press the] key to increase the size of the brush. (The options bar displays the brush size; we used 300 px at first.) Then, begin brushing along the top of the hair, high enough to include the spikes. Press the [key to decrease the brush size by about half. Then, paint along the right side of the head, where the hair is a solid color, to pick up any small, fine hairs that protrude.

As you paint, Photoshop refines the mask edge, including the hair, but eliminating most of the background. If you were painting on a layer mask, the background would be included. The Refine Mask feature is good, but it's not perfect. You'll clean up any areas of background that are included with the hair.

13 Select the Erase Refinements tool (), hidden behind the Refine Radius tool in the Refine Mask dialog box. Click once or twice in each area where background color shows. When you erase an area, the Refine Mask feature erases similar colors, cleaning up more of the mask for you. Be careful not to erase the refinements you made to the hair edge. You can undo a step or use the Refine Radius tool to restore the edge if necessary.

14 Select Decontaminate Colors, and move the Amount slider to 85%. Choose New Layer With Layer Mask from the Output menu. Then click OK.

15 In the Layers panel, make the Magazine Background layer visible. The model appears in front of an orange patterned background.

Creating a quick mask

You'll create a quick mask to change the color of the glasses frames. First, you'll clean up the Layers panel.

1   Hide the Magazine Background layer so you can focus on the model. Then delete the Layer 0 and Layer 0 copy layers. Click Yes or Delete to confirm deletion of the layers or their masks, if prompted; you do not need to apply the mask to the current layer because Layer 0 copy 2 already has the mask applied.

2 Double-click the Layer 0 copy 2 layer name, and rename it **Model**.

3 Click the Edit In Quick Mask Mode button in the Tools panel. (By default, you have been working in Standard mode.)

In Quick Mask mode, a red overlay appears as you make a selection, masking the area outside the selection the way a rubylith, or red acetate, was used to mask images in traditional print shops. You can apply changes only to the unprotected area that is visible and selected. Notice that the highlight for the selected layer in the Layers panel appears gray instead of blue, indicating you're in Quick Mask mode.

4 In the Tools panel, select the Brush tool (✏).

5 In the options bar, make sure that the mode is Normal. Open the Brush pop-up panel, and select a small brush with a diameter of **13** px. Click outside the panel to close it.

6 Paint the earpiece of the glasses frames. The area you paint will appear red, creating a mask.

7 Continue painting with the Brush tool to mask the earpiece of the frames and the frame around the lenses. Reduce the brush size to paint around the lenses. Don't worry about the part of the earpiece that is overlapped by hair; the color change won't affect that area.

In Quick Mask mode, Photoshop automatically defaults to Grayscale mode, with a foreground color of black, and a background color of white. When using a painting or editing tool in Quick Mask mode, keep these principles in mind:

- Painting with black adds to the mask (the red overlay) and decreases the selected area.
- Painting with white erases the mask (the red overlay) and increases the selected area.
- Painting with gray partially adds to the mask.

8   Click the Edit In Standard Mode button to exit Quick Mask Mode.

The unmasked area is selected. Unless you save a quick mask as a more permanent alpha-channel mask, Photoshop discards the temporary mask once it is converted to a selection.

9   Choose Select > Inverse to select the area you originally masked.

10 Choose Image > Adjustments > Hue/Saturation.

11 In the Hue/Saturation dialog box, change the Hue to **70**. The new green color fills the glasses frame. Click OK.

12 Choose Select > Deselect.

13 Save your work so far.

Manipulating an image with Puppet Warp

The Puppet Warp feature gives you flexibility in manipulating an image. You can reposition areas, such as hair or an arm, just as you might pull the strings on a puppet. You place pins where you want to control movement. You'll use Puppet Warp to tilt the model's head back, so he appears to be looking up.

1 With the Model layer selected in the Layers panel, choose Edit > Puppet Warp.

A mesh appears over the visible areas in the layer—in this case, the mesh appears over the model. You'll use the mesh to place pins where you want to control movement (or to ensure there is no movement).

2 Click around the edges of the shirt. Each time you click, Puppet Warp adds a pin. Approximately 10 pins should work.

The pins you've added around the shirt will keep it in place as you tilt the head.

3 Select the pin at the nape of the neck. A white dot appears in the center of the pin to indicate that it's selected.

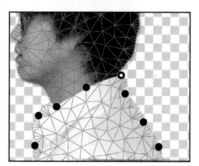

4 Press Alt (Windows) or Option (Mac OS). A larger circle appears around the pin and a curved double arrow appears next to it. Continue pressing Alt or Option as you drag the pointer to rotate the head backwards. You can see the angle of rotation in the options bar; you can enter **135** there to rotate the head back.

5 When you're satisfied with the rotation, click the Commit Puppet Warp button (✔) in the options bar, or press Enter or Return.

6 Save your work so far.

Working with channels

Just as different information in an image is stored on different layers, channels also let you access specific kinds of information. Alpha channels store selections as gray-scale images. Color information channels store information about each color in an image; for example, an RGB image automatically has red, green, blue, and composite channels.

To avoid confusing channels and layers, think of channels as containing an image's color and selection information; think of layers as containing painting and effects.

You'll use an alpha channel to create a shadow for the model. Then, you'll convert the image to CMYK mode and use the Black channel to add color highlights to the hair.

Using an alpha channel to create a shadow

You've already created a mask of the model. To create a shadow, you want to essentially duplicate that mask and then shift it. You'll use an alpha channel to make that possible.

1   In the Layers panel, Ctrl-click (Windows) or Command-click (Mac OS) the layer icon in the Model layer. The masked area is selected.

2   Choose Select > Save Selection. In the Save Selection dialog box, make sure New is chosen in the Channel menu. Then name the channel **Model Outline,** and click OK.

Nothing changes in the Layers panel or in the image window. However, a new channel named Model Outline has been added to the Channels panel.

3   Click the Create A New Layer icon at the bottom of the Layers panel. Drag the new layer below the Model layer. Then double-click its name, and rename it **Shadow**.

4   With the Shadow layer selected, choose Select > Refine Edge. In the Refine Edge dialog box, move the Shift Edge slider to **+36**%. Then click OK.

5   Choose Edit > Fill. In the Fill dialog box, choose Black from the Use menu, and then click OK.

The Shadow layer displays a filled-in black outline of the model. Shadows aren't usually as dark as the person that casts them. You'll reduce the layer opacity.

6   In the Layers panel, change the layer opacity to **30**%.

The shadow is in exactly the same position as the model, where it can't be seen. You'll shift it.

7 Choose Select > Deselect to remove the selection.

8 Choose Edit > Transform > Skew. Rotate the shadow by hand, or enter **-15°** in the Rotate field in the options bar. Then drag the shadow to the left, or enter **845** in the X field in the options bar. Click the Commit Transform button (✔) in the options bar, or press Enter or Return, to accept the transformation.

9 Choose File > Save to save your work so far.

About alpha channels

If you work in Photoshop very long, you're bound to work with alpha channels. It's a good idea to know a few things about them.

- An image can contain up to 56 channels, including all color and alpha channels.
- All channels are 8-bit grayscale images, capable of displaying 256 levels of gray.
- You can specify a name, color, mask option, and opacity for each channel. (The opacity affects the preview of the channel, not the image.)
- All new channels have the same dimensions and number of pixels as the original image.
- You can edit the mask in an alpha channel using the painting tools, editing tools, and filters.
- You can convert alpha channels to spot-color channels.

Adjusting an individual channel

You're almost done with the magazine cover image. All that remains is to add color highlights to the model's hair. You'll convert the image to CMYK mode so you can take advantage of the Black channel to do just that.

1 Select the Model layer in the Layers panel.

2 Choose Image > Mode > CMYK Color. Click Don't Merge in the dialog box that appears, because you want to keep your layers intact. Click OK if you're prompted about color profiles.

3 Alt-click (Windows) or Option-click (Mac OS) the visibility icon for the Model layer to hide the other layers.

4 Select the Channels tab. In the Channels panel, select the Black channel. Then choose Duplicate Channel from the Channels panel menu. Name the channel **Hair**, and click OK.

Individual channels appear in grayscale. If more than one channel is visible in the Channels panel, the channels appear in color.

5 Make the Hair channel visible, and hide the Black channel. Then select the Hair channel, and choose Image > Adjustments > Levels.

6 In the Levels dialog box, adjust the levels to move Black to **85**, Midtones to **1**, and White to **165**. Click OK.

7 With the Hair channel still selected, choose Image > Adjustments > Invert. The channel appears white against a black background.

8 Select the Brush tool, and click the Switch Foreground And Background Colors icon in the Tools panel to make the Foreground color black. Then paint over the glasses, eyes, and anything in the channel that isn't hair.

9 Click the Load Channel As Selection icon at the bottom of the Channels panel.

10 Select the Layers tab. In the Layers panel, select the Model layer.

11 Choose Select > Refine Edge. In the Refine Edge dialog box, move the Feather slider to **1.2** px, and then click OK.

12 Choose Image > Adjustments > Hue/Saturation. Select Colorize, and then move the sliders as follows, and click OK:

- Hue: **230**
- Saturation: **56**
- Lightness: **11**

13 Choose Image > Adjustments > Levels. In the Levels dialog box, move the sliders so that the Black slider is positioned where the blacks peak, the White slider where the whites peak, and the Midtones in between. Then click OK.
We used the values 58, 1.65, 255, but your values may vary.

14 In the Layers panel, make the Shadow and Magazine Background layers visible.

15 Choose Select > Deselect.

16 Choose File > Save.

Your magazine cover is ready to go!

About masks and masking

Alpha channels, channel masks, clipping masks, layer masks, vector masks—what's the difference? In some cases, they're interchangeable: A channel mask can be converted to a layer mask, a layer mask can be converted to a vector mask, and vice versa.

Here's a brief description to help you keep them all straight. What they have in common is that they all store selections, and they all let you edit an image nondestructively, so you can return at any time to your original.

- An **alpha channel**—also called a *mask* or *selection*—is an extra channel added to an image; it stores selections as grayscale images. You can add alpha channels to create and store masks.

- A **layer mask** is like an alpha channel, but it's attached to a specific layer. A layer mask controls which part of a layer is revealed or hidden. It appears as a blank thumbnail next to the layer thumbnail in the Layers panel until you add content to it; a black outline indicates that it's selected.

- A **vector mask** is essentially a layer mask made up of vectors, not pixels. Resolution-independent, vector masks have crisp edges and are created with the pen or shape tools. They don't support transparency, so their edges can't be feathered. Their thumbnails appear the same as layer mask thumbnails.

- A **clipping mask** applies to a layer. It confines the influence of an effect to specific layers, rather than to everything below the layer in the layer stack. Using a clipping mask clips layers to a base layer; only that base layer is affected. Thumbnails of a clipped layer are indented with a right-angle arrow pointing to the layer below. The name of the clipped base layer is underlined.

- A **channel mask** restricts editing to a specific channel (for example, a Cyan channel in a CMYK image). Channel masks are useful for making intricate, fringed, or wispy-edged selections. You can create a channel mask based on a dominant color in an image or a pronounced contrast in an isolated channel, for example, between the subject and the background.

Review questions

1 What is the benefit of using a quick mask?

2 What happens to a quick mask when you deselect it?

3 When you save a selection as a mask, where is the mask stored?

4 How can you edit a mask in a channel once you've saved it?

5 How do channels differ from layers?

Review answers

1 Quick masks are helpful for creating quick, one-time selections. In addition, using a quick mask is an easy way to edit a selection using the painting tools.

2 The quick mask disappears when you deselect it.

3 Masks are saved in channels, which can be thought of as storage areas for color and selection information in an image.

4 You can paint on a mask in a channel using black, white, and shades of gray.

5 Channels are used as storage areas for saved selections. Unless you explicitly display a channel, it does not appear in the image or print. Layers can be used to isolate various parts of an image so that they can be edited as discrete objects with the painting or editing tools or other effects.

7 TYPOGRAPHIC DESIGN

Lesson overview

In this lesson, you'll learn how to do the following:

- Use guides to position text in a composition.

- Make a clipping mask from type.

- Merge type with other layers.

- Format text.

- Distribute text along a path.

- Create and apply type styles.

- Control type and positioning using advanced features.

 This lesson will take less than an hour to complete. Copy the Lesson07 folder onto your hard drive if you haven't already done so. As you work on this lesson, you'll preserve the start files. If you need to restore the start files, copy them from the *Adobe Photoshop CS6 Classroom in a Book* DVD.

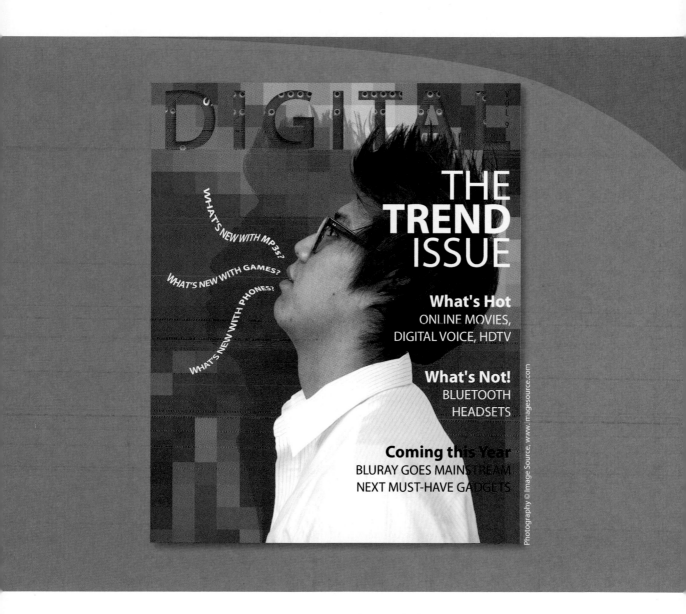

Photoshop provides powerful, flexible text tools so you can add type to your images with great control and creativity.

About type

Type in Photoshop consists of mathematically defined shapes that describe the letters, numbers, and symbols of a typeface. Many typefaces are available in more than one format, the most common formats being Type 1 or PostScript fonts, TrueType, and OpenType (see "OpenType in Photoshop" later in this lesson).

When you add type to an image in Photoshop, the characters are composed of pixels and have the same resolution as the image file—zooming in on characters shows jagged edges. However, Photoshop preserves the vector-based type outlines and uses them when you scale or resize type, save a PDF or EPS file, or print the image to a PostScript printer. As a result, you can produce type with crisp, resolution-independent edges, apply effects and styles to type, and transform its shape and size.

Getting started

In this lesson, you'll work on the layout for the cover of a technology magazine. You'll start with the artwork you created in Lesson 6: The cover has a model, his shadow, and the orange background. You'll add and stylize type for the cover, including warping the text.

You'll start the lesson by viewing an image of the final composition.

1 Start Photoshop, and then immediately hold down Ctrl+Alt+Shift (Windows) or Command+Option+Shift (Mac OS) to restore the default preferences. (See "Restoring default preferences" on page 4.)

2 When prompted, click Yes to delete the Adobe Photoshop Settings file.

3 Choose File > Browse In Bridge to open Adobe Bridge.

4 In the Favorites panel on the left side of Bridge, click the Lessons folder, and then double-click the Lesson07 folder in the Content panel.

5 Select the 07End.psd file. Increase the thumbnail size to see the image clearly by dragging the thumbnail slider to the right.

● **Note:** Though this lesson starts where Lesson 6 left off, use the 07Start.psd file. We've included a path and a sticky note in the start file that won't be in the 06Working.psd file you saved.

You'll apply the type treatment in Photoshop to finish the magazine cover. All of the type controls you need are available in Photoshop, so you don't have to switch to another application to complete the project.

6 Double-click the 07Start.psd file to open it in Photoshop.

7 Choose File > Save As, rename the file **07Working.psd**, and click Save.

8 Click OK if the Photoshop Format Options dialog box appears.

9 Choose Typography from the Workspace Switcher in the options bar.

The Typography workspace displays the Character, Paragraph, Paragraph Styles, Layers, and Paths panels that you'll use in this lesson.

Creating a clipping mask from type

A *clipping mask* is an object or a group of objects whose shape masks other artwork so that only areas that lie within the clipping mask are visible. In effect, you are clipping the artwork to conform to the shape of the object (or mask). In Photoshop, you can create a clipping mask from shapes or letters. In this exercise, you'll use letters as a clipping mask to allow an image in another layer to show through the letters.

Adding guides to position type

The 07Working.psd file includes a background layer, which will be the foundation for your typography. You'll start by zooming in on the work area and using ruler guides to help position the type.

1 Choose View > Fit On Screen to see the whole cover clearly.

2 Choose View > Rulers to display rulers along the left and top borders of the image window.

3 Drag a vertical guide from the left ruler to the center of the cover (4.25").

Adding point type

Now you're ready to add type to the composition. Photoshop lets you create horizontal or vertical type anywhere in an image. You can enter *point type* (a single letter, word, or line) or *paragraph type*. You will do both in this lesson. First, you'll create point type.

1 In the Layers panel, select the Background layer.

2 Select the Horizontal Type tool (T), and, in the options bar, do the following:

- Choose a sans serif typeface, such as Myriad Pro, from the Font Family pop-up menu, and choose Semibold from the Font Style pop-up menu.

- Type **144 pt** for the Size, and press Enter or Return.

- Click the Center Text button.

3 In the Character panel, change the Tracking value to **100**.

4 Click on the center guide you added to set an insertion point, and type **DIGITAL** in all capital letters. Then click the Commit Any Current Edits button (✔) in the options bar.

● **Note:** After you type, you must commit your editing in the layer by clicking the Commit Any Current Edits button or switching to another tool or layer. You cannot commit to current edits by pressing Enter or Return; doing so merely creates a new line of type.

The word "DIGITAL" is added to the cover, and it appears in the Layers panel as a new type layer, DIGITAL. You can edit and manage the type layer as you would any other layer. You can add or change the text, change the orientation of the type, apply anti-aliasing, apply layer styles and transformations, and create masks. You can move, restack, and copy a type layer, or edit its layer options, just as you would for any other layer.

5 Press Ctrl (Windows) or Command (Mac OS), and drag the "DIGITAL" text to move it to the top of the cover, if it's not there already.

6 Choose File > Save to save your work so far.

Making a clipping mask and applying a shadow

You added the letters in black, the default text color. However, you want the letters to appear to be filled with an image of a circuit board, so you'll use the letters to make a clipping mask that will allow another image layer to show through.

1 Open the circuit_board.tif file, which is in the Lesson07 folder. You can open it using Bridge or by choosing File > Open.

2 In Photoshop, choose Window > Arrange > 2-Up Vertical. The circuit_board.tif and 07Working.psd files appear onscreen together. Click the circuit_board.tif file to ensure that it's the active window.

3 Select the Move tool. Then, hold down the Shift key as you drag the Background layer from the Layers panel in the circuit_board.tif file onto the center of the 07Working.psd file. Pressing Shift as you drag centers the circuit_board.tif image in the composition.

A new layer—Layer 1— appears in the Layers panel for the 07Working.psd file. This new layer contains the image of the circuit board, which will show through the type. But before you make the clipping mask, you'll resize the circuit board image, as it's currently too large for the composition.

4 Close the circuit_board.tif file without saving any changes to it.

5 In the 07Working.psd file, select Layer 1, and then choose Edit > Transform > Scale.

6 Grab a corner handle on the bounding box for the circuit board. Press Shift as you resize it to approximately the same width as the area of text. Pressing Shift retains the image proportions. Reposition the circuit board so that the image covers the text.

7 Press Enter or Return to apply the transformation.

8 Double-click the Layer 1 name, and change it to **Circuit Board**. Then press Enter or Return, or click away from the name in the Layers panel, to apply the change.

▶ **Tip:** You can also make a clipping mask by holding down the Alt (Windows) or Option (Mac OS) key and clicking between the Circuit Board and DIGITAL type layers.

9 Select the Circuit Board layer, if it isn't already selected, and choose Create Clipping Mask from the Layers panel menu (▾≡).

The circuit board now shows through the DIGITAL letters. A small arrow in the Circuit Board layer and the underlined type layer name indicate the clipping mask is applied. Next, you'll add an inner shadow to give the letters depth.

10 Select the DIGITAL layer to make it active, click the Add A Layer Style button (*fx*) at the bottom of the Layers panel, and then choose Inner Shadow from the pop-up menu.

11 In the Layer Style dialog box, change the Blending Mode to Multiply, Opacity to **48**%, Distance to **18**, Choke to **0**, and Size to **16**. Then click OK.

12 Choose File > Save to save your work so far.

Julieanne Kost is an official Adobe Photoshop evangelist.

Tool tips from the Photoshop evangelist

Type tool tricks

- Shift-click in the image window with the Type tool (T) to create a new type layer—in case you're close to another block of type and Photoshop tries to autoselect it.

- Double-click the thumbnail icon on any type layer in the Layers panel to select all of the type on that layer.

- With any text selected, right-click (Windows) or Control-click (Mac OS) on the text to access the context menu. Choose Check Spelling to run a spell check.

Creating type on a path

In Photoshop, you can create type that follows along a path you create with a pen or shape tool. The direction the type flows depends on the order in which anchor points were added to the path. When you use the Horizontal Type tool to add text to a path, the letters are perpendicular to the baseline of the path. If you change the location or shape of the path, the type moves with it.

You'll create type on a path to make it look as if questions are coming from the model's mouth. We've already created the path for you.

1   In the Layers panel, select the Background layer.

2   Select the Paths tab in the Layers panel group.

3   In the Paths panel, select the path named Speech Path. The path appears to be coming out of the model's mouth.

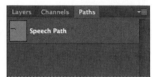

4   Select the Horizontal Type tool.

5   In the Character panel, select the following settings:

   • Font Family: Myriad Pro

   • Font Style: Regular

   • Font Size (𝕋): **16** pt

   • Tracking (🗛): **-10**

   • Color: White

   • All Caps (TT)

6   Move the Type tool over the path. When a small slanted line appears across the I-bar, click the beginning of the path, and type **What's new with Games?**

7 Select the word "GAMES," and change its font style to Bold. Click the Commit Any Current Edits button (✔) in the options bar.

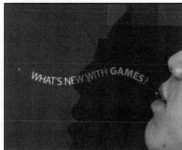

8 In the Layers panel, select the What's New with Games layer, and then choose Duplicate Layer from the Layers panel menu. Name the new layer **What's new with MP3s?**

9 With the Type tool, select "Games," and replace it with **MP3s**. Click the Commit Any Current Edits button in the options bar.

10 Choose Edit > Free Transform. Rotate the left side of the path approximately 30 degrees, and then shift the path up above the first path. Click the Commit Transform button in the options bar.

11 Repeat steps 8–10, replacing the word "GAMES" with **PHONES**. Rotate the left side of the path approximately -30 degrees, and move it below the original path.

12 Choose File > Save to save your work so far.

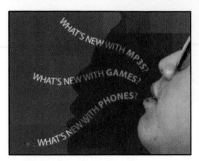

Warping point type

The text on a path is more interesting than straight lines would be, but you'll warp the text to make it more playful. *Warping* lets you distort type to conform to a variety of shapes, such as an arc or a wave. The warp style you select is an attribute of the type layer—you can change a layer's warp style at any time to change the overall shape of the warp. Warping options give you precise control over the orientation and perspective of the warp effect.

1 Scroll or use the Hand tool (🖑) to move the visible area of the image window so that the sentences to the left of the model are in the center of the screen.

2 Right-click (Windows) or Control-click (Mac OS) the What's new with Games? layer in the Layers panel, and choose Warp Text from the context menu.

3 In the Warp Text dialog box, choose Wave from the Style menu, and select the Horizontal option. Specify the following values: Bend, +**33**%; Horizontal Distortion, -**23**%; and Vertical Distortion, +**5**%. Then click OK.

 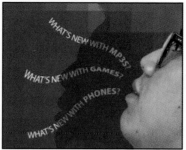

The words "What's new with games?" appear to float like a wave on the cover. Repeat steps 2 and 3 to warp the other two text layers you typed on a path.

4 Save your work.

Designing paragraphs of type

All of the text you've written on this cover so far has been a few discrete words or lines—point type. However, many designs call for full paragraphs of text. You can design complete paragraphs of type in Photoshop; you can even apply paragraph styles. You don't have to switch to a dedicated page layout program for sophisticated paragraph type controls.

Using guides for positioning

You will add paragraphs to the cover in Photoshop. First, you'll add some guides to the work area to help you position the paragraph, and create a new paragraph style.

1 Drag a guide from the left vertical ruler, placing it approximately ¼" from the right side of the cover.

2 Drag a guide down from the top horizontal ruler, placing it approximately 2" from the top of the cover.

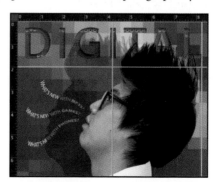

Adding paragraph type from a sticky note

You're ready to add the text. In a real design environment, the text might be provided to you in a word-processing document or the body of an email message, which you could copy and paste into Photoshop. Or you might have to type it in. Another easy way to add a bit of text is for the copywriter to attach it to the image file in a sticky note, as we've done for you here.

1   Double-click the yellow sticky note in the lower right corner of the image window to open the Notes panel. Expand the Notes panel, if necessary, to see all the text.

2   In the Notes panel, select all the text. Press Ctrl+C (Windows) or Command+C (Mac OS) to copy the text to the clipboard. Close the Notes panel.

▶ **Tip:** If you accidentally select the "DIGITAL" text, press Shift as you start to drag the text box, and then release it to continue to drag. Pressing Shift ensures that Photoshop creates a new text layer.

3   Select the Model layer. Then, with the Horizontal Type tool (T), drag a text box on the right side of the magazine cover. The text box should be about 4 inches by 8 inches, about ¼" from the right edge of the cover. Align the top and right edges using the guides you just added.

4   Press Ctrl+V (Windows) or Command+V (Mac OS) to paste the text. The new text layer is at the top of the Layers panel, so the text appears in front of the model.

The pasted text is huge, because your default is set to 144 pt text. You'll change it all to a readable size before stylizing it.

5   Click in the pasted text, and press Ctrl+A (Windows) or Command+A (Mac OS) to select all the text. Then change its size to 18 pt in the Character panel.

6 Select the first three lines ("The Trend Issue"), and then apply the following settings in the Character panel:

- Font Family: Myriad Pro (or another sans serif font)
- Font Style: Regular
- Font Size (⫪T): **70** pt
- Leading (⊼Ａ): **55** pt
- Color: White

7 Click the Paragraph tab in the Character panel group to make the Paragraph panel active.

8 With "The Trend Issue" still selected, click the Right Align Text option.

9 Click the Character tab to open the Character panel again. Then select just the word "Trend," and change the Font Style to Bold.

10 Click the Commit Any Current Edits button (✔) in the options bar.

11 Click in the blank area of the Layers panel to ensure that no layers are selected.

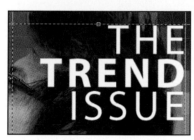

You've formatted the title.

Creating paragraph styles

You'll create a paragraph style to format the rest of the text. A paragraph style is a collection of type attributes that you can apply to an entire paragraph with a single click. Paragraph styles in Photoshop are similar to styles in page layout applications such as Adobe InDesign and popular word-processing applications, but you'll probably notice some differences in the way they work. By default, all text you create in Photoshop has the Basic paragraph style applied.

1 Click the Create New Paragraph Style button () at the bottom of the Paragraph Styles panel.

2 Double-click Paragraph Style 1 to change its attributes.

3 In the Paragraph Style Options dialog box, specify the following settings:

- Style Name: **Cover Teasers**
- Font Family: Myriad Pro
- Font Style: Bold
- Font Size: **28** pt
- Leading: **28** pt
- Color: White

4 Select Indents And Spacing from the list on the left in the Paragraph Style Options dialog box.

5 Choose Right from the Alignment menu, and then click OK.

You've created a style that you can apply to quickly format the teaser titles on the cover. You'll create another style for the subheadings, which should be smaller.

6 Click the Create New Paragraph Style button at the bottom of the Paragraph Styles panel again.

7 Double-click Paragraph Style 1, and then specify the following:

- Style Name: **Teaser subheads**
- Font Family: Myriad Pro
- Font Style: Regular
- Font Size: **22** pt
- Leading: **28** pt
- Color: White

8 Select Indents And Spacing from the list on the left in the Paragraph Style Options dialog box.

9 Choose Right from the Alignment menu, and then click OK.

Applying paragraph styles

Applying a paragraph style is easy. With the text selected, simply click the style name. If the text has been changed from the Basic paragraph style, Photoshop retains those overrides and applies only the attributes of the style that do not conflict with the overrides. In that case, clear overrides to apply all the style's attributes.

1 Select the "What's Hot" text, and then select Cover Teasers in the Paragraph Styles panel.

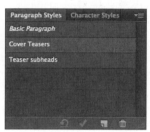

Photoshop applies some of the Cover Teasers attributes to the paragraph, but not all of them because there were style overrides in effect when you applied the style.

2 Click the Clear Override button (⬛) at the bottom of the Paragraph Styles panel.

3 Select the text beneath "What's Hot," and then select Teaser subheads in the Paragraph Styles panel. Click the Clear Override button again.

4 Repeat steps 1–3 for the "What's Not" and "Coming this year" sections.

Now there is just one more change to make to specific areas of the text.

5 Select "Coming this year" and all the text that follows it. Then, in the Character panel, change the text color to Black.

6 Finally, click the Commit Any Current Edits button to accept the type changes.

OpenType in Photoshop

OpenType is a cross-platform font file format developed jointly by Adobe and Microsoft. The format uses a single font file for both Mac OS and Windows, so you can move files from one platform to another without font substitution or reflowed text. OpenType offers widely expanded character sets and layout features, such as swashes and discretionary ligatures, that aren't available in traditional PostScript and TrueType fonts. This, in turn, provides richer linguistic support and advanced typography control. Here are some highlights of OpenType.

The OpenType menu The Character panel menu includes an OpenType submenu that displays all available features for a selected OpenType font, including ligatures, alternates, and fractions. Dimmed features are unavailable for that typeface; a check mark appears next to features that have been applied.

Discretionary ligatures To add a discretionary ligature to two OpenType letters, such as to "th" in the Bickham Script Standard typeface, select them in the image, and choose OpenType > Discretionary Ligatures from the Character panel menu.

Swashes Adding swashes or alternate characters works the same way. Select the letter, such as a capital "T" in Bickham Script, and choose OpenType > Swash to change the ordinary capital into a dramatically ornate swash T.

Creating true fractions Type fractions as usual—for example, 1/2—and then select the characters, and from the Character panel menu, choose OpenType > Fractions. Photoshop applies the true fraction (½).

▶ **Tip:** Use the Adobe Illustrator Glyphs panel to preview OpenType options: Copy your text in Photoshop and paste it into an Illustrator document. Then, choose Window > Type > Glyphs. Select the text you want to change, and choose Show > Alternates For Current Selection. Double-click a glyph to apply it, and when you've finished, copy and paste the new type into your Photoshop file.

Adding vertical type

You're almost done with the text for the magazine cover. All that remains to do is to add the volume number in the upper right corner. You'll use vertical type to add it.

1   Choose Select > Deselect Layers. Then select the Vertical Type tool (↓T), which is hidden under the Horizontal Type tool.

2   Press the Shift key, and begin dragging in the upper right corner of the cover, near the letter "L." Release the Shift key, and drag a vertical rectangle.

Pressing the Shift key as you begin dragging ensures that you create a new text box instead of selecting the title.

3   Type **VOL 9**.

4 Select the letters either by dragging or triple-clicking them, and then, in the Character panel, select the following:

- Font Family: a serif typeface, such as Myriad Pro
- Font Style: a light or narrow style, such as Light Condensed
- Font size: **15** pt
- Tracking: **150**
- Color: Black

5 Click the Commit Any Current Edits button (✔) in the options bar. Your vertical text now appears as the layer named VOL 9. Use the Move tool (▶✛) to drag it to the right, if necessary.

Now, you'll clean up a bit.

6 Click the note to select it. Then right-click (Windows) or Control-click (Mac OS) and choose Delete Note from the context menu; click Yes to confirm that you want to delete the note.

7 Hide the guides: Choose the Hand tool (✋), and then press Ctrl+; (Windows) or Command+; (Mac OS). Then zoom out to get a nice look at your work.

8 Choose File > Save to save your work.

Congratulations! You've added and stylized all of the type on the Digital magazine cover. Now that the magazine cover is ready to go, you'll flatten it and prepare it for printing.

9 Choose File > Save As, rename the file **07Working_flattened**, and click Save. Click OK if you see the Photoshop Format Options dialog box.

Keeping a layered version lets you return to the 07Working.psd file in the future to edit it.

10 Choose Layer > Flatten Image.

11 Choose File > Save, and then close the image window.

Review questions

1 How does Photoshop treat type?

2 How is a text layer the same as or different from other layers in Photoshop?

3 What is a clipping mask, and how do you make one from type?

4 What is a paragraph style?

Review answers

1 Type in Photoshop consists of mathematically defined shapes that describe the letters, numbers, and symbols of a typeface. When you add type to an image in Photoshop, the characters are composed of pixels and have the same resolution as the image file. However, Photoshop preserves the vector-based type outlines and uses them when you scale or resize type, save a PDF or EPS file, or print the image to a PostScript printer.

2 Type that is added to an image appears in the Layers panel as a text layer that can be edited and managed in the same way as any other kind of layer. You can add and edit the text, change the orientation of the type, and apply anti-aliasing as well as move, restack, copy, and change the options for layers.

3 A clipping mask is an object or group whose shape masks other artwork so that only areas that lie within the shape are visible. To convert the letters on any text layer to a clipping mask, select both the text layer and the layer you want to show through the letters, and then choose Create Clipping Mask from the Layers panel menu.

4 A paragraph style is a collection of type attributes that you can quickly apply to an entire paragraph.

8 VECTOR DRAWING TECHNIQUES

Lesson overview

In this lesson, you'll learn how to do the following:

- Differentiate between bitmap and vector graphics.

- Draw straight and curved paths using the Pen tool.

- Convert a path to a selection, and convert a selection to a path.

- Save paths.

- Draw and edit shape layers.

- Draw custom shapes.

- Import and edit a Smart Object from Adobe Illustrator.

This lesson will take about 90 minutes to complete. Copy the Lesson08 folder onto your hard drive if you haven't already done so. As you work on this lesson, you'll preserve the start files. If you need to restore the start files, copy them from the *Adobe Photoshop CS6 Classroom in a Book* DVD.

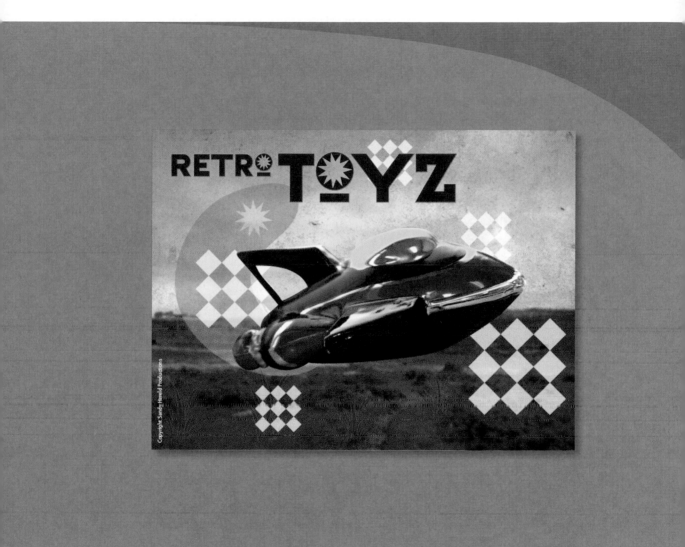

Unlike bitmap images, vector images retain their crisp edges when you enlarge them to any size. You can draw vector shapes and paths in your Photoshop images and add vector masks to control what is shown in an image.

About bitmap images and vector graphics

Before working with vector shapes and vector paths, it's important to understand the basic differences between the two main categories of computer graphics: *bitmap images* and *vector graphics*. You can use Photoshop to work with either type of graphic; in fact, you can combine both bitmap and vector data in an individual Photoshop image file.

Bitmap images, technically called *raster images*, are based on a grid of dots known as *pixels*. Each pixel is assigned a specific location and color value. In working with bitmap images, you edit groups of pixels rather than objects or shapes. Because bitmap graphics can represent subtle gradations of shade and color, they are appropriate for continuous-tone images such as photographs or artwork created in painting programs. A disadvantage of bitmap graphics is that they contain a fixed number of pixels. As a result, they can lose detail and appear jagged when scaled up onscreen or printed at a lower resolution than they were created for.

Vector graphics are made up of lines and curves defined by mathematical objects called *vectors*. These graphics retain their crispness whether they are moved, resized, or have their color changed. Vector graphics are appropriate for illustrations, type, and graphics such as logos that may be scaled to different sizes.

Logo drawn as vector art

Logo rasterized as bitmap art

About paths and the Pen tool

In Photoshop, the outline of a vector shape is a *path*. A path is a curved or straight line segment you draw using the Pen tool, Freeform Pen tool, or a shape tool. The Pen tool draws paths with the greatest precision; shape tools draw rectangles, ellipses, and other shape paths; the Freeform Pen tool draws paths as if you were drawing with a pencil on paper.

Julieanne Kost is an official Adobe Photoshop evangelist.

Tool tips from the Photoshop evangelist

Accessing tools quickly

Each tool in the Tools panel has a single-letter keyboard shortcut. Type the letter, get the tool. Press Shift with the shortcut key to cycle though any nested tools in a group. For example, press P to select the Pen tool, and press Shift+P to toggle between the Pen and Freeform Pen tools.

Paths can be open or closed. An open path (such as a wavy line) has two distinct endpoints. A closed path (such as a circle) is continuous. The type of path you draw affects how it can be selected and adjusted.

Paths that have no fill or stroke do not print when you print your artwork. This is because paths are vector objects that contain no pixels, unlike the bitmap shapes drawn by the Pencil tool and other painting tools.

Getting started

Before you begin, you'll view the image you'll be creating—a poster for a fictitious toy company.

1   Start Photoshop, and then immediately hold down Ctrl+Alt+Shift (Windows) or Command+Option+Shift (Mac OS) to restore the default preferences. (See "Restoring default preferences" on page 4.)

2   When prompted, click Yes to delete the Adobe Photoshop Settings file.

Note: If you open the 08End.psd file in Photoshop, you might be prompted to update type layers. If so, click Update. You may need to update type layers when files are transferred between computers, especially between operating systems.

3   Click the Mini Bridge tab to open the Mini Bridge panel. If Bridge isn't running in the background, click Launch Bridge.

4   In the Mini Bridge panel, choose Favorites from the pop-up menu on the left. Double-click the Lessons folder, and then double-click the Lesson08 folder.

5   Select the 08End.psd file, and press the spacebar to see it in full-screen view.

To create this poster, you'll work with an image of a toy spaceship, and practice making paths and selections using the Pen tool. As you create the background shapes and type, you'll learn more about shape layers and vector masks, as well as ways to use Smart Objects.

6   When you've finished looking at 08End.psd, press the spacebar again. Then double-click the 08Start.psd file to open it in Photoshop.

7   Choose File > Save As, rename the file **08Working.psd**, and click Save. Click OK in the Photoshop Format Options dialog box.

Using paths with artwork

You'll use the Pen tool to select the toy spaceship. The spaceship has long, smooth, curved edges that would be difficult to select using other methods.

You'll draw a path around the spaceship, and create another path inside it. You'll convert the paths to selections, and then subtract one selection from the other so that only the spaceship and none of the background is selected. Finally, you'll make a new layer from the spaceship image, and change the image that appears behind it.

When drawing a freehand path using the Pen tool, use as few points as possible to create the shape you want. The fewer points you use, the smoother the curves are—and the more efficient your file is.

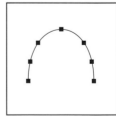

Correct number of points   Too many points

Creating paths with the Pen tool

You can use the Pen tool to create paths that are straight or curved, open or closed. If you're unfamiliar with the Pen tool, it can be confusing to use at first. Understanding the elements of a path and how to create them with the Pen tool makes paths much easier to draw.

To create a straight path, click the mouse button. The first time you click, you set the starting point. Each time that you click thereafter, a straight line is drawn between the previous point and the current point. To draw complex straight-segment paths with the Pen tool, simply continue to add points.

To create a curved path, click to place an anchor point, drag to create a direction line for that point, and then click to place the next anchor point. Each direction line ends in two direction points; the positions of direction lines and points determine the size and shape of the curved segment. Moving the direction lines and points reshapes the curves in a path.

Creating a straight line

Smooth curves are connected by anchor points called *smooth points*. Sharply curved paths are connected by *corner points*. When you move a direction line on a smooth point, the curved segments on both sides of the point adjust simultaneously, but when you move a direction line on a corner point, only the curve on the same side of the point as the direction line is adjusted.

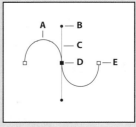

A. Curved line segment
B. Direction point
C. Direction line
D. Selected anchor point
E. Unselected anchor point

Path segments and anchor points can be moved after they're drawn, either individually or as a group. When a path contains more than one segment, you can drag individual anchor points to adjust individual segments of the path, or select all of the anchor points in a path to edit the entire path. Use the Direct Selection tool to select and adjust an anchor point, a path segment, or an entire path.

Creating a closed path differs from creating an open path in the way that you end it. To end an open path, click the Pen tool in the Tools panel. To create a closed path, position the Pen tool pointer over the starting point, and click. Closing a path automatically ends the path. After the path closes, the Pen tool pointer appears with a small x, indicating that your next click will start a new path.

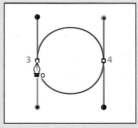

Creating a closed path

As you draw paths, a temporary storage area named Work Path appears in the Paths panel. It's a good idea to save work paths, and it's essential if you use multiple discrete paths in the same image file. If you deselect an existing Work Path in the Paths panel and then start drawing again, a new work path will replace the original one, which will be lost. To save a work path, double-click it in the Paths panel, type a name in the Save Path dialog box, and click OK to rename and save the path. The path remains selected in the Paths panel.

Drawing the outline of a shape

▶ **Tip:** If you're not familiar with the Pen tool, it can be a little confusing. To make the task of outlining the spaceship easier, we've included a video of these steps in the Lesson08/Video folder. Double-click the Paths.mp4 file to follow along.

You'll use the Pen tool to connect the dots from point A to point S, and then back to point A. You'll set straight segments, smooth curve points, and corner points.

The first step is to configure the Pen tool options and the work area. Then you'll trace the outline of a spaceship using a template.

1 Double-click the Mini Bridge tab to close the panel and free up more of the workspace.

2 In the Tools panel, select the Pen tool (✐).

3 In the options bar, select or verify the following settings:

• Choose Path from the Tool Mode pop-up menu.

• From the Path Operations menu, choose Combine Shapes.

• In the Pen Options menu, make sure that Rubber Band is not selected.

• Make sure that the Auto Add/Delete option is selected.

A. Tool Mode menu **B.** Path Operations menu **C.** Pen Options menu

4 Click the Paths tab to bring that panel to the front of the Layers panel group.

The Paths panel displays thumbnail previews of the paths you draw. Currently, the panel is empty, because you haven't started drawing.

5 If necessary, zoom in so that you can easily see the lettered points and red dots on the shape template. Make sure you can see the whole template in the image window, and be sure to reselect the Pen tool after you zoom.

6 Click point A (the blue dot at the top of the spaceship), and release the mouse. You've set the first anchor point.

7 Click point B, and drag the cursor to the red dot labeled b. Release the mouse. You've set the direction of the curve.

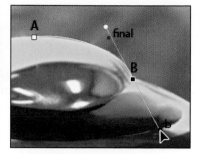

Creating the first anchor point at A   Setting a smooth point at B

At the corner of the cockpit (point B), you'll need to convert the smooth point to a corner point to create a sharp transition between the curved segment and the straight one.

8 Alt-click (Windows) or Option-click (Mac OS) point B to convert the smooth point into a corner point and remove one of the direction lines.

9 Click point C, and drag to the red dot labeled c. Do the same for points D and E.

Converting the smooth point   Adding a segment   Rounding the corner
to a corner point

If you make a mistake while you're drawing, choose Edit > Undo to undo the step. Then resume drawing.

10 Click point F, and release the mouse without dragging a handle.

11 Click point G, and drag over from point G to its red dot.

12 Click point H, and drag up to its dot. Then Alt-click or Option-click to create another corner point at point H.

13 Click point I, and drag up to its dot in the yellow area. Then Alt-click or Option-click to create a corner point at point I.

14 Click point J, and drag to its dot. Then create a corner point at point J.

15 Click point K, and drag to its dot; click point L and drag to its dot; and then create a corner point at point L.

16 Click point M, drag to its dot, create a corner point at point M, and then click point N, and drag to its dot.

17 Click points O and P, leaving straight lines. Click Point Q, and drag the handle to the corresponding red dot to create the curve around the tail of the fin.

18 Click at points R and S without dragging to create straight lines.

19 Move the pointer over point A so that a small circle appears in the pointer icon, indicating that you are about to close the path. (The small circle may be difficult to see.) Drag from point A to the red dot labeled "final," and then release the mouse button to draw the last curved line.

20 In the Paths panel, double-click Work Path, type **Spaceship** in the Save Path dialog box, and click OK to save it.

21 Choose File > Save to save your work.

Converting selections to paths

Now, you'll create a second path using a different method. First you'll use a selection tool to select a similarly colored area, and then you'll convert the selection to a path. (You can convert any selection made with a selection tool into a path.)

1 Click the Layers tab to display the Layers panel, and then drag the Template layer to the Delete button at the bottom of the panel. You no longer need this layer.

2 Select the Magic Wand tool (✻) in the Tools panel, hidden under the Quick Selection tool.

3 In the options bar, make sure the Tolerance value is **32**.

4 Carefully click the green area inside the spaceship's vertical fin.

5 Click the Paths tab to bring the Paths panel forward. Then, click the Make Work Path From Selection button (⬥) at the bottom of the panel.

The selection is converted to a path, and a new work path is created.

6 Double-click the path named Work Path, name it **Fin**, and then click OK to save the path.

7 Choose File > Save to save your work.

Converting paths to selections

Just as you can convert selection borders to paths, you can convert paths to selections. With their smooth outlines, paths let you make precise selections. Now that you've drawn paths for the spaceship and its fin, you'll convert those paths to a selection and apply a filter to the selection.

1   In the Paths panel, click the Spaceship path to make it active.

▶ **Tip:** You can also click the Load Path As Selection button at the bottom of the Paths panel to convert the active path to a selection.

2   Choose Make Selection from the Paths panel menu, and then click OK to convert the Spaceship path to a selection.

Next, you'll subtract the Fin selection from the Spaceship selection so that you can see the background through the vacant areas in the fin.

3   In the Paths panel, click the Fin path to make it active. Then, from the Paths panel menu, choose Make Selection.

4   In the Operation area of the Make Selection dialog box, select Subtract From Selection, and click OK.

The Fin path is simultaneously converted to a selection and subtracted from the Spaceship selection.

Leave the paths selected, because you'll use them in the next exercise.

Converting the selection to a layer

Now you'll see how creating the selection with the Pen tool can help you achieve interesting effects. Because you've isolated the spaceship, you can create a duplicate of it on a new layer. Then, you can copy it to another image file—specifically, to the image that's the background for the toy-store poster.

1 Make sure that you can still see the selection outline in the image window. If you can't, repeat the previous exercise, "Converting paths to selections."

2 Choose Layer > New > Layer Via Copy.

3 Click the Layers tab to bring the Layers panel to the front. A new layer appears in the Layers panel, called Layer 2. The Layer 2 thumbnail shows that the layer contains only the image of the spaceship, not the background of the original layer.

4 In the Layers panel, rename Layer 2 **Spaceship**, and press Enter or Return.

5 Choose File > Open, and double-click the 08Landscape.psd file in the Lessons/ Lesson08 folder.

The 08Landscape.psd file contains the landscape that you'll use as the background for the spaceship.

6 Choose Window > Arrange > 2 Up Vertical so that you can see both the open files. Click the 08Working.psd image to make it active.

7 Select the Move tool (▸✛), and drag the spaceship from the 08Working.psd image window to the 08Landscape.psd image window so that the spaceship appears to be hovering over the planet.

8 Close the 08Working.psd image without saving changes, leaving the 08Landscape.psd file open and active.

Now you'll position the spaceship more precisely over the poster background.

9 Select the Spaceship layer in the Layers panel, and choose Edit > Free Transform.

A bounding box appears around the spaceship.

● **Note:** If you accidentally distort the spaceship instead of rotating it, press Esc and start over.

10 Position the pointer near any corner handle until it turns into the rotate cursor (↻), and then drag to rotate the spaceship until its angle is about -12 degrees. For precise rotation, you can enter the value in the Rotate box in the options bar. When you're satisfied, press Enter or Return.

11 Make sure the Spaceship layer is still selected, and then use the Move tool to drag the ship so that it grazes the top of the planet, as in the third image.

12 Choose File > Save As, rename the file **08B_Working.psd**, and click Save. Click OK in the Photoshop Format Options dialog box.

Creating vector objects for the background

Many posters are designed to be scalable, either up or down, while retaining a crisp appearance: a good use for vector shapes. Next, you'll create vector shapes with paths, and use masks to control what appears in the poster. Because they're vectors, the shapes can be scaled in future design revisions without a loss of quality or detail.

Drawing a scalable shape

You'll begin by creating a white kidney-shaped object for the backdrop of the poster.

1 Choose View > Rulers to display the horizontal and vertical rulers.

2 Drag the tab for the Paths panel out of the Layers panel group so that it floats independently. Since you'll be using the Layers and Paths panels frequently in this exercise, it's convenient to have them separated.

3 Toggle the eye icons in the Layers panel to show the Retro Shape Guide and Background layers, and to hide the other two layers. Select the Background layer to make it active.

The guide layer will serve as a template as you draw the kidney shape.

4 In the Tools panel, select the Pen tool (✐).

5 In the options bar, choose Shape from the pop-up menu, and then click the Fill color. Select white for the fill color.

● **Note:** If you have trouble, open the spaceship image again and practice drawing the path around the spaceship shape until you get more comfortable with drawing curved path segments. Also, be sure to read the sidebar, "Creating paths with the Pen tool."

6 Create the shape by clicking and dragging as follows:

- Click point A, drag a direction line up to point B, and then release.

- Click point C, drag a direction line to point D, and then release.

- Continue to draw curved segments in this way around the shape until you return to point A, and then click point A to close the path. Don't worry if the shape flips in on itself; it will right itself as you continue.

Notice that as you drew, Photoshop automatically created a new layer, Shape 1, just above the active layer (the Background layer) in the Layers panel.

7 Double-click the Shape 1 layer name, rename the layer **Retro Shape**, and press Enter or Return.

8 Hide the Retro Shape Guide layer in the Layers panel.

Deselecting paths

You may need to deselect paths to see the appropriate options in the options bar when you select a vector tool. Deselecting paths can also help you view certain effects that might be obscured if a path is highlighted.

Notice that the border between the white kidney shape and the background has a grainy quality. What you see is actually the path itself, which is a nonprinting item. This is a visual clue that the Retro Shape layer is still selected. Before proceeding to the next exercise, you'll make sure that all paths are deselected.

1 In the Paths panel, click in the empty area beneath the path to deselect all paths.

2 Choose File > Save to save your work.

Changing the fill color of a shape layer

You created the shape with a white fill so that it was easy to see. But for the poster, you'll change the color of the shape to blue.

1 Select the Pen tool in the Tools panel, if it's not already selected.

2 In the options bar, click the Fill color. Select the Light Cyan Blue color.

The fill color of the shape changes to the blue you selected.

Subtracting shapes from a shape layer

After you create a shape layer (vector graphic), you can set options to subtract new shapes from the vector graphic. You can also use the Path Selection tool and the Direct Selection tool to move, resize, and edit shapes. You'll add some interest to the retro shape by subtracting a star shape from it, allowing the outer-space background to show through. To help you position the star, you'll refer to the Star Guide layer, which has been created for you. Currently, that layer is hidden.

1 In the Layers panel, show the Star Guide layer, but leave the Retro Shape layer selected. The Star Guide layer is now visible in the image window.

2 In the Paths panel, select the Retro Shape shape path.

3 In the Tools panel, select the Polygon tool (⬡), hidden under the Rectangle tool (▢).

4 On the options bar, do the following:

- For Sides, type **11**.

- From the Path Operations pop-up menu, choose Subtract Front Shape. The pointer now appears as cross-hairs with a small minus sign (✛).

- Click the Settings icon to the left of the Sides option to display the Polygon Options window. Select Star, and type **50%** in the Indent Sides By box. Then click an empty area of the options bar to close the window.

● **Note:** As you drag, you can rotate the star by dragging the pointer to the side.

5 Click on the orange dot in the center of the orange circle in the image window, and drag outward until the tips of the star rays touch the circle's perimeter.

When you release the mouse button, the star shape becomes a cutout, allowing the sky to show through.

Notice that the star has a grainy outline, reminding you that the shape is selected. Another indication that the shape is selected is that the Retro Shape shape path is selected in the Paths panel.

6 In the Layers panel, hide the Star Guide layer.

Notice that the thumbnails in both the Layers panel and Paths panel show the retro shape with the star-shaped cutout.

7 Click in the area beneath the path in the Paths panel to deselect the path.

The path is now deselected, and the grainy path lines have disappeared, leaving a sharp edge between the blue areas and the sky. Also, the Retro Shape shape path is no longer highlighted in the Paths panel. That shape is pretty bright, though, and may overpower the spaceship. You'll make the shape semitransparent.

8 In the Layers panel, reduce the opacity of the Retro Shape layer to **40**%.

9 Choose File > Save to save your work.

Working with defined custom shapes

Another way to use shapes in your artwork is to draw a custom or preset shape. Doing so is as easy as selecting the Custom Shape tool, picking a shape from the Custom Shape Picker, and dragging in the image window. You'll do just that to add checkerboard patterns and clumps of grass to the background of your poster for the toy store.

1   Make sure the Retro Shape layer is selected in the Layers panel. Then click the New Layer button (⬜) to add a layer above it. Rename the new layer **Pattern**, and then press Enter or Return.

2   In the Tools panel, select the Custom Shape tool (⬚), which is hidden under the Polygon tool (⬡).

3   In the options bar, choose Pixels from the Tool Mode menu.

● **Note:** The options in the options bar change depending on what you choose from the Tool Mode menu. When you work in Shape mode, you can select a fill or stroke in the options bar; in Pixels mode, those options aren't available.

4   In the options bar, click the arrow next to the Shape option to open the Custom Shape Picker.

5   Double-click the checkerboard preset in the Custom Shape Picker (you may need to scroll or drag the corner of the picker to see it) to select it and close the picker.

6   Make sure that the foreground color is white. Then press Shift and drag diagonally in the image window to draw and size the shape so that it's about 2 inches square.

Pressing Shift constrains the shape to its original proportions.

7 Add five more checkerboards of various sizes until your poster resembles the figure below.

8 In the Layers panel, reduce the opacity of the Pattern layer to **75%**.

9 In the Layers panel, show the Spaceship layer so you can see the whole composition.

You'll use the Custom Shape tool to add clumps of grass to the background. You can apply a fill and stroke to shapes when you work in Shape mode.

10 With the Custom Shape tool still selected, open the Custom Shape Picker, and double-click the clump of grass (called Grass 2).

11 Choose Shape from the Tool Mode menu. Then, select Dark Yellow Green for the Fill color, select Darker Green Cyan for the Stroke color, and enter **.75** for the stroke width.

▶ **Tip:** If the clumps of grass are on separate layers, you weren't holding down the Shift key as you drew them. Delete the grass, and repeat steps 12–13.

12 Press Shift as you draw four clumps of grass in the lower left corner of the background and an additional clump in the lower right corner.

Pressing Shift as you draw ensures that all the shapes are on the same layer.

13 Select the Path Selection tool (▶) in the Tools panel, and then Shift-select all five clumps of grass.

14 Choose Distribute Widths from the Path Alignment menu in the options bar.

Photoshop distributes the grass clumps evenly across the bottom of the background.

15 Rename the layer **Grass**, change its opacity to **60%**, and drag the layer just above the Background layer in the Layers panel.

16 Deselect the layer, and then choose File > Save to save your work so far.

Importing a Smart Object

Smart Objects are layers that you can edit in Photoshop nondestructively; that is, changes you make to the image remain editable and don't affect the actual image pixels, which are preserved. Regardless of how often you scale, rotate, skew, or otherwise transform a Smart Object, it retains its sharp, precise edges.

You can import vector objects from Adobe Illustrator as Smart Objects. If you edit the original object in Illustrator, the changes will be reflected in the placed Smart Object in your Photoshop image file. You'll work with a Smart Object now by placing text created in Illustrator into the toy-store poster.

Adding the title

The toy-store name was created in Illustrator. You'll add it to the poster now.

1   Select the Move tool (▶✛) in the Tools panel. Then select the Spaceship layer, and choose File > Place. Navigate to the Lessons/Lesson08 folder, select the Title.ai file, and click Place. Click OK in the Place PDF dialog box that appears.

The Retro Toyz text is added to the middle of the composition, inside a bounding box with adjustable handles. A new layer, Title, appears in the Layers panel.

2   Drag the Retro Toyz object to the upper left corner of the poster, and then press Shift and drag a corner to make the text object proportionally larger—so that it fills the top portion of the poster, as in the following figure. When you've finished, either press Enter or Return, or click the Commit Transform button (✔) in the options bar.

When you commit to the transformation, the layer thumbnail icon changes to reflect that the title layer is a Smart Object.

As with any shape layer or Smart Object, you can continue to edit its size and shape if you'd like. Simply select the layer, choose Edit > Free Transform to access the control handles, and drag to adjust them. Or, select the Move tool (▶✛), and select Show Transform Controls in the options bar. Then adjust the handles.

Adding a vector mask to a Smart Object

For a fun effect, you'll turn the center of each letter "O" in the title into a star that matches the cutout you created earlier. You'll use a vector mask, which you can link to a Smart Object in Photoshop.

1 Select the Title layer, and then choose Layer > Vector Mask > Reveal All.

2 Select the Polygon tool (⬤), hidden beneath the Custom Shape tool (✿). The options you used earlier to create the star should still be in effect: settings for an 11-sided star with a 50% indent. The Polygon tool holds your settings until you change them again.

3 Choose Path from the Tool Mode menu in the options bar. Make sure Subtract From Front is still selected from the Path Operations menu. Then select the vector mask thumbnail in the Title layer.

4 Click in the center of the "O" in "Toyz," and drag the cursor outward until the star covers the center of the "O."

5 Repeat step 4 to add a star in the small "O" in Retro.

Rotating the canvas (OpenGL only)

You've been working with the image with "Retro Toyz" at the top of the work area and the ground at the bottom. But if your video card supports OpenGL, you can rotate the work area to draw, type, or position objects from a different perspective. You'll rotate the view as you add a copyright statement along the side of the image. (If your video card doesn't support OpenGL, skip this section.)

First, you'll type the text.

1 Choose Window > Character to open the Character panel. Select a serif font such as Myriad Pro with a small size such as 10 pt, and set the color to white.

2 Select the Horizontal Type tool, and then click in the lower left corner of the image. Type **Copyright YOUR NAME Productions**, substituting your own name.

You want the copyright to run along the left side of the image. You'll rotate the canvas to make it easier to place.

3 Select the Rotate View tool (⊙), hidden beneath the Hand tool (✋).

4 Press the Shift key as you drag the tool in an arc to rotate the canvas 90 degrees clockwise. Pressing the Shift key restrains the rotation to 45-degree increments.

▶ **Tip:** You can also enter a value in the Rotation Angle box in the options bar.

5 Select the Copyright text layer, and then choose Edit > Transform > Rotate 90° CCW.

6 Use the Move tool to align the text along the top edge of the image, which will be the left edge when it is in its usual position.

7 Select the Rotate View tool again, and then click Reset View in the options bar.

8 Choose File > Save to save your work.

Finishing up

As a final step, clean up the Layers panel by deleting your guide template layers.

1 Make sure that the Copyright, Title, Spaceship, Pattern, Retro Shape, Grass, and Background layers are the only visible layers in the Layers panel.

2 Choose Delete Hidden Layers from the Layers panel menu, and then click Yes to confirm the deletion.

3 Choose File > Save to save your work.

Congratulations! You've finished the poster. It should look similar to the following image.

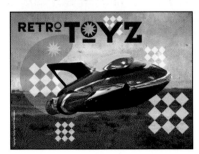

Review questions

1 How can the Pen tool be useful as a selection tool?

2 What is the difference between a bitmap image and a vector graphic?

3 What is a shape layer?

4 What tools can you use to move and resize paths and shapes?

5 What are Smart Objects, and what is the benefit of using them?

Review answers

1 If you need to create an intricate selection, it can be easier to draw the path with the Pen tool and then convert the path to a selection.

2 Bitmap, or raster, images are based on a grid of pixels and are appropriate for continuous-tone images such as photographs or artwork created in painting programs. Vector graphics are made up of shapes based on mathematical expressions and are appropriate for illustrations, type, and drawings that require clear, smooth lines.

3 A shape layer is a vector layer that contains either a shape (including fill and stroke), pixels, or a path.

4 You use the Path Selection tool and the Direct Selection tool to move, resize, and edit shapes. You can also modify and scale a shape or path by choosing Edit > Free Transform Path.

5 Smart Objects are vector objects that you can place and edit in Photoshop without a loss of quality. Regardless of how often you scale, rotate, skew, or otherwise transform a Smart Object, it retains sharp, precise edges. A great benefit of using Smart Objects is that you can edit the original object in the authoring application, such as Illustrator, and the changes will be reflected in the placed Smart Object in your Photoshop image file.

9 ADVANCED COMPOSITING

Lesson overview

In this lesson, you'll learn how to do the following:

- Add guides to help you place and align images precisely.

- Save selections and load them as masks.

- Apply color effects only to unmasked areas of an image.

- Apply filters to selections to create various effects.

- Add layer styles to create editable special effects.

- Record and play back an action to automate a series of steps.

- Blend images to create a panorama.

 This lesson will take about 90 minutes to complete. Copy the Lesson09 folder onto your hard drive if you haven't already done so. As you work on this lesson, you'll preserve the start files. If you need to restore the start files, copy them from the *Adobe Photoshop CS6 Classroom in a Book* DVD.

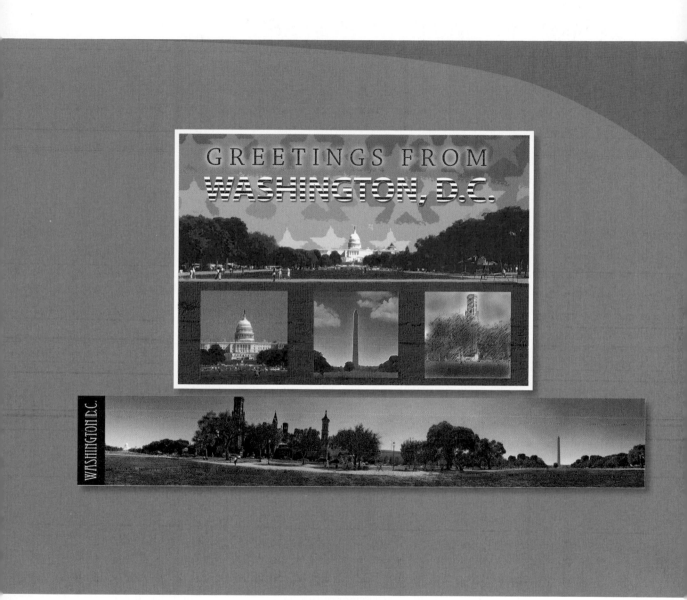

Filters can transform ordinary images into extraordinary digital artwork. Choose from filters that blur, bend, sharpen, or fragment images, or that simulate a traditional artistic medium, such as watercolor. You can also use adjustment layers and painting modes to vary the look of your artwork.

Getting started

In this lesson, you'll create souvenirs from a vacation to Washington, D.C. You'll assemble a montage of images for a postcard, and then stitch together a panorama to create a poster. First, look at the final projects to see what you'll be creating.

1 Start Photoshop, and then immediately hold down Ctrl+Alt+Shift (Windows) or Command+Option+Shift (Mac OS) to restore the default preferences. (See "Restoring default preferences" on page 4.)

2 When prompted, click Yes to delete the Adobe Photoshop Settings file.

3 Click the Mini Bridge tab at the bottom of the application window to open the Mini Bridge panel. If Bridge is not running in the background, click Launch Bridge to start it.

4 In the Mini Bridge panel, choose Favorites from the menu on the left, and then double-click the Lessons folder. Select the Lesson09 folder.

5 View the 09A_End.psd thumbnail, and press the spacebar for a full-screen view.

This file is a postcard that comprises four photos. Each image has had a specific filter or effect applied to it.

6 Press the spacebar to return to Photoshop. Then, select the 09B_End.psd thumbnail, and press the spacebar to see a full-screen view of it.

This file is a poster with a panoramic image and text. You'll create the postcard with multiple images first.

7 Press the spacebar to return to Photoshop. Then, double-click the 09A_Start.jpg thumbnail to open the file in Photoshop.

Assembling a montage of images

The postcard is a montage of four different images. You'll crop each image, and add them as separate layers to a composite image. Using guides, you'll align the images precisely with minimal effort. Before you make additional changes to the images, you'll add the text and apply effects to it.

Opening and cropping the images

The images you'll use in the insets are larger than you need, so you'll crop them before combining them in a composite file. Cropping images involves aesthetic choices about where and how much of the image to crop. The 09A_Start.jpg file is already open, so you'll start with it.

1   Select the Crop tool (⊠). In the options bar, choose Size & Resolution from the Select A Preset Aspect Ratio menu. Then, in the Crop Image Size & Resolution dialog box, enter **500** pixels for the Width, **500** pixels for the Height, and **300** pixels/inch for the Resolution. Click OK.

● **Note:** Be sure to enter 500 pixels, not 500 inches!

The cropped image will be 500 pixels by 500 pixels.

2   Resize and reposition the crop box so that the Smithsonian Institution is the focus of the cropped area. You can use the Right Arrow and Left Arrow keys on your keyboard to nudge the crop box into position if necessary.

3   When you're satisfied with the crop area, select Delete Cropped Pixels in the options bar, and then press Enter or Return to apply the crop.

Because you're working with several files, you'll give the 09A_Start.jpg file a descriptive name, so that it will be easy to identify. You'll also save the file in the Photoshop format, because each time you edit and then resave a JPEG file, its quality degrades.

4 Choose File > Save As, choose Photoshop for the Format, and name the cropped image **Museum.psd**. Make sure it's in the Lesson09 folder, and click Save.

5 In the Mini Bridge panel, double-click the Capitol_Building.jpg and then the Washington_Monument.jpg file to open them.

The image files open in Photoshop, each with its own tab.

6 Select the Washington_Monument.jpg file, and choose File > Save As. Choose Photoshop for the Format, and rename the file **Monument.psd**. Then click Save.

7 Select the Capitol_Building.jpg tab. Choose File > Save As, choose Photoshop for the Format, and rename the file **Capitol.psd**. Then click Save.

8 Repeat steps 1–3 to crop the Capitol.psd and Monument.psd files. Then save each file.

Cropped versions of Museum.psd, Capitol.psd, and Monument.psd

9 In Mini Bridge, double-click the Background.jpg file to open it in Photoshop.

10 Select the Move tool to remove the crop window.

11 Choose File > Save As. Choose Photoshop for the Format, and rename the file **09A_Working.psd**. Then click Save. Double-click the Mini Bridge tab to close the panel, but leave all four files open for the next exercise.

Positioning images using guides

Guides are nonprinting lines that help you align elements in your document, either horizontally or vertically. If you choose a Snap To command, the guides behave like magnets: When you drag an object close to a guide and then release the mouse button, the object snaps into place along the guide. You'll add guides to the background image that you'll use as the basis for the composite.

1 Choose View > Rulers. Rulers appear along the top and left edges of the window.

2 Choose Window > Info to open the Info panel.

3 From the horizontal ruler, drag a guide to the middle of the image, and release the mouse when the Y coordinate value in the Info panel is 3.000 inches. A blue guide line appears across the image.

● **Note:** If the ruler units are marked in a unit other than inches, right-click or Control-click a ruler, and choose Inches from the context menu.

4 Drag another guide, this time from the vertical ruler, and release the mouse when X = 3.000 inches.

5 Choose View > Snap To, and make sure Guides is selected.

6 Drag another guide from the vertical ruler to the middle of the image. Though you could move it further, it snaps into place at the exact midpoint of the image.

▶ **Tip:** If you need to adjust a ruler guide, use the Move tool. You may need to zoom in to move the ruler to a precise coordinate.

7 Choose Window > Arrange > 4-Up. All four images are visible, each in its own window.

8 Select the Move tool (⊕), and then drag the Museum.psd image onto the 09A_Working.psd image. Photoshop places the Museum.psd image on its own layer in the 09A_Working.psd file.

9 Drag the Monument.psd and Capitol.psd images onto the 09A_Working.psd file.

10 Close the Monument.psd, Capitol.psd, and Museum.psd files without saving them.

11 Rename the layers in the Layers panel to correspond with the appropriate images: **Museum**, **Monument**, and **Capitol**. If you dragged them in the order listed above, rename Layer 1 **Museum**, Layer 2 **Monument**, and Layer 3 **Capitol**.

12 Click the Create A New Group button at the bottom of the Layers panel, and name the group **Montage images**.

13 Drag the Capitol, Monument, and Museum layers into the Montage images group.

14 Select the Monument layer, and then select the Move tool (⊕) in the Tools panel. Move the Monument layer to the center of the canvas, with its top edge aligned to the horizontal guide.

15 Select the Capitol layer, and then drag it to the left of the monument so that the top of the image snaps onto the horizontal guide. Space it evenly between the image of the monument and the left edge of the postcard. Do the same for the Museum layer, placing it to the right of the monument image.

16 Choose View > Show > Guides to hide the guides. Then choose View > Rulers to hide them.

17 Choose File > Save to save your work so far. Click OK if the Photoshop Format Options dialog box appears.

Extra credit

It was easy to align the images using centered guides, but for greater precision, Smart Guides are an excellent way to align photos and objects. Using your working file as it is after the "Positioning images using guides" exercise, you can try another way to align these photos; or continue with the lesson and try this technique some other time.

1 Select the Museum layer in the Layers panel. In the image window, use the Move tool to move the image out of alignment.

2 Choose View > Show > Smart Guides.

3 Using the Move tool, drag the Museum image in the image window to align its top edge with the top edge of the monument.

4 Choose View > Show > Smart Guides to hide the Smart Guides.

Adding text to a montage

You'll add text to the postcard, and then apply some effects to it.

1 Select the Background layer, so that the text layer will be right above it.

2 Select the Horizontal Type tool (T). Then click in the sky area and type **Greetings From**. Click the Commit Any Current Edits button in the options bar to accept the text. Photoshop creates a new text layer.

3 With the Greetings From text layer selected, choose Window > Character, and then enter the following settings in the Character panel:

- Font: Chapparal Pro, Regular
- Font size: **36** pt
- Tracking: **220**
- Color: Red
- All Caps (TT)
- Anti-Aliasing: Smooth

4 Select the Move tool (✛), and then move the text across the center of the top of the canvas. It snaps into place when it's centered even though the guides are hidden, because Snap To Guides is still selected.

5 Select the Text tool again, click on the canvas, and type **Washington, D.C.** Then click the Commit Any Current Edits button.

Photoshop used the current settings in the Character panel for the new text.

6 Enter the following settings in the Character panel:

- Font: Myriad Pro, Bold
- Font Size: **48** pt
- Tracking: **0**
- Color: White

(Leave All Caps selected, and Anti-Aliasing set to Smooth.)

7 Use the Move tool to drag the Washington, D.C. text to the center of the canvas, just below the other text.

8 Select the Greetings From text layer in the Layers panel. Click the Add A Layer Style button (fx) at the bottom of the Layers panel, and choose Outer Glow.

9 Apply these settings in the Outer Glow area of the Layer Style dialog box:

- Blend Mode: Screen

- Opacity: **40**%

- Color: White

- Spread: **14**%

- Size: **40** px

10 Click OK to accept the layer style.

11 In the Tools panel, click the Foreground Color swatch, and then select red from the Color Picker dialog box. Click OK.

You'll use the foreground color to create stripes in the lower text.

12 Select the Washington, D.C. text layer, click the Add A Layer Style button (*fx*), and choose Gradient Overlay.

13 In the Gradient Overlay area of the Layer Style dialog box, click the arrow next to the Gradient swatch to open the Gradient pop-up menu. Select the gradient that looks like red and transparent stripes (the next-to-last one in the menu). You'll use the defaults for the other settings.

14 Click Drop Shadow in the list on the left to add another effect to the same text. In the Drop Shadow area of the dialog box, change the Opacity to **45**% and the Distance to **9** px. Leave the other settings unchanged.

15 Click OK to apply the effects and close the Layer Style dialog box. Then choose File > Save to save your work so far.

Applying filters

Photoshop includes many filters for creating special effects. The best way to learn about them is to test different filters with various options on your files. You can use the Filter Gallery to preview a filter's effect on your image without committing to it.

You've used filters in some earlier lessons. In this lesson, you'll apply the Graphic Pen filter to the museum image for a hand-sketched effect.

Improving performance with filters

Some filter effects can be memory-intensive, especially when applied to a high-resolution image. You can use these techniques to improve performance:

*   Test filters and settings on a small portion of an image.

*   Apply the effect to individual channels—for example, to each RGB channel—if the image is large and you're having problems with insufficient memory. (Note, however, that some filters may produce different results when you apply them to individual channels rather than the composite image, especially if the filter randomly modifies pixels.)

*   Free up memory before running the filter by using the Purge commands in the Edit menu.

*   Close other open applications to free more memory for Photoshop. If you're using Mac OS, allocate more RAM to Photoshop.

*   Try changing settings to improve the speed of memory-intensive filters such as Lighting Effects, Cutout, Stained Glass, Chrome, Ripple, Spatter, Sprayed Strokes, and Glass filters. For example, with the Stained Glass filter, you might increase cell size. With the Cutout filter, try increasing Edge Simplicity, decreasing Edge Fidelity, or both.

*   If you plan to print to a grayscale printer, convert a copy of the image to grayscale before applying filters. However, applying a filter to a color image and then converting to grayscale may not have the same effect as applying the filter to a grayscale version of the image.

1 Select the Museum layer in the Layers panel.

2 In the Tools panel, click the Default Foreground And Background Colors button (🖿) to return the foreground color to black.

The Graphic Pen filter uses the foreground color.

3 Choose Filter > Filter Gallery.

The Filter Gallery includes a preview window, lists of available filters, and the settings for the selected filter. This is a great place to test filter settings on your image before you decide which settings to apply.

4 Click the triangle next to Sketch to expand the section. Then, select Graphic Pen. The image preview immediately changes to reflect the default values for that filter.

5 In the rightmost pane, set the Light/Dark Balance to **25**. Leave the other options at their default settings (Stroke Length 15, Stroke Direction Right Diagonal). The preview updates.

6 Click OK to apply the filter and close the Filter Gallery.

7 Choose File > Save to save your work so far.

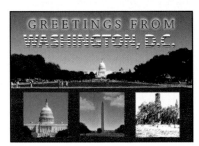

Using filters

As you consider which filter to use and the effect it might have, keep in mind the following:

- The last filter chosen appears at the top of the Filter menu.
- Filters are applied to the active, visible layer.
- Filters cannot be applied to bitmap-mode or indexed-color images.
- Some filters work only on RGB images.
- Some filters are processed entirely in RAM.
- To apply more than one filter in the Filter Gallery, click the New Filter button at the bottom of the filters list, and then select a filter.
- See "Using filters" in Photoshop Help for a list of filters that can be used with 16- and 32-bit-per-channel images.
- Photoshop Help provides specific information on individual filters.

Julieanne Kost is an official Adobe Photoshop evangelist.

Tool tips from the Photoshop evangelist

Using filter shortcuts

These powerful shortcuts can save time when working with filters:

- To reapply the most recently used filter with its last values, press Ctrl+F (Windows) or Command+F (Mac OS).
- To display the dialog box for the last filter you applied, press Ctrl+Alt+F (Windows) or Command+Option+F (Mac OS).
- To reduce the effect of the last filter you applied, press Ctrl+Shift+F (Windows) or Command+Shift+F (Mac OS).

Hand-coloring selections on a layer

Before the days of color photography, artists painted color onto black-and-white images. You can create the same effect by hand-coloring selections on a layer. In this exercise, you'll hand-color the museum image, and then add stars to the sky in the background image.

Applying painting effects

You'll use different brushes, with varying opacities and blending modes, to add color to the sky, grass, and building in the museum image.

1   In the Layers panel, Ctrl-click (Windows) or Command-click (Mac OS) the image thumbnail on the Museum layer. The contents of the layer are selected.

You can paint only within the selection, so you don't need to worry about painting the background image or the other images. Just make sure you see the selection border around the image before you start painting.

2   Zoom in on the museum image so that you can see it clearly.

▶ **Tip:** You can change the brush opacity by pressing a number on the keypad from 0 to 9 (where 1 is 10%, 9 is 90%, and 0 is 100%).

3   Select the Brush tool (✏). In the options bar, select a **90**-pixel brush with a hardness of **0**. Choose Darken from the Mode menu. Set the brush opacity to **20**%.

4   Click the Foreground Color swatch in the Tools panel, and select a color of bright blue (not too light). You'll use this color to paint the sky.

▶ **Tip:** To change the brush size as you paint, press the bracket keys on your keyboard. The Left Bracket key ([) decreases the brush size; the Right Bracket ([]) increases it.

5   Paint the sky in the museum image. Because the opacity is set to 20%, you can paint over the same area again to darken it. Don't be afraid to paint near the borders; nothing outside the image border is affected by the paintbrush. You can change the brush size and opacity as you paint; for example, you may need a smaller brush to paint the areas between treetops. If you make a mistake, press Ctrl+Z (Windows) or Command+Z (Mac OS) to undo it. But remember that you're going for a handpainted look; it doesn't need to be perfect.

6 Paint the trees and grass the same way. Change the foreground color to green, and then set up a **70**-pixel soft brush, using the Darken blending mode, and **80%** opacity. It's fine to paint over the black sketched areas; only the white areas show much color.

Tip: When hand-coloring an image, work from the background forward, so that you can overpaint any stray marks.

7 Next, paint the museum façade a dark red color. Start with a **40**-pixel brush, using the Lighten blending mode, and **80%** opacity.

Using the Lighten blending mode affects the black lines rather than the white areas.

8 When you're satisfied with the painting, choose Select > Deselect to deselect the image. Then choose File > Save to save your work.

Saving selections

In order to fill the background sky with handpainted stars, you need to save a selection of the sky. First, you'll save the background image as a Smart Object so that you can apply Smart Filters to it later.

1 In the Layers panel, close the Montage images folder to make things tidier. Then, right-click (Windows) or Control-click (Mac OS) the Background layer, and choose Convert To Smart Object. (The Background layer is at the bottom of the layer stack.)

The layer name changes to Layer 2. An icon appears in the layer thumbnail, indicating that the layer is now a Smart Object. Filters, called *Smart Filters*, are applied to Smart Objects nondestructively, so that you can continue to edit them later.

2 Rename Layer 2 **Capitol and Mall**.

3 Double-click the image thumbnail on the Capitol and Mall layer; click OK in the informational message.

The Smart Object opens in its own image window. You can edit it without affecting any other objects.

4 Select the Quick Selection tool (✐), and use it to select the sky. If you need to remove an area of the selection, click the Subtract From Selection button in the options bar, and then click the area you need to deselect. Don't worry about making the selection perfect.

For help using the Quick Selection tool and other selection tools, see Lesson 3, "Working with Selections."

5 With the sky selected, click Refine Edge in the options bar. Change the following settings, and click OK:

- Smooth: **25**
- Feather: **30**
- Shift Edge: **-20**

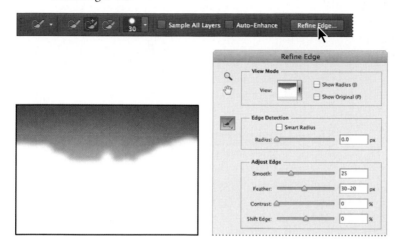

These settings feather the edge of the skyline so that the selection does not have a hard edge.

6 Choose Select > Save Selection. In the Save Selection dialog box, name the selection **Sky**, and click OK.

7 Choose Select > Deselect.

Painting with a special effects brush

You'll add stars to the sky you just selected, using a star-shaped brush.

1 Press D to restore the default foreground and background colors to the Tools panel. Then press X to switch them, so that white is the foreground color.

You'll paint white stars on the sky, so the foreground color needs to be white.

2 Select the Brush tool ( ). In the options bar, open the Brush Preset picker.

3 From the Options menu ( )in the upper right corner, choose Assorted Brushes, and then click Append.

You'll use a star-shaped brush, which is in the Assorted Brushes set.

4 Scroll down in the Brush Preset picker, and select a Star brush. Increase its size to **300** pixels, choose Normal from the Mode menu, and select **100%** opacity.

Now that you have your brush set up, you need to load the selection you saved.

5 Choose Select > Load Selection. In the Load Selection dialog box, choose Sky from the Channel menu, and click OK.

6 In the Layers panel, click the New Layer button. Rename the layer **Paint**.

7 Click the brush to paint stars in the sky. You can paint near the edges, because only the selection will be affected. Just make sure the selection remains active.

● **Note:** If you want to start over, just delete the Paint layer and create a new layer. To delete a layer, drag it to the Delete Layer button in the Layers panel.

8 When you're satisfied with the arrangement of the stars, change the Opacity of the Paint layer to **50**% in the Layers panel. Then, in the Layers panel, choose Overlay from the Blending Mode menu.

9 Choose File > Save, and then close the Smart Object. When Photoshop returns you to the 09A_Working.psd image, choose View > Fit On Screen so you can see the entire postcard.

The stars have been added to your postcard. You can edit the stars at any time by double-clicking the image thumbnail in the Layers panel to open the Smart Object.

10 Choose File > Save to save your work.

Applying Smart Filters

Unlike regular filters, which permanently change an image, Smart Filters are non-destructive: They can be adjusted, turned off and on, and deleted. However, you can apply Smart Filters only to a Smart Object.

You already converted the Capitol and Mall layer to a Smart Object. You'll apply several Smart Filters to the layer, and then add some layer styles.

1   Select the Capitol and Mall layer in the Layers panel. Then choose Filter > Filter Gallery.

Photoshop opens the Filter Gallery.

2   In the Filter Gallery, expand the Artistic folder, and then select Cutout.

The Cutout filter makes an image appear as if it were constructed from roughly cut pieces of colored paper.

3   On the right side of the dialog box, change the Number Of Levels to **8**, leave Edge Simplicity at **4**, and move the Edge Fidelity slider to **3**. Then click OK.

Smart Filters appear with the Smart Object in the Layers panel. An icon appears to the right of a layer name if filter effects are applied to a layer.

4   Double-click the Filter Gallery in the Layers panel to open the Filter Gallery again. Click the New Effect Layer button (◥) at the bottom of the applied filters list, and then select any filter. Experiment with the settings until you're satisfied, but don't click OK yet.

We chose Film Grain from the Artistic folder, and used the following settings: Grain 2, Highlight Area 6, and Intensity 1.

You can mix and match Smart Filters and turn them off and on.

5 In the applied filters list in the Filter Gallery, drag the Cutout filter above the second filter you applied to see how the effect changes. Click OK to close the Filter Gallery.

The order in which you apply filters can change the effect. You can also hide an effect by clicking the eye icon (👁) next to its name in the filter list.

You'll use filters to give the other inset images a handpainted look without going to all the trouble of painting them manually. First, you'll convert them to Smart Objects.

6 Open the Montage images folder again, and select the Capitol layer. Then choose Filter > Convert For Smart Filters. Click OK in the informational dialog box.

The Capitol layer is now a Smart Object.

7 Select the Monument layer, and choose Filter > Convert For Smart Filters to convert it to a Smart Object, too.

8 Select the Capitol layer, and then choose Filter > Filter Gallery, and select a filter you like. Experiment with the settings until you find an effect you like. Then click OK to apply the filter.

We chose the Crosshatch filter (in the Brush Strokes folder), with a Stroke Length of 12, Sharpness of 9, and Strength of 1.

9 Select the Monument layer, and choose Filter > Filter Gallery. Select a filter you like, and then click OK to apply it.

You can apply almost any filter, including third-party filters, as a Smart Filter. The only exceptions are the Extract, Liquify, Pattern Maker, and Vanishing Point filters, because those require access to the original image pixels. In addition to filters, you can apply the Shadows/Highlights and Variations adjustments to Smart Objects.

10 Choose File > Save to save your work.

Adding drop shadows and a border

You're almost done with the postcard. To make the inset images stand out a little more, you'll add drop shadows to them. Then, you'll add a border around the entire postcard.

1 Select the Capitol layer, and click the Add A Layer Style button (*fx*) at the bottom of the Layers panel. Choose Drop Shadow.

2 In the Layer Style dialog box, change the Opacity to **40**%, Distance to **15** px, Spread to **9**%, and the Size to **9** px. Then click OK.

3 In the Layers panel, press Alt (Windows) or Option (Mac OS) as you drag the Drop Shadow effect from the Capitol layer onto the Monument layer.

4 Alt-drag or Option-drag the same Drop Shadow effect onto the Museum layer.

5 Close the Montage images folder again.

Now you'll expand the canvas so that you can add a border without covering any of your image.

6 Choose Image > Canvas Size, and enter **7** inches for the Width and **5** inches for the Height. Click OK.

A transparent border appears around the image. You'll make that border appear white.

7 Press D to return the foreground and background colors to the defaults in the Tools panel, so that the background layer is white.

8 In the Layers panel, click the Create A New Layer button (🖺), and then drag the new layer to the bottom of the layer stack. Name it **Border**.

9 With the Border layer selected, choose Select > All.

10 Choose Edit > Fill. In the Fill dialog box, choose Background Color from the Use menu, and click OK.

11 Choose File > Save to save the postcard.

The postcard is ready to print and mail. It's a standard U.S. Postal Service postcard size.

12 Close the 09A_Working.psd file. You'll use different files to create the panorama.

Matching color schemes across images

You'll be combining six images into a panorama for the poster. To provide continuity in the panorama, you'll harmonize the color schemes in the images by matching the target image to the dominant colors in a source. First, you'll open the document that you'll use as the source for the color matching.

1 Open the Mini Bridge tab to open the panel, and then double-click the IMG_1441.psd file to open it.

There are six sequentially numbered images in the same folder. You'll match the colors for these files.

2 In the Mini Bridge panel, double-click the IMG_1442.psd file to open it.

The IMG_1442.psd file is overexposed in some areas, and a little washed out. You'll use the Match Color feature to match its colors to those in the IMG_1441.psd file.

3 With the IMG_1442.psd file active, choose Image > Adjustments > Match Color. In the Match Color dialog box, do the following:

- Select the Preview option, if it's not already selected.

- Choose IMG_1441.psd from the Source menu.

- Choose the Background layer from the Layer menu. You can select any layer in the source image, but this image has only one layer.

- Experiment with the Luminance, Color Intensity, and Fade settings.

- When the color scheme unifies the colors in the images, click OK.

4 Choose File > Save to save the IMG_1442.psd file with the new colors. Then double-click the Mini Bridge tab to close the Mini Bridge panel.

You can use Match Color with any source file to create interesting and unusual effects. The Match Color feature is also useful for certain color corrections (such as skin tones) in some photographs. The feature can also match the color between different layers in the same image. See Photoshop Help for more information.

Automating a multistep task

An *action* is a set of one or more commands that you record and then play back to apply to a single file or a batch of files. In this exercise, you'll use actions to color match, sharpen, and save the images you'll combine in a panorama.

Using actions is one of several ways that you can automate tasks in Adobe Photoshop. To learn more about recording actions, see Photoshop Help.

You've already matched the color for one of the images. Now, you'll sharpen one image using the Unsharp Mask filter, and save it to a new Ready For Panorama folder.

1 With the IMG_1442.psd file active, choose Filter > Sharpen > Unsharp Mask.

2 In the Unsharp Mask dialog box, change the Radius to **1.2**, leave the other settings unchanged, and click OK.

3 Choose File > Save As. Choose TIFF for the Format, use the same name (IMG_1442), and save it to a new folder called **Ready For Panorama**. Then click Save.

4 In the Image Compression area of the TIFF Options dialog box, select LZW, and click OK.

5 Close the IMG_1442.tif file.

Preparing to record an action

You use the Actions panel to record, play, edit, and delete individual actions. You also use the Actions panel to save and load action files. First, you'll open the Actions panel and open the additional files you'll be using.

1 Choose Window > Actions to open the Actions panel.

2 In the Actions panel, click the Create New Set button (▣). Name the new set **My Actions**, and click OK.

3 Choose File > Open. In the Open dialog box, navigate to the Lesson09 folder. Shift-select the IMG_1443.psd, IMG_1444.psd, IMG_1445.psd, and IMG_1446.psd files. Then click Open.

Now there are five tabs, representing five open files in Photoshop.

Recording actions

You'll record the steps for matching colors, sharpening, and saving the images as an action.

1   Select the IMG_1443.psd tab. Then, in the Actions panel, click the New Action button (■).

2   In the New Action dialog box, name the action **color match and sharpen**, and make sure that My Actions is selected in the Set menu. Then click Record.

Don't let the fact that you're recording rush you. Take all the time you need to do this procedure accurately. The speed at which you work has no influence on the amount of time required to play a recorded action.

3   Choose Image > Adjustments > Match Color.

4   In the Match Color dialog box, select IMG_1441.psd from the Source menu, select Background from the Layer menu, and make any other changes that you made when you matched color for IMG_1442.psd. Click OK.

● **Note:** You must finish all steps in this procedure without interruption. If you need to start over, skip ahead to step 8 to stop the recording, and then drag the action onto the Delete button in the Actions panel. Use the History panel to delete any states after you opened the files. Then start again at step 1.

5 Choose Filter > Sharpen > Unsharp Mask. The settings in the Unsharp Mask dialog box should be the settings you used for the IMG_1442.psd file. Click OK.

Photoshop preserves your most recent settings in filter dialog boxes until you change them again.

6 Choose File > Save As. In the Save As dialog box, choose TIFF for the Format, keep the same name (IMG_1443), and save the file to the Ready For Panorama folder. Click Save. In the TIFF Options dialog box, make sure LZW is selected, and click OK.

7 Close the image.

8 Click the Stop button (■) at the bottom of the Actions panel to stop recording.

The action you just recorded is now saved in the Actions panel. Click the arrows to expand different sets of steps. You can examine each recorded step and the specific selections you made.

Playing an action

You'll apply the color match and sharpen action to one of the other three image files that you opened.

1 Click the IMG_1444.psd tab to make that image active.

2 In the Actions panel, select the color match and sharpen action in the My Actions set, and then click the Play button (▶).

The IMG_1444.psd image is automatically color matched, sharpened, and saved as a TIFF, and it now matches the IMG_1443.tif image for these properties. Because you recorded closing the file, the file has also been closed.

Batch-playing an action

Applying actions is a timesaving process for performing routine tasks on files, but you can streamline your work even further by applying actions to all open files. Two more files in this project need to be prepared for the panorama, so you'll apply your automated action to them simultaneously.

1 Make sure that the IMG_1445.psd and IMG_1446.psd files are open. Close the IMG_1441.psd file, and then open it again to ensure that it's the third tab.

2 Choose File > Automate > Batch.

3 In the Play area of the Batch dialog box, choose My Actions from the Set menu, and choose color match and sharpen from the Action menu.

4 Choose Opened Files from the Source menu. Leave Destination set to None, and click OK.

● **Note:** If the IMG_1441.psd file is not the third tab, it will close before the color can be matched for one or both of the other images. Match Color requires that the source file be open. Simply rearranging the tabs doesn't change the order in which Photoshop applies the action.

The action is applied to both IMG_1445.psd and IMG_1446.psd, so the files have the same color matching and sharpening and are saved as TIFF files. The same action was applied to IMG_1441.psd, even though its color was matched with itself.

In this exercise, you batch-processed three files instead of making all the same changes in each of them; this was a mild convenience. But creating and applying actions can save significant amounts of time and tedium when you have dozens or even hundreds of files that require any routine, repetitive work.

Stitching a panorama

The files have been color matched, sharpened, and saved to prevent unsightly inconsistencies in your panorama. Now you're ready to stitch the images together! Then, you'll add a border with lettering to complete the poster.

1   With no files open in Photoshop, choose File > Automate > Photomerge.

2   In the Layout area of the dialog box, select Auto. Then, in the Source Files area, click Browse, and navigate to the Lesson09/Ready For Panorama folder. Shift-select all the images in the folder, and click OK or Open.

3   At the bottom of the Photomerge dialog box, select Blend Images Together, Vignette Removal, and Geometric Distortion Correction. Then click OK.

Photoshop creates the panorama image. It's a complex process, so you may have to wait several minutes while Photoshop works. When it's finished, you should see an image that looks similar to the one below, with six layers in the Layers panel—one for each of the images. Photoshop has found the overlapping areas of the images and matched them, correcting any angular discrepancies. In the process, it left some empty areas. You'll make the panorama tidy by adding a little sky to fill in some of the empty area, and by cropping the image.

4 Select all the layers in the Layers panel, and then choose Layer > Merge Layers.

5 Choose File > Save As. Choose Photoshop for the Format, and name the file
   09B_Working.psd. Save the file in the Lesson09 folder. Click Save, and then
   click OK in the Photoshop Format Options dialog box.

6 Select the Crop tool (⊟). In the options bar, choose Unconstrained to remove
   any aspect ratio values, so you can crop to any size. Then drag the crop box to
   include the area from the edge of the grass (where its bottom edge is highest) to
   the highest point of the image (just above the highest museum tower). Crop out
   all the transparent areas on the sides. When you are satisfied with your cropped
   area, press Enter or Return, or click the Commit Current Crop Operation button
   (✔) in the options bar.

7 Select the Magic Wand tool (🪄), hidden beneath the Quick Selection tool in the Tools panel.

8 Click in the transparent area on the right to select it, and then Shift-click in the transparent area on the left to add it to the selection.

9 Choose Edit > Fill.

10 In the Fill dialog box, choose Content-Aware from the Use menu, and click OK.

Photoshop fills the transparent area with color that blends with the existing sky.

11 Choose Select > Deselect.

12 Choose File > Save to save your work so far.

Finishing the image

The panorama looks great, but because of the wide angle, some of the lines are a little off. For example, several buildings lean unrealistically. You'll use the Adaptive Wide Angle filter to correct the perspective, and then add lettering on the side for the final touch.

1 Choose Filter > Adaptive Wide Angle.

2 In the Adaptive Wide Angle dialog box, select the Constraint tool (⬉). The Constraint tool lets you define the straight areas in the image; the filter adjusts the rest of the image to match the perspective you specify.

3 Click a point on the ground beneath the first tower, and then click another point at the base of the large tree, effectively drawing a straight line.

▶ **Tip:** If transparent areas appear along the edge of the image, use the Scale option in the Adaptive Wide Angle filter to scale the image.

As you release the mouse from the second point, the filter adjusts the perspective of the image. Next, you'll adjust the ground under the Washington Monument so that it stands vertically.

4 Click in the center of the trees next to the monument, and then click again in the grass to the right of the momument, drawing a diagonal line, as in the image below.

5 If you want to adjust the angle, click the rotation handle on the line you drew, and drag it up a few degrees.

You can continue to adjust the rotation on any line you drew until you close the filter dialog box.

6 When you're satisfied, click OK to accept the changes and apply the filter to the image.

The poster needs only the lettering on the side to be complete.

7 Choose File > Open, navigate to the Lesson09 folder, and double-click the DC_Letters.psd file to open it.

8 Choose Window > Arrange > 2 Up Vertical so that you can see both files. Then, use the Move tool (✛) to drag the DC_Letters.psd image onto the Panorama image. Close the DC_Letters.psd file without saving it.

9 With the Move tool, position the lettering and red background along the left side of the image.

Because you're preparing this poster for printing, you'll convert it to CMYK.

10 Choose Image > Mode > CMYK Color. Click Merge to merge layers. Click OK if you see a color profile informational dialog box.

11 Choose Layer > Flatten Image to reduce the image size.

12 Choose File > Save to save your work.

You've created two photographic souvenirs by combining images. You created a montage of several images, and you blended images into a panorama. You're ready to create montages and panoramas from your own images.

Review questions

1 What is the purpose of saving selections?

2 How can you preview filter effects before you commit to them?

3 What are the differences between using a Smart Filter and a regular filter to apply effects to an image?

4 Describe one use for the Match Color feature.

Review answers

1 By saving a selection, you can create and reuse time-consuming selections and uniformly select artwork in an image. You can also combine selections or create new selections by adding to or subtracting from existing selections.

2 Use the Filter Gallery to test different filters with different settings to see the effect they'll have on your image.

3 Smart Filters are nondestructive: They can be adjusted, turned off and on, and deleted at any time. In contrast, regular filters permanently change an image; once applied, they cannot be removed. Smart Filters can be applied only to a Smart Object layer.

4 You can use the Match Color feature to match color between different images, such as to adjust the facial skin tones in photographs—or to match color between different layers in the same image. You can also use the feature to create unusual color effects.

10 EDITING VIDEO

Lesson overview

In this lesson, you'll learn how to do the following:

- Create a video timeline in Photoshop.

- Add media to a video group in the Timeline panel.

- Add motion to video clips and still images.

- Animate type and effects using keyframes.

- Add transitions between video clips.

- Include audio in a video file.

- Render a video.

 This lesson will take about 90 minutes to complete. Copy the Lesson10 folder onto your hard drive if you haven't already done so. As you work on this lesson, you'll preserve the start files. If you need to restore the start files, copy them from the *Adobe Photoshop CS6 Classroom in a Book* DVD.

Now you can edit video files in Photoshop using many of the same effects you use to edit image files. You can create a movie from video files, still images, Smart Objects, audio files, and type layers; apply transitions; and animate effects using keyframes.

Getting started

In this lesson, you'll edit a video that was shot using a camera phone. You'll create a video timeline, import clips, add transitions and other video effects, and render the final video. First, look at the final project to see what you'll be creating.

1 Start Photoshop, and then immediately hold down Ctrl+Alt+Shift (Windows) or Command+Option+Shift (Mac OS) to restore the default preferences. (See "Restoring default preferences" on page 4.)

2 When prompted, click Yes to delete the Adobe Photoshop Settings file.

3 Choose File > Browse In Bridge.

4 In Bridge, select the Lessons folder in the Favorites panel. Then, double-click the Lesson10 folder in the Content panel.

5 Double-click the 10End.mp4 file to open it in QuickTime.

6 Click the Play button in QuickTime to view the final video.

The short video is a compilation of clips from a day at the beach. It includes transitions, layer effects, animated text, and a musical.

7 Close QuickTime and return to Bridge.

8 Double-click the 10End.psd file to open it in Photoshop.

Photoshop displays the Timeline panel, and there are guidelines across the document window. The guidelines identify the area that would be visible if the video is broadcast. The Timeline panel includes all the video clips and the audio track.

9 When you've finished exploring the end file, close it.

Creating a new video project

Working with video is a little different from working with still images in Photoshop. You may find it easiest to create the project first, and then import the assets you'll be using. You'll choose the video preset for this project, and then add nine video and image files to include in your movie.

Creating a new file

Photoshop CS6 includes several film and video presets for you to choose from. You'll create a new file and select an appropriate preset.

1 Choose File > New.

2 Name the file **10Start.psd**.

3 Choose Film & Video from the Preset menu.

4 Choose HDV/HDTV 720p/29.97 from the Size menu.

5 Accept the default settings for the other options, and click OK.

● **Note:** The video in this lesson was shot using an Apple iPhone, so one of the HDV presets is appropriate. The 720P preset provides good quality without providing too much data for easy streaming online.

6 Choose File > Save As, and save the file in the Lesson10 folder.

Importing assets

Photoshop CS6 includes tools specifically for working with video, such as the Timeline panel. The Timeline panel may already be open because you previewed the end file earlier. You use the Timeline panel to arrange layers in a video, animate their properties, set the start and end points for each layer, and apply transitions. To ensure you have access to the resources you need, you'll select the Motion workspace and organize your panels before you import files for the video.

1 Choose Window > Workspace > Motion.

2 Pull the top edge of the Timeline panel up so that the panel occupies the bottom half of the workspace.

3 Select the Zoom tool (🔍), and then click Fit Screen in the options bar so that you can see the entire canvas within the top half of the screen.

4 Click Create Video Timeline. Photoshop creates a new video timeline, including two default tracks: Layer 0 and Audio Track.

5 Click the Video menu in the Layer 0 track, and choose Add Media.

● **Note:** When you use the Add Media button with an unspecified canvas, Photoshop determines the project size based on the size of the first video file it finds—or, if you're importing only images, based on the image size.

6 Navigate to the Lesson10 folder.

7 Shift-select the video and photo assets numbered 1–9, and click Open.

Photoshop imports all nine of the assets you selected onto the same track, now named Video Group 1, in the Timeline panel. It displays still images with a purple background and video clips with a blue background. In the Layers panel, the assets appear as individual layers in the layer group named Video Group 1. You don't need the Layer 0 layer, so you'll delete it.

8 Select Layer 0 in the Layers panel, and click the Delete Layer button at the bottom of the panel. Click Yes if you're prompted to confirm the deletion.

Changing the duration of clips in the timeline

The clips are of very different lengths, meaning they'd play for different amounts of time. For this video, you want all the clips to be the same length, so you'll shorten them all to 3 seconds. The length of a clip (its *duration*) is measured in seconds and frames: 03:00 is 3 seconds; 02:25 is 2 seconds and 25 frames.

1 Drag the Control Timeline Magnification slider to the right at the bottom of the Timeline panel to zoom in to the timeline. You want to be able to see a thumbnail of each clip, and enough detail in the time ruler that you can accurately change the duration of each clip.

2 Drag the right edge of the first clip (1_Family) to 03:00 on the time ruler. Photoshop displays the end point and the duration as you drag so that you can find the right stopping point.

● **Note:** You're shortening each clip to the same length here, but you can have clips of varying lengths, depending on what's appropriate for the project.

3 Drag the right edge of the second clip (2_BoatRide) to a duration of 03:00.

Shortening a video clip doesn't compress it; it removes part of the clip from the video. In this case, you want to use the first three seconds of each clip. If you wanted to use a different portion of a video clip, you might want to shorten the clip from each end.

4 Repeat step 3 for each of the remaining clips, so that each has a duration of 3 seconds.

The clips are now the right duration, but some of the images are the wrong size for the canvas. You'll resize the first image before continuing.

5 Select the 1_Family layer in the Layers panel. The clip is also selected in the Timeline panel.

▶ **Tip:** The arrow on the left side of a clip (next to the clip's thumbnail) reveals the attributes you can animate using keyframes. The arrow on the right side of a clip opens the Motion dialog box.

6 Click the triangle in the upper right corner of the 1_Family clip in the Timeline panel to open the Motion dialog box.

7 Choose Pan & Zoom from the menu, and make sure Resize To Fill Canvas is selected. Then click in an empty area of the Timeline panel to close the Motion dialog box.

The image resizes to fit the canvas, which is what you wanted. However, you don't actually want to pan and zoom. You'll remove the effect.

8 Open the Motion dialog box from the 1_Family clip again, and choose No Motion from the menu. Click in an empty area of the Timeline panel to close the Motion dialog box.

9 Choose File > Save. Click OK in the Photoshop Format Options dialog box.

Animating text with keyframes

Keyframes let you control animation, effects, and other changes that occur over time. A keyframe marks the point in time where you specify a value, such as a position, size, or style. To create a change over time, you must have at least two keyframes: one for the state at the beginning of the change and one for the state at the end. Photoshop interpolates the values for the positions in between so that the change takes effect smoothly over the specified time. You'll use keyframes to animate a movie title (Beach Day) from left to right over the opening image.

1 Click the Video pop-up menu in the Video Group 1 track, and choose New Video Group. Photoshop adds Video Group 2 to the Timeline panel.

2 Select the Horizontal Type tool (T), and then click on the left edge of the image, about halfway down from the top. Photoshop creates a new type layer, named Layer 1, in the Video Group 2 track.

3 In the options bar, select a sans serif font such as Myriad Pro, set the type size to **600 pt**, and select white for the type color.

4 Type **BEACH DAY**.

The text is large enough that it doesn't all fit on the image. That's okay; you'll animate it to move across the image.

5 In the Layers panel, change the opacity for the BEACH DAY layer to **25%**.

6 In the Timeline panel, drag the end point of the type layer to 03:00, so that it has the same duration as the 1_Family layer.

7 Click the arrow next to the thumbnail in the BEACH DAY clip to display the clip's attributes.

8 Make sure the playhead is at the beginning of the time ruler.

9 Click the stopwatch icon next to the Transform property to set an initial keyframe for the layer. The keyframe appears as a yellow diamond in the timeline.

10 Select the Move tool (▶♦), and then use it to drag the type layer over the canvas so that it is centered vertically. Drag it to the right so that only the left edge of the letter "B" in the word "BEACH" is visible on the canvas.

▶ **Tip:** Photoshop displays the playhead's location in the lower left corner of the Timeline panel.

11 Move the playhead to the last frame of the first clip (02:29f).

12 Press the Shift key as you drag the type layer to the left over the canvas so that only the right edge of the "Y" in the word "DAY" is visible. Pressing the Shift key ensures the type remains level as you move it across.

Photoshop creates a new keyframe because you've changed the position.

13 Move the playhead across the first three seconds of the time ruler to preview the animation. The title moves across the image.

14 Choose File > Save to save your work so far.

Creating effects

One of the benefits of working with video files in Photoshop is that you can create effects using adjustment layers, styles, and simple transformations.

Adding adjustment layers to video clips

You've used adjustment layers with still images throughout this book. They work just as well on video clips. When you apply an adjustment layer in a video group, Photoshop applies it only to the following layer.

1 Select the 3_DogAtBeach layer in the Layers panel.

2 In the Timeline panel, move the playhead to the beginning of the 3_DogAtBeach layer so you can see the effect as you apply it.

3 In the Adjustments panel, click the Black & White button.

4 In the Properties panel, leave the default preset, and select Tint. The default tint color creates a sepia effect that works well for this clip. You can experiment with the sliders and the tint color to modify the black-and-white effect to your taste.

● **Note:** If you had imported the video file using the Place command, so that it was not in a video group, you would need to create a clipping layer to limit the adjustment layer to a single layer.

5 Move the playhead across the 3_DogAtBeach clip in the Timeline panel to preview the effect.

Animating a zoom effect

Even simple transformations become interesting effects when you animate them. You'll use animation to zoom in on the 4_Dogs clip.

1 Move the playhead to the beginning of the 4_Dogs clip in the Timeline panel (09:01). The image is so large that all that appears is a white portion of the sky.

2 Click the arrow in the 4_Dogs clip to display the Motion dialog box.

3 Choose Zoom from the pop-up menu, choose Zoom In from the Zoom menu, and make sure Resize To Fill Canvas is selected. Then click in an empty area of the Timeline panel to close the Motion dialog box.

4 Drag the playhead across the clip to preview the effect. You'll enlarge the image in the last keyframe to make the zoom more dramatic.

5 Click the arrow on the left side of the 4_Dogs clip to reveal the attributes for the clip.

► **Tip:** You can move
to the next keyframe by
clicking the right arrow
next to the attribute
in the Timeline panel.
Click the left arrow to
move to the previous
keyframe.

6 Click the right arrow next to the Transform attribute to select the last keyframe, and choose Edit > Free Transform. Then enter **100%** for the Width and Height in the options bar. Press Enter or Return to confirm the transformation.

7 Drag the playhead across the 4_Dogs clip in the time ruler to preview the animation again.

8 Choose File > Save.

Animating style effects

You can apply layer styles to clips in the Timeline panel. First, you'll resize the image to fit the canvas. Then you'll apply a style and remove it, twice, so that it appears to be blinking on and off in the video.

1 Move the playhead to the beginning of the 6_Avery clip (15:01). The image is too large for the canvas.

2 Open the Motion dialog box for the clip, and choose Pan & Zoom from the pop-up menu. Make sure Resize To Fill Canvas is selected. Then click an empty area of the Timeline panel to close the Motion dialog box and resize the image.

3 Open the Motion dialog box again, and choose No Motion from the pop-up menu, since you don't actually want to pan and zoom in this image. Click an empty area of the Timeline panel to close the dialog box.

4 Choose Window > Styles to open the Styles panel.

5 Click the arrow next to the thumbnail in the 6_Avery clip to show its attributes in the Timeline panel, and then click the stopwatch icon for the Style keyframe.

6 Move the playhead about a quarter of the way through the clip. Then, in the Styles panel, select the Negative Image style.

Photoshop adds a keyframe.

7 Move the playhead to the middle of the clip. Select the Default style to remove the effect. Photoshop adds another keyframe.

8 Move the playhead three-quarters of the way through the clip, and apply the Negative Image style again. Photoshop adds a fourth keyframe.

9 Move the playhead to the end of the clip (17:29), and select the Default style. Photoshop adds a final keyframe for the clip.

10 Move the playhead across the time ruler to preview the effect.

Animating an image to create a motion effect

You'll animate another transformation to create the appearance of motion. You want the image to begin with the diver's legs and end with his hands.

1 Move the playhead to the end of the 7_jumping clip (20:29). The diver is in the final position.

2 Display the attributes for the clip, and click the stopwatch icon for the Position attribute to add a keyframe.

3 Move the playhead to the beginning of the clip (18:01). Press Shift while you move the image up so that the feet are near the bottom of the canvas.

Photoshop adds a keyframe.

4 Move the playhead across the time ruler to preview the animation.

5 Choose File > Save to save your work so far.

Adding pan & zoom effects

You can easily add features similar to the pan and zoom effects used in documentaries. You'll add them to the sunsets to bring the video to a dramatic close.

1 Move the playhead to the beginning of the 8_Sunset clip.

2 Open the Motion dialog box, and choose Pan from the pop-up menu. Make sure Resize To Fill Canvas is selected, and then select an empty area of the Timeline panel to close the Motion dialog box.

3 Move the playhead to the beginning of the 9_Sunset2 clip.

4 Open the Motion dialog box for the clip. Choose Pan & Zoom from the pop-up menu, choose Zoom Out from the Zoom menu, and make sure Resize To Fill Canvas is selected. Then select an empty area of the Timeline panel to close the Motion dialog box.

5 Move the playhead across the last two clips to preview the effects.

Adding transitions

A transition moves a scene from one shot to the next. Simply drag and drop to add transitions to clips in Photoshop.

1 Click the Go To First Frame button (⏮) in the upper left corner of the Timeline panel to return the playhead to the beginning of the time ruler.

2 Click the Transitions button (◩) in the upper left corner of the Timeline panel. Select Cross Fade, and change the Duration value to **.25 s** (for a quarter of a second).

3 Drag the Cross Fade transition between the 1_Family and 2_BoatRide clips.

Photoshop adjusts the ends of the clips to apply the transition and adds a small white icon in the lower corner of the second clip.

4 Drag Cross Fade transitions between each of the other clips.

5 Drag a Fade With Black transition onto the end of the final clip.

6 To make the transition smoother, extend the Fade With Black transition by stretching its left side to about one-third the total length of the clip.

7 Choose File > Save.

Adding audio

You can add a separate audio track to a video file in Photoshop. In fact, the Timeline panel includes an audio track by default. You'll add an MP3 file to play as the soundtrack for this short video.

Tip: You can also add an audio track by clicking the + sign at the far-right end of the track in the Timeline panel.

1 Click the note icon in the Audio Track at the bottom of the Timeline panel, and choose Add Audio from the pop-up menu.

2 Select the Beachsong.mp3 file from the Lesson10 folder, and click Open.

The audio file is added to the timeline, but it's much longer than the video. You'll use the Split At Playhead tool to shorten it.

3 Move the playhead to the end of the 9_Sunset2 clip (25:02), and then click the Split At Playhead tool. The audio file is clipped at that point, becoming two audio clips.

4 Select the second audio file segment, the one that begins after the end of the 9_Sunset2 clip.

5 Press the Delete key on your keyboard to delete the selected audio clip.

Now the audio file is the same length as the video. You'll add a fade so that it ends smoothly.

6 Click the small arrow at the right edge of the audio clip to open the Audio dialog box, and enter **5** seconds for Fade Out.

Muting unwanted audio

So far, you've previewed portions of the video by moving the playhead across the time ruler. Now you'll preview the entire video using the Play button in the Timeline panel, and then mute any extraneous audio from the video clips.

1 Click the Play button (▶) in the upper left corner of the Timeline panel to preview the video so far.

It's looking good, but there is some unwanted background noise from a few of the video clips. You'll mute that extra sound.

▶ **Tip:** To create a smoother preview, disable the audio playback button in the Timeline panel the first time you play the video. With audio playback disabled, Photoshop can create a more complete cache, resulting in a more accurate preview.

2 Click the small triangle at the right end of the 2_BoatRide clip.

3 Click the Audio tab to see audio options, and then select Mute Audio. Click an empty area of the Timeline panel to close the dialog box.

4 Repeat steps 2–3 for the 3_DogAtBeach and 5_BoatRide2 layers.

5 Play the video again. Now the only sound is the audio file you added.

6 Choose File > Save to save your work so far.

Rendering video

You're ready to render your project to video. Photoshop provides several rendering options. You'll select options appropriate for streaming video to share on the Vimeo website. For information about other rendering options, see Photoshop Help.

1 Choose File > Export > Render Video, or click the Render Video button (➡) in the lower left corner of the Timeline panel.

2 Name the file **10Final.mp4**.

3 Click Select Folder, and then navigate to the Lesson10 folder, and click OK or Choose.

4 From the Preset menu, choose Vimeo HD 720p 25.

5 Click Render.

Photoshop displays a progress bar as it exports the video. Depending on your system, the rendering process may take several minutes.

Depending on your system, this may take a while.

6 Locate the 10Final.mp4 file in the Lesson10 folder in Bridge. Double-click it to view the video you made.

Review questions

1 What is a keyframe, and how do you create one?

2 How do you add a transition between clips?

3 How do you render a video?

Review answers

1 A keyframe marks the point in time where you specify a value, such as a position, size, or style. To create a change over time, you must have at least two keyframes: one for the state at the beginning of the change and one for the state at the end. To create an initial keyframe, click the stopwatch icon next to the attribute you want to animate for the layer. Photoshop creates additional keyframes each time you change the values of that attribute.

2 To add a transition, click the Transition icon in the upper left corner of the Timeline panel, and then drag a transition onto a clip.

3 To render a video, choose File > Export > Render Video, or click the Render Video button in the lower left corner of the Timeline panel. Then select the video settings that are appropriate for your intended output.

11 PAINTING WITH THE MIXER BRUSH

Lesson overview

In this lesson, you'll learn how to do the following:

- Customize brush settings.

- Clean the brush.

- Mix colors.

- Use an erodible tip.

- Create a custom brush preset.

- Use wet and dry brushes to blend color.

 This lesson will take about an hour to complete. Copy the Lesson11 folder onto your hard drive if you have not already done so. As you work on this lesson, you'll preserve the start files. If you need to restore the start files, copy them again from the *Adobe Photoshop CS6 Classroom in a Book* DVD.

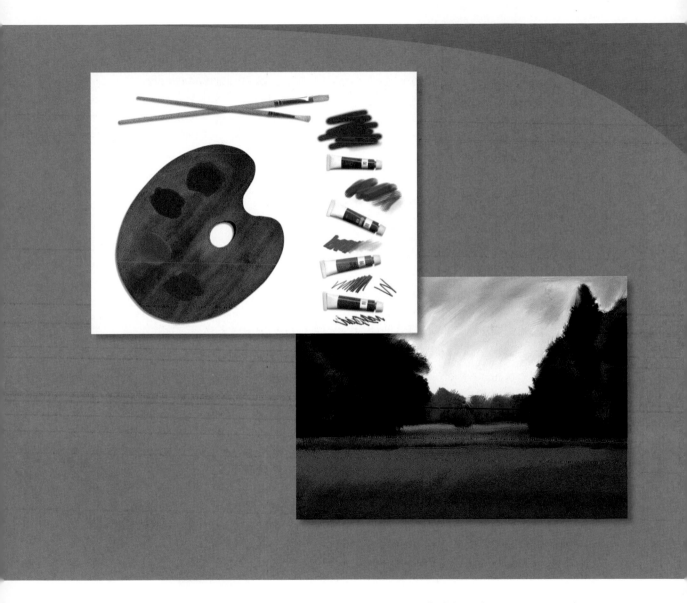

The Mixer Brush tool gives you flexibility, color-mixing abilities, and brush strokes as if you were painting on a physical canvas.

About the Mixer Brush

In previous lessons, you've used brushes in Photoshop to perform various tasks. The Mixer Brush is unlike other brushes in that it lets you mix colors with each other. You can change the wetness of the brush and how it mixes the brush color with the color already on the canvas.

Photoshop brushes have realistic bristles, so you can add textures that resemble those in paintings you might create in the physical world. While this is a great feature in general, it's particularly useful when you're using the Mixer Brush. In Photoshop CS6, you can also use an erodible tip to achieve the effects you might get with charcoal pencils and pastels in the physical world. Combining different bristle settings and brush tips with different wetness, paint-load, and paint-mixing settings gives you opportunities to create exactly the look you want.

Getting started

In this lesson, you'll get acquainted with the Mixer Brush as well as the brush tip and bristle options available in Photoshop CS6. Start by taking a look at the final projects you'll create.

1 Start Photoshop, and then immediately hold down Ctrl+Alt+Shift (Windows) or Command+Option+Shift (Mac OS) to restore the default preferences. (See "Restoring default preferences" on page 4.)

2 When prompted, click Yes to delete the Adobe Photoshop Settings file.

3 Choose File > Browse In Bridge to open Adobe Bridge.

4 In Bridge, click Lessons in the Favorites panel. Double-click the Lesson11 folder in the Content panel.

5 Preview the Lesson11 end files. You'll use the palette image to explore brush options and learn to mix colors. You'll then apply what you've learned to transform the landscape image into a watercolor.

● **Note:** If you plan to do a lot of painting in Photoshop, consider using a tablet, such as a Wacom tablet, instead of a mouse. Photoshop can sense the way you hold and use the pen to change the brush width, strength, and angle on the fly.

6 Double-click 11Palette_start.psd to open the file in Photoshop.

7 Choose File > Save As, and name the file **11Palette_working.psd**. Click OK if the Photoshop Format Options dialog box appears.

Selecting brush settings

The image includes a palette and four tubes of color, which you'll use to sample the colors you're working with. You'll change settings as you paint different colors, exploring brush tip settings and wetness options.

1 Select the Zoom tool (🔍), and zoom in to see the tubes of paint.

2 Select the Eyedropper tool (🖊), and sample the red color from the red tube. The foreground color changes to red.

● **Note:** If you have OpenGL enabled, Photoshop displays a sampling ring so you can preview the color you're picking up.

3 Select the Mixer Brush tool (🖌), hidden under the Brush tool (🖌).

4 Choose Window > Brush to open the Brush panel. Select the first brush.

The Brush panel contains brush presets and several options for customizing brushes.

Experiment with wetness options and brushes

The effect of the brush is determined by the Wet, Load, and Mix fields in the options bar. Wet controls how much paint the brush picks up from the canvas. Load controls how much paint the brush holds when you begin painting (as with a physical brush, it runs out of paint as you paint with it). Mix controls the ratio of paint from the canvas and paint from the brush.

You can change these settings separately. However, it's faster to select a standard combination from the pop-up menu.

1 In the options bar, choose Dry from the pop-up menu of blending brush combinations.

When you select Dry, Wet is set to 0%, Load to 50%, and Mix is not applicable. With the Dry preset, you paint opaque color; you cannot mix colors on a dry canvas.

2 Paint in the area above the red tube. Solid red appears. As you continue painting without releasing the mouse, the paint eventually fades and runs out.

3 Sample the blue color from the blue tube of paint. You can use the Eyedropper tool or Alt-click (Windows) or Option-click (Mac OS) to sample the color. If you use the Eyedropper tool, return to the Mixer Brush tool after you sample the color.

4 In the Brush panel, select the round fan-shaped brush. Choose Wet from the pop-up menu in the options bar.

5 Paint above the blue tube. The paint mixes with the white background.

6 Choose Dry from the menu in the options bar, and then paint again above the blue tube. A much darker, more opaque blue appears, and doesn't mix with the white background.

The bristles from the fan brush you selected are much more apparent than the bristles you used originally. Changing bristle qualities makes a big difference in the texture you paint.

7 In the Brush panel, decrease the number of bristles to **40**%. Paint a little more with the blue brush to see the change in texture. The bristles are much more obvious in the stroke.

> ▶ **Tip:** The Bristle Brush Preview shows you the direction of the bristles as you paint. To show or hide the Bristle Brush Preview, click the Toggle The Bristle Brush Preview button at the bottom of the Brush or Brush Presets panel. The Bristle Brush Preview is available only with OpenGL enabled.

● **Note:** When you use
Alt-click or Option-click
to load paint from the
canvas, the brush picks
up any color variation
in the sample area. If
you want to sample
only solid colors, select
Load Solid Colors Only
in the Current Brush
Load menu in the
options bar.

8 Sample the yellow color from the yellow paint tube. In the Brush panel, select the flat-point brush with fewer bristles (the one to the right of the fan brush). Choose Dry from the menu in the options bar, and then paint in the area over the yellow paint tube.

9 Choose Very Wet from the menu in the options bar, and then paint some more. Now the yellow mixes with the white background.

Use an erodible tip

In Photoshop CS6, you can choose an erodible tip, so that the width of the brush changes as you paint. Erodible tips are represented in the Brush panel by pencil icons, because in the physical world, pencils and pastels have erodible tips. You'll experiment with erodible point and flat tips.

1 Sample the green color from the green paint tube, and choose Dry, Heavy Load in the options bar.

2 Select an Erodible Point brush. Change its Size to **9 px**, and Softness to **100%**.

The Softness value determines how quickly the tip erodes. A higher value results in faster erosion.

3 Draw a zig-zag line above the green paint tube.

The line gets thicker as the tip erodes.

4 Click Sharpen Tip in the Brush panel, and then draw a line next to the one you just drew.

The sharper tip draws a much narrower line.

5 Choose Erodible Triangle from the Shape menu in the Brush panel, and draw a zig-zag line with it.

You can choose from several erodible tips, depending on the effect you want.

Mixing colors

You've used wet and dry brushes, changed brush settings, and mixed the paint with the background color. Now, you'll focus more on mixing colors with each other as you add paint to the painter's palette.

1 Zoom out just enough to see the full palette and the paint tubes.

2 Select the Paint mix layer in the Layers panel, so the color you paint won't blend with the brown palette on the Background layer.

The Mixer Brush tool mixes colors only on the active layer unless you select Sample All Layers in the options bar.

● **Note:** Depending on the complexity of your project, you may need to be patient. Mixing colors can be a memory-intensive process.

3 Sample the red color from the red paint tube. Select the round blunt brush in the Brush panel (the fifth brush). Then select Wet from the pop-up menu in the options bar, and paint in the top circle on the palette.

4 Click the Clean Brush After Every Stroke icon in the options bar to deselect it.

5 Sample the blue color from the blue paint tube, and then paint in the same circle, mixing the red with the blue to make purple.

6 Paint in the next circle. You're painting in purple because the paint stays on the brush until you clean it.

7 In the options bar, choose Clean Brush from the Current Brush Load pop-up menu. The preview changes to indicate transparency, meaning the brush has no paint loaded.

To remove the paint load from a brush, you can choose Clean Brush in the options bar. To replace the paint load in a brush, sample a different color.

If you want Photoshop to clean the brush after each stroke, select the Clean Brush icon in the options bar. To load the brush with the foreground color after each stroke, select the Load Brush icon in the options bar. By default, both of these options are selected.

8 Choose Load Brush from the Current Brush Load pop-up menu in the options bar to load the brush with blue paint. Paint blue in half of the next circle.

9 Sample the yellow color from the yellow paint tube, and paint over the blue with a wet brush to mix the two colors.

10 Fill the last circle with yellow and red paint, mixing the two with a wet brush to create an orange color.

11 Hide the Circles layer in the Layers panel to remove the outlines on the palette.

12 Choose File > Save.

Tool tips from the Photoshop evangelist

Mixer Brush shortcuts

There are no default keyboard shortcuts for the Mixer Brush tool, but you can create your own.

To create custom keyboard shortcuts:

1   Choose Edit > Keyboard Shortcuts.

2   Choose Tools from the Shortcuts For menu.

3   Scroll down to the bottom of the list.

4   Select a command, and then enter a custom shortcut. You can create shortcuts for the following commands:

- Load Mixer Brush
- Clean Mixer Brush
- Toggle Mixer Brush Auto-Load
- Toggle Mixer Brush Auto-Clean

Creating a custom brush preset

Photoshop includes numerous brush presets, which are very handy. But if you need to tweak a brush for your project, you might find it easier to create your own preset. You'll create a brush preset to use in the following exercise.

1   In the Brush panel, select the following settings:

- Size: **36** px
- Shape: Round Fan
- Bristles: **35**%
- Length: **32**%
- Thickness: 2%
- Stiffness: **75**%
- Angle: **0**%
- Spacing: **2**%

2 Choose New Brush Preset from the Brush panel menu.

3 Name the brush **Landscape**, and click OK.

4 Click Brush Presets in the Brush panel to open the Brush Presets panel.

The Brush Presets panel displays samples of the strokes created by different brushes. If you know which brush you want to use, it can be easier to find by name. You'll list them by name now, so you can find your preset for the next exercise.

5 Choose Large List from the Brush Presets panel menu.

6 Scroll to the bottom of the list. The preset you created, named Landscape, is the last preset in the list.

7 Close the 11Palette_working.psd file.

Mixing colors with a photograph

Earlier, you mixed colors with a white background and with each other. Now, you'll use a photograph as your canvas. You'll add colors and mix them with each other and with the background colors to transform a photograph of a landscape into a watercolor.

1 Choose File > Open. Double-click the 11Landscape_Start.jpg file in the Lesson11 folder to open it.

2 Choose File > Save As. Rename the file **11Landscape_working.jpg**, and click Save. Click OK in the JPEG Options dialog box.

You'll paint the sky first. Start by setting up the color and selecting the brush.

3 Click the Foreground color swatch in the Tools panel. Select a medium-light blue color (we chose R=185, G=204, B=228), and then click OK.

4 Select the Mixer Brush tool (✔), if it isn't already selected. Choose Dry from the pop-up menu in the options bar. Then select the Landscape brush from the Brush Presets panel.

Presets are saved on your system, so they're available when you work with any image.

5 Paint over the sky, moving in close to the trees. Because you're using a dry brush, the paint isn't mixing with the colors beneath it.

6 Select a darker blue color (we used R=103, G=151, B=212), and add darker color at the top of the sky, still using the dry brush.

7 Select a light blue color again, and choose Very Wet, Heavy Mix from the pop-up menu in the options bar. Use this brush to scrub diagonally across the sky, blending the two colors in with the background color. Paint in close to the trees, and smooth out the entire sky.

Adding a darker color with a dry brush   Blending colors with a wet brush

When you're satisfied with the sky, move on to the grass and trees.

8 Select a light green (we used R=92, G=157, B=13). Choose Dry from the pop-up menu in the options bar. Then, paint along the top section of the grass to highlight it.

9 Sample a darker green from the grass itself. Choose Very Wet, Heavy Mix in the options bar. Then paint using diagonal strokes to blend the colors in the grass.

▶ **Tip:** Remember that you can Alt-click (Windows) or Option-click (Mac OS) to sample a color instead of using the Eyedropper tool. To sample only solid colors using the keyboard shortcut, choose Load Solid Colors from the Current Brush Load pop-up menu in the options bar.

Adding light green with a dry brush   Blending colors with a wet brush

10 Sample a light green, and then use a dry brush to highlight the lighter areas of the trees and the small tree in the middle of the landscape. Then select a dark green (we used R=26, G=79, B=34), and choose Very Wet, Heavy Mix in the options bar. Paint with the wet brush to mix together the colors in the trees.

Highlighting the trees   Mixing the colors

▶ **Tip:** For different
effects, paint in dif-
ferent directions. With
the Mixer Brush tool,
you can go wherever
your artistic instincts
lead you.

So far, so good. The background trees and the brown grasses are all that remain
to be painted.

11 Select a bluer color for the background trees (we used R=65, G=91, B=116).
    Paint with a dry brush to add the blue at the top. Then choose Wet in the
    options bar, and paint to mix the blue into the trees.

12 Sample a brown color from the tall grasses, and then select Very Wet, Heavy
    Mix in the options bar. Paint along the top of the tall grass with up-and-down
    strokes for the look of a field. Across the back area, behind the small center tree,
    paint back and forth to create smooth strokes.

Voilà! You've created a masterpiece with your paints and brushes, and there's
no mess to clean up.

Brush variations

You can go beyond the settings in these projects to explore numerous variations in brush tips and settings. In particular, you may want to play with Brush Pose and Shape Dynamics options.

Brush Pose settings change the tilt, rotation, and pressure of the brush. In the Brush panel, select Brush Pose from the list on the left. Move the Tilt X slider to tilt the brush from left to right. Move the Tilt Y slider to tilt the brush forward and backward. Change the Rotation value to rotate the bristles. (Rotation is more obvious when using a flat fan-shaped brush, for example.) Change the Pressure setting to determine how much effect the brush has on the artwork.

Shape Dynamics settings affect the steadiness of the stroke. Move the sliders up to increase the variability in the stroke.

If you're using a Wacom tablet, Photoshop recognizes the angle and pressure of the pen you're using and applies them to the brush. You can use the pen to control such things as Size Jitter; choose Pen Pressure or Pen Tilt from the Control menu in the Shape Dynamics settings to determine how the value changes.

There are many more options—some subtle, some not so subtle—to create variety in brush effects. Which options are available depend on the brush tip shape you've selected. For more information about all the options, see Photoshop Help.

Painting gallery

The painting tools and brush tips in Photoshop CS6 let you create all kinds of painting effects.

Erodible brush tips give an added realism to your art. The following pages show examples of art created with the new brush tips and tools in Photoshop CS6.

Image © sholby, www.sholby.net

Image © Lynette Kent, www.LynetteKent.com

Image © Victoria Pavlov

Image © Janet Stoppee

Image © Brian Stoppee

Image © John Derry

Image © sholby, www.sholby.net

Image © John Derry

Review questions

1 What does the Mixer Brush do that other brushes don't?

2 How do you load a mixer brush?

3 How do you clean a brush?

4 How can you display the names of brush presets?

5 What is the Bristle Brush Preview, and how can you hide it?

6 What is an erodible tip?

Review answers

1 The Mixer Brush mixes the color of the paintbrush with colors on the canvas.

2 You can load a mixer brush by sampling a color, either by using the Eyedropper tool or keyboard shortcuts (Alt-click or Option-click). Or, you can choose Load Brush from the pop-up menu in the options bar to load the brush with the foreground color.

3 To clean a brush, choose Clean Brush from the pop-up menu in the options bar.

4 To display brush presets by name, open the Brush Presets panel, and then choose Large List (or Small List) from the Brush Presets panel menu.

5 The Bristle Brush Preview shows you the direction the brush strokes are moving. It's available if OpenGL is enabled. To hide or show the Bristle Brush Preview, click the Toggle The Bristle Brush Preview icon at the bottom of the Brush panel or the Brush Presets panel.

6 An erodible tip erodes, changing thickness, as you paint or draw. It's similar to the way a pencil or pastel tip changes shape as it erodes.

12 WORKING WITH 3D IMAGES

Lesson overview

In this lesson, you'll learn how to do the following:

- Create a 3D shape from a layer.

- Import a 3D object.

- Create 3D text.

- Apply the 3D postcard effect.

- Manipulate 3D objects using the 3D Axis widget.

- Adjust the camera view.

- Set coordinates in the Properties panel.

- Adjust light sources.

- Animate a 3D file.

This lesson will take about 90 minutes to complete. Copy the Lesson12 folder onto your hard drive if you have not already done so. As you work on this lesson, you'll preserve the start files. If you need to restore the start files, copy them again from the *Adobe Photoshop CS6 Classroom in a Book* DVD.

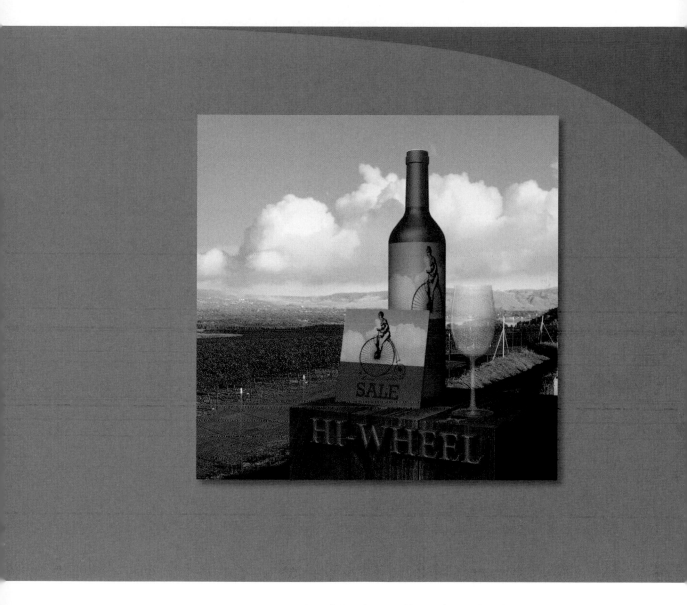

Traditional 3D artists spend hours, days, and weeks creating photo-realistic images. The 3D capabilities in Photoshop let you create sophisticated, precise 3D images easily—and you can change them easily, too.

Getting started

● **Note:** If you're using Windows XP, or if your video card does not support OpenGL 2.0, you won't be able to work with 3D features in Photoshop.

This lesson explores 3D features, which are available only if OpenGL 2.0 is supported by your video card and enabled on your computer. To learn about your video card, choose Edit > Preferences > Performance (Windows) or Photoshop > Preferences > Performance (Mac OS). Information about your video card is in the Graphics Processor Settings area of the dialog box.

In this lesson, you'll create a three-dimensional scene for a wine advertisement. First, you'll view the finished scene.

1 Start Photoshop, and then immediately hold down Ctrl+Alt+Shift (Windows) or Command+Option+Shift (Mac OS) to restore the default preferences. (See "Restoring default preferences" on page 4.)

2 When prompted, click Yes to delete the Adobe Photoshop Settings file.

3 Choose File > Browse In Bridge to open Adobe Bridge.

4 In Bridge, click Lessons in the Favorites panel. Double-click the Lesson12 folder in the Content panel.

5 View the 12End.psd file in Bridge. A three-dimensional wine bottle, wine glass, and sale card sit atop a wooden box with 3D lettering.

6 Double-click the 12End.mp4 file to view the movie in which light has been animated to simulate a sunrise. When you're done viewing the movie, exit QuickTime.

7 Double-click the 12Start.psd file to open it in Photoshop.

The file contains an image of a vineyard, a black background layer, and two additional layers.

Creating a 3D shape from a layer

Photoshop includes several 3D shape presets, representing geometric shapes and the shapes of everyday objects, such as a wine bottle or ring. When you create a 3D shape from a layer, Photoshop wraps the layer onto the 3D object preset. You can then rotate, reposition, and resize the 3D object—you can even light it from various angles with a number of colored lights.

First, you'll create the table for the wine bottle, glass, and card. To make the table, you'll wrap a 3D cube with the layer that contains the image of wood.

1 Choose File > Save As. Navigate to the Lesson12 folder, and save the file as **12Working.psd**. Click OK if the Photoshop Format Options dialog box appears.

2 In the Layers panel, make the Wood layer visible, and then select it.

3 Choose 3D > New Mesh From Layer > Mesh Preset > Cube Wrap.

4 Click Yes when asked whether you want to switch to the 3D workspace.

The 3D workspace includes the 3D panel, the Layers panel, and the Properties panel. You'll want to have all of these panels handy as you work with 3D objects. It also displays the ground plane, a grid that reflects the position of the ground relative to the 3D object, and the Secondary View window that lets you see the 3D object from a different perspective.

Photoshop wraps the wood image around a cube. You're viewing the front of the cube. You'll save the file now so you can easily return to this state after you've had a chance to experiment with the 3D tools.

5 Choose File > Save to save the file at this point.

Manipulating 3D objects

The advantage to working with 3D objects is, obviously, that you can work with them in three dimensions. You can also return to a 3D layer at any time to change lighting, color, material, or position without having to re-create a lot of the art. Photoshop CS6 includes several basic tools that make it easy to rotate, resize, and position 3D objects. The 3D tools in the options bar manipulate the object itself. The Camera widget in the lower left corner of the application window manipulates the camera so you can view a 3D scene from different angles.

You can use the 3D tools whenever a 3D layer is selected in the Layers panel. A 3D layer behaves like any other layer—you can apply layer styles, mask it, and so on. However, a 3D layer can be quite complex.

Unlike a regular layer, a 3D layer contains one or more *meshes*. A mesh defines the 3D object. In the layer you just created, the mesh is the cube wrap shape. Each mesh, in turn, includes one or more *materials*—the appearance of a part or all of the mesh. Each material includes one or more *maps*, which are the components of the appearance. There are nine typical maps, and there can be only one of each kind; however, you can also use custom maps. Each map contains one *texture*—the image that defines what the maps and materials look like. The texture may be a simple bitmap graphic or a set of layers. The same texture might be used by many different maps and materials. In the layer you just created, the image of the wood composes the texture.

In addition to meshes, a 3D layer also includes one or more *lights*, which affect the appearance of 3D objects and remain in a fixed position as you spin or move the object. A 3D layer also includes *cameras*, which are saved views with the objects in a particular position. The *shader* creates the final appearance based on the materials, object properties, and renderer.

That may all sound complicated, but the most important thing to remember is that the 3D tools in the options bar move an object in 3D space and the Camera widget moves the cameras that view the object.

1 In the Tools panel, select the Move tool (⊹).

All the 3D capabilities are embedded into the Move tool, which recognizes when a 3D layer is selected and enables the 3D tools.

2 Select the Drag The 3D Object tool in the 3D Mode area of the options bar.

3 Click on the wood, and drag it to move it from side to side or up and down.

4 Select the Roll The 3D Object tool in the options bar, and then click and drag the cube.

5 Experiment with the other tools to see how they affect the object.

When you select a 3D object, Photoshop displays the colorful 3D Axis widget, with green, red, and blue representing different axes. Red represents the x axis, green represents the y axis, and blue represents the z axis. (Hint: Think of RGB color to remember the order.) If you hover the mouse over the center box until it turns yellow, you can click the box and drag to scale the object uniformly. Click an arrow to move the object along that axis; click the curved handle just before the arrow to rotate on that axis; and click the smaller handle to scale along that axis.

6 Rotate, scale, and move the cube using the widget.

▶ **Tip:** As you move the object, the 3D Axis widget shifts, too. For example, the x and y axis arrows may be available, while the z axis is pointing directly into the scene. The yellow center box may also be obscured by an axis.

7 Right-click (Windows) or Control-click (Mac OS) the Camera widget in the lower left corner of the application window (it has two axes visible), and choose Top.

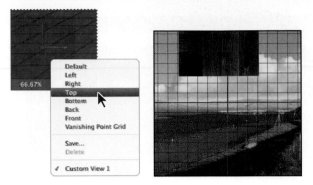

Options in the Camera menu determine the angle from which you see the object. The camera angle changes, but the object itself does not. Don't be fooled by its relationship to the background image; that image is not 3D, so Photoshop leaves it in place when it moves the camera for the 3D object.

8 Choose other camera views to see how they affect the perspective.

9 When you're done experimenting, choose File > Revert. You should see the front view of the wood cube again.

Adding 3D objects

The wooden cube is just one of five 3D elements in the scene. You'll create all of the 3D objects, and then merge them onto a single 3D layer, where you can work with them as a group. On one layer, they'll share cameras and lights.

Creating a 3D postcard

In Photoshop CS6, you can transform a 2D object into a 3D postcard that you can manipulate in perspective in a 3D space. It's called a 3D postcard because it's as if your image became a postcard you could turn over in your hand.

You'll use a 3D postcard to create the card that leans on the wine bottle.

1 Click the Layers tab to bring the Layers panel forward.

2 Make the Card layer visible, and select it.

3 Choose 3D > New Mesh From Layer > Postcard.

The card doesn't look much different, because you're viewing the front of it. When you manipulate it later, it will be much more obvious that it's a 3D postcard. Meanwhile, you can be sure it's a 3D object because Photoshop switches to the 3D panel, displays the Secondary View window in the upper left corner, enables the 3D tools in the options bar, and displays the Camera widget in the lower left corner of the application window.

Creating a 3D mesh from a new layer

You used a 3D mesh preset to wrap the wood layer around a cube, but you can also use a mesh preset with a new, empty layer. You'll do that to create a wine bottle.

1 Bring the Layers panel forward, and make sure the Card layer is selected.

2 Click the Create A New Layer button at the bottom of the Layers panel.

A new layer, named Layer 1, appears above the Card layer.

3 With Layer 1 selected, choose 3D > New Mesh From Layer > Mesh Preset > Wine Bottle.

A gray wine bottle shape appears in front of the card. Later, you'll apply materials to the shape to make it look like a glass wine bottle.

4 In the Layers panel, rename the layer **Bottle**.

Importing a 3D file

In Photoshop CS6, you can open and work with 3D files exported from various applications, such as Collada, 3DS, KMZ (Google Earth) or U3D. You can also work with files saved in Collada format, a file interchange format supported by Autodesk, for example. When you add a 3D file as a 3D layer, it includes the 3D model and a transparent background. The layer uses the dimensions of the existing file, but you can resize it.

You'll import a 3D wine glass that was created in another application.

1 Choose 3D > New 3D Layer From File.

2 Navigate to the Lesson12/Assets folder, and double-click the WineGlass.obj file.

The wine glass shape appears in front of the bottle, centered in the document window.

3 Choose File > Save to save your work so far.

Creating 3D text

Even text can be three-dimensional. When you've created 3D text, you can rotate it, scale it, move it, apply materials to it, change its lighting (and the accompanying shadows), and extrude it. You'll create 3D text for the front of the wooden table.

1 Select the Horizontal Type tool (T) in the Tools panel.

2 Drag a marquee across the middle of the window.

3 In the options bar, select a serif font such as Minion Pro, Bold for the font style, and **72 pt** for the font size.

4 Type **HI-WHEEL**, in all capital letters.

You've created text, but it's not three-dimensional yet. You'll convert it now.

5 Click the Update 3D Associated With This Text button in the options bar.

Now the text is 3D, and Photoshop displays its ground plane and the rest of the 3D work environment.

Merging 3D layers to share the same 3D space

You can include multiple 3D meshes in the same 3D layer. Meshes in the same layer can share lighting effects and be rotated in the same 3D space (also called the *scene*), creating a more realistic 3D effect.

You'll merge the 3D layers you created so that all the 3D objects are part of the same scene.

1   Bring the Layers panel forward.

2   Press Shift while you select the HI-WHEEL, WineGlass, Bottle, Card, and Wood layers.

All five 3D layers are selected. Now you'll merge them. Be sure to press Shift while you merge them in order to retain their alignment.

3   Hold down the Shift key while you choose 3D > Merge 3D Layers.

Photoshop merges the layers into one layer, named Wood. Because you pressed Shift while you merged the layers, the objects' positions are unchanged.

4 Choose File > Save to save your work so far.

▶ **Tip:** If your merged layers don't look like this image, you probably released the Shift key before the layers were merged. Choose Edit > Undo Merge Layers, and try again.

Positioning objects in a scene

The objects are all there, but it's not a very attractive arrangement. You'll use on-canvas widgets and the Properties panel to resize and reposition each of the 3D objects to compose an appealing scene.

Changing the camera view

The Secondary View window can show you the scene from different perspectives. You'll use it to see the objects, and then change the camera view to get a better look at them as you reposition them.

1 Pan to see the objects below the wooden block in the Secondary View window in the upper left corner of the document window.

The current camera view for the Secondary View window is from the top. The objects you created are in front of the wooden box.

● **Note:** The camera view in the Secondary View window is independent of the camera view for the scene. You can change the view in the Secondary View window to see the scene from different angles without changing its appearance in Photoshop.

2 Click the Select View/Camera button at the top of the Secondary View window, and choose Left.

Now you can see the objects clearly. You'll use this camera view for the scene.

3 Right-click (Windows) or Control-click (Mac OS) the Camera widget in the lower left corner of the document window, and choose Left.

Moving objects with the 3D Axis widget

▶ **Tip:** We've included a video of these steps in the Lesson12/Video folder. Double-click the PositioningObjects.mp4 file to follow along.

The wine glass, wine bottle, and card need to sit atop the wooden table, not beside it. You can manipulate individual 3D objects within a 3D layer by selecting their folders in the 3D panel. You'll use the 3D Axis widget to move the objects on top of the table.

1 Bring the 3D panel forward in the Layers panel group.

2 Press the Shift key as you select the Card_Layer, Bottle_Layer, and WineGlass_Layer folders.

3 Hover the cursor over the tip of the green arrow until you see the Move On Y Axis tool tip.

4 Click the tip of the green arrow, and drag the objects up until the bottom of the wine bottle is level with the top of the wooden cube.

5 Click the tip of the blue arrow, and drag the objects to the left until they are centered on the cube. You can use the green arrow to drag the objects up or down again. The positioning doesn't have to be perfect; you'll have the opportunity to make adjustments later.

▶ **Tip:** You can change the size of the 3D Axis widget. Press Shift as you hover the cursor over the yellow scaling cube. Then click and drag to make the 3D Axis widget smaller or larger.

You've moved the card, bottle, and glass. Now you'll move the text, which is currently a small black square off to the side of the box.

6 In the 3D panel, expand the HI-WHEEL_Layer folder, and select the HI-WHEEL text.

7 Drag the HI-WHEEL text so that it is just in front of the cube, using the green and blue arrows in the 3D Axis widget.

Remember that the camera view is from the left. To move the text in front of the box, it needs to appear to be to the right of the box in this view.

8 Right-click (Windows) or Control-click (Mac OS) the Camera widget, and choose Default.

The camera angle changes to display the scene from the front.

9 In the 3D panel, select Environment.

10 Select the Drag The 3D Object tool in the options bar, and then drag the entire set of objects toward the lower right area of the canvas, as in the image below.

Using the Properties panel to position 3D objects

You've done some good work, but the objects aren't in their final positions yet. You'll change coordinates in the Properties panel to move them into place.

1 Select Scene in the 3D panel.

Changes you make while Scene is selected affect the entire 3D scene.

2 In the Properties panel, click the Coordinates button to change the options available.

3 Type **-30** in the Y Rotation box.

▶ **Tip:** Press V to switch between panes in the Properties panel.

The entire 3D scene rotates 30 degrees against the background. Next, you'll scale the wine glass and align it with the bottle.

4 In the 3D panel, select objMesh, inside the WineGlass_Layer folder.

5 In the Properties panel, enter **55%** for the X Scale, Y Scale, and Z Scale values.

6 In the 3D panel, Shift-select the Bottle_Layer and WineGlass_Layer folders.

7 Click the Align Bottom Edges button in the Photoshop options bar to align the bottom edges of the two objects (so that they both rest on the cube).

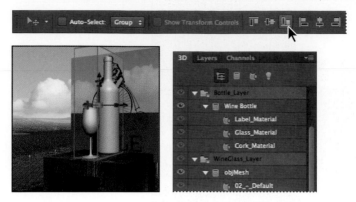

The wine glass is more proportionate with the bottle, and aligned with it. Now you'll move it to the right of the bottle, and then move the bottle to the left side of the box.

▶ **Tip:** If you'd rather, you can position the wine glass and the bottle using the 3D Axis widget.

8 Select ObjMesh in the WineGlass_Layer folder in the 3D panel. Then enter the following values in the Position boxes in the Properties panel: X: **217.1**, Y: **274.2**, and Z: **81.8**.

9 Select the Wine Bottle mesh in the Bottle_Layer folder in the 3D panel. Then enter the following values in the Position boxes in the Properties panel: X: **102.4**, Y: **388.8**, and Z: **4.8**.

10 In the Properties panel, enter **120%** for the X Scale, Y Scale, and Z Scale.

11 Choose File > Save to save your work so far.

Scaling and rotating objects with widgets

The wine glass and bottle are in position now, but the text and card are still out of place. You'll use the 3D Axis widget to scale and position them appropriately.

1 In the 3D panel, expand the HI-WHEEL_Layer folder, and select the HI-WHEEL text.

2 Select the Rotate The 3D Object tool in the options bar.

3 Use the red arrow on the 3D Axis widget to pull the text back and forth until it's centered on the front of the box. Use the green and blue arrows to move the text up and down, and forward and backward, as needed.

4 Hover the mouse over the center of the 3D Axis widget until the center cube turns yellow. Then drag the widget to scale the text so that it fits the width of the cube (about 135% of its original size, as reported in the hint text as you drag).

● **Note:** If you prefer to enter coordinates, type **57%** for the X Scale, Y Scale, and Z Scale values. The starting scale is about 42%; 57 is roughly 135% of 42.

The text is in place. Now you'll resize and position the card.

5 In the 3D panel, close the HI-WHEEL folder, and expand the Card_Layer folder.

6 Select Card Mesh in the 3D panel, and then use the 3D Axis widget to scale it to about 25% of its original size.

7 Drag the tip of the blue arrow on the 3D Axis widget to move the card forward along the Z axis until the front of the card and the front of the cube are even.

8 Drag the tip of the green arrow to pull the card down so it rests on the cube.

9 Use the blue curved handle to rotate the top of the card back so that it appears to lean against the bottle. Make any further adjustments to the card's position using the blue, green, and red arrows, as necessary.

Everything's in position!

9 Choose File > Save to save your work.

Applying materials to 3D objects

One of the benefits of working with 3D objects is that you can quickly change the appearance of the objects. You'll apply materials to the text to make it stand out. Then you'll make the bottle and wine glass look much more realistic.

Changing the appearance of 3D text

You'll change the shape of the text, extrude it, and then apply materials to each surface of the 3D text.

1 In the 3D panel, expand the HI-WHEEL_Layer folder, and select the HI-WHEEL text.

2 Press V to change panes in the Properties panel, cycling through the Mesh, Deform, Cap, and Coordinates panels. The on-canvas widgets change for different panes.

3 Click the Deform button in the Properties panel to see the Deform properties.

4 In the Properties panel, choose Bevel from the Shape Preset menu. (Bevel is the middle option in the top row.)

5 Click the center of the on-canvas Deform widget and drag until the extrusion depth is approximately 23.

▶ **Tip:** When the Deform properties are shown, the on-canvas widget lets you extrude, taper, bend, or twist the selected object mesh.

6 Press V to display the Cap properties in the Properties panel.

7 Drag the on-canvas widget upwards until the inflation strength is 4.75.

The bevel looks great. Now you'll apply a material to make the text shiny.

8 In the 3D panel, Shift-select the five material components of the HI-WHEEL text: HI-WHEEL Front Inflation Material, HI-WHEEL Front Bevel Material, HI-WHEEL Extrusion Material, HI-WHEEL Back Bevel Material, and HI-WHEEL Back Inflation Material.

9 In the Properties panel, open the Materials picker.

10 Choose Default (For Ray Tracer) from the settings menu. Click OK when you're prompted to replace the materials, and click Don't Save if you're prompted to save the current materials.

A different set of materials appears in the Materials picker.

11 In the Materials picker, select Metal Gold, the middle option in the fourth row.

Every aspect of the 3D text is now gold. You'll use the same process to apply materials to the bottle and wine glass.

12 Hide the contents of the HI-WHEEL_Layer folder in the 3D panel.

Applying materials to objects

You'll use similar techniques to apply materials to the wine bottle's cork and glass, and then apply an imported label. Next, you'll make the wine glass look much more realistic than it does now.

1 Select the Cork_Material component in the Bottle_Layer folder in the 3D panel.

This material applies to only the cork area of the bottle.

2 In the Properties panel, open the Materials picker, and then select Metal Brass (Solid) from the middle of the third row.

The bottle appears to have a foil wrapper around its cork.

3 Select the Glass_Material component in the 3D panel, and then select Gemstone Emerald from the Materials picker.

4 In the Properties panel, click the Diffuse color swatch, select a very dark green, and click OK. Then change the Ambient color swatch to a similar dark green.

5 Change the sliders in the Properties panel to the following settings:

- Shine: **45%**
- Reflection: **55%**
- Bump: **10%**
- Opacity: **91%**
- Refraction: **1.5**

6 Select the Label_Material component in the 3D panel, and then click the icon next to the Diffuse swatch in the Properties panel. Choose Replace Texture. Navigate to the Lesson12/Assets folder, and double-click Label.psd. (In Windows, choose Photoshop (*.PSD, *.PDD) from the Files Of Type menu to see the Label.psd file; you may have to scroll up to see the option.)

7 Select the Wine Bottle mesh in the 3D panel. Then select the Coordinates button at the top of the Properties panel, and change the Y Rotation value to -**34** degrees so that the label is more visible.

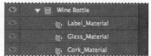

8 In the 3D panel, expand the WineGlass_Layer folder, and then select the 02_ Default material component under objMesh.

9 In the Materials picker, select Glass Smooth (the first option in the third row).

10 Change the sliders in the Properties panel to apply the following settings:

- Shine: **96%**

- Reflection: **83%**

- Roughness: **0%**

- Bump:**10**

- Opacity: **22%**

- Refraction: **1**

11 Choose File > Save.

Lighting a 3D scene

You can adjust the default light for a scene, and add new lights. How you adjust the lights determines the shadows, the highlights, and the mood of the scene.

1 In the 3D panel, select Infinite Light 1, the last item in the panel.

By default, Photoshop creates one infinite light when you create a 3D scene. When you select the light, an on-canvas widget appears to help you direct the light. Move the large knob to make sweeping changes; adjust the small knob for more precise lighting shifts.

2 Use the small knob to position the light in the upper left corner (at about the 11:00 position on a clock), so that there's a tall highlight along the center of the neck of the bottle.

● **Note:** The size of the light widget depends on the screen magnification. Yours might be larger or smaller than the one shown here.

3 Right-click (Windows) or Control-click (Mac OS) the light itself (the white round icon) to open the Infinite Light 1 panel. Then change the color to a faint gold color (we used R=251, G=242, B=203), and change the Intensity to **75%**.

● **Note:** You can make changes in the Infinite Light 1 panel or in the Properties panel.

4 Click the Add New Light To Scene button at the bottom of the 3D panel, and choose New Infinite Light.

5 With Infinite Light 2 selected, change the color to a similar light gold color in the Properties panel. Then change the Intensity value to **30%**.

6 With Infinite Light 2 still selected in the 3D panel, move the knob on the on-canvas widget to position the light at about the 1:00 position on the clock, so that there's a nice highlight on the edge of the bottle.

7 Click the Add New Light To Scene button at the bottom of the 3D panel, and choose New Point Light.

8 Select Point Light 1 in the 3D panel, and then change its Intensity to 30% in the Properties panel.

9 Use the on-canvas widget to pull the light onto the center of the wine glass.

10 Choose File > Save to save your work so far.

Rendering a 3D scene

▶ **Tip:** You can change the number of passes Photoshop makes when it renders the scene. Choose Edit > Preferences > 3D (Windows) or Photoshop > Preferences > 3D (Mac OS) and then change the High Quality Threshold value in the Ray Tracer area.

As you build a scene in Photoshop, you can get a pretty good idea of what it will look like. But it's only when you render it that you know how realistic the final project will look. You can render small areas of the scene at any time, but wait until you think you're close to done to render the entire scene. Rendering is a time-consuming process, and once you've rendered the scene, every change you makes triggers re-rendering.

You can render the scene now, or, if you're planning to do the Extra Credit project, wait and render the animated scene.

1 Choose File > Save As, and save the file as **12_render.psd**. Click OK if the Photoshop Format Options dialog box appears.

Saving a separate file for rendering ensures that you'll be able to make changes to the original more quickly.

2 In the 3D panel, select Scene to ensure that the entire scene is selected.

3 Click the Render button at the bottom of the Properties panel.

Depending on your system, this may take a while.

Photoshop renders the file. Depending on your system, this can take anywhere from a few minutes to half an hour or more.

▶ **Tip:** If you need to interrupt the rendering, or believe that the quality is sufficient, click anywhere on the image to stop the rendering process.

Extra credit

Animating lighting for a 3D scene

You can simulate a time-lapse video of daybreak by setting different states for the lighting and opacity of the background. For more information about animating properties using the Timeline panel, see Lesson 10, "Editing Video."

1   Click the Timeline tab at the bottom of the application window to open the Timeline panel.

2   Click Create Video Timeline.

Photoshop adds the document layers to the timeline.

3   Shorten the duration of the Wood layer by dragging the end of the clip to the left until it matches the Landscape layer (05:00f).

4   Display the properties for the Landscape layer. Move the playhead to the end of the time ruler, and then click the stopwatch for the Opacity property to create a keyframe.

5   Move the playhead to the beginning of the time ruler.

6   Bring the Layers panel forward. In the Layers panel, change the opacity for the Landscape layer to **0%**.

(continues on next page)

Extra Credit (continued)

7 In the Timeline panel, hide the properties for the Landscape layer, expand the properties for the Wood layer, and then expand the 3D Lights under the Wood layer.

8 Move the playhead to the end of the time ruler, and click the stopwatch icons for all three 3D Node properties.

9 Move the playhead back to the beginning of the time ruler.

10 Bring the 3D panel forward, and select Infinite Light 1. Use the on-canvas widget to direct the light downward. Then select Infinite Light 2, and move its light downward, too.

11 Select Point Light 1, and drag its light to the bottom of the scene.

12 Click Play in the Timeline panel to preview the animation, and then make any adjustments you want to make.

13 In the 3D panel, select Scene to ensure that the entire scene is selected.

14 Choose Render Video from the Timeline panel menu.

15 At the bottom of the Render Video dialog box, choose Interactive from the 3D Quality menu if you have a slower computer; otherwise, choose Ray Traced Draft.

16 Leave all other options at their default settings, and click Render.

17 When Photoshop has finished rendering the movie, double-click the 12Working.mp4 file in the Lesson12/Assets folder to view it.

Review questions

1 How does a 3D layer differ from other layers in Photoshop?

2 How can you change the camera view?

3 How do you apply materials to an object?

4 Which color represents each axis on the 3D Axis widget?

5 How do you render a 3D scene?

Review answers

1 A 3D layer behaves like any other layer—you can apply layer styles, mask it, and so on. However, unlike a regular layer, a 3D layer also contains one or more meshes, which define 3D objects. You can work with meshes and the materials, maps, and textures they contain. You can also adjust the lighting for a 3D layer.

2 To change the camera view, you can move the Camera widget, or right-click (Windows) or Control-click (Mac OS) the widget to choose a camera view preset.

3 To apply materials, select the material component in the 3D panel, and then select materials and settings in the Properties panel.

4 In the 3D Axis widget, the red arrow represents the X axis; the green arrow represents the Y axis, and the blue arrow represents the Z axis.

5 To render a 3D scene, select Scene in the 3D panel, and then click the Render button at the bottom of the Properties panel.

13 PREPARING FILES FOR THE WEB

Lesson overview

In this lesson, you'll learn how to do the following:

- Slice an image in Photoshop.

- Distinguish between user slices and auto slices.

- Link user slices to other HTML pages or locations.

- Optimize images for the web and make good compression choices.

- Export large, high-resolution files that tile for zooming and panning.

- Showcase your images in a media gallery.

 This lesson will take about an hour to complete. Copy the Lesson13 folder onto your hard drive if you have not already done so. As you work on this lesson, you'll preserve the start files. If you need to restore the start files, copy them again from the *Adobe Photoshop CS6 Classroom in a Book* DVD.

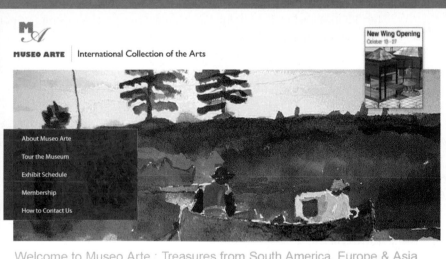

MA
MUSEO ARTE | International Collection of the Arts

New Wing Opening
October 13 - 27

About Museo Arte

Tour the Museum

Exhibit Schedule

Membership

How to Contact Us

Welcome to Museo Arte : Treasures from South America, Europe & Asia

Museo Arte, founded in 1864, and located in the heart of Madrid's cultural district offers a dazzling array of art works from Spanish masters, as well as from other areas of Europe, and from Asia. The permanent collection at Museo Arte includes paintings, drawings, ceramics, and sculptural works.

Current Exhibits
Museo Arte is currently showing a travelling exhibit of **Watercolors by Spanish Contemporary Artists** Other current exhibits include a **Sculpture Show in the Sculpture Garden Courtyard**, and **Road to Morrisy: An Installation by Jaime Nelson** For more information on exhibits at Museo Arte, visit Exhibits.

Special Events
Museo Arte holds special events throughout the year for general public, as well as special groups. Facilities are also available for charity events, weddings, and private gatherings.

Web users expect to click linked graphics to jump to another site or page, and to activate built-in animations. You can prepare a file for the web in Photoshop by adding slices to link to other pages or sites.

Getting started

For this lesson, you will need to use a web browser application such as Firefox, Netscape, Internet Explorer, or Safari. You do not need to connect to the Internet.

You'll fine-tune graphics for the home page of a Spanish art museum's website. You'll add hypertext links to the topics, so that website visitors can jump to other prebuilt pages on the site.

First, you'll explore the final HTML page that you will create from a single Photoshop file.

1　Start Photoshop, and then immediately hold down Ctrl+Alt+Shift (Windows) or Command+Option+Shift (Mac OS) to restore the default preferences. (See "Restoring default preferences" on page 4.)

2　When prompted, click Yes to delete the Adobe Photoshop Settings file.

3　Choose File > Browse In Bridge.

4　In Bridge, click Lessons in the Favorites panel. Double-click the Lesson13 folder in the Content panel, double-click the 13End folder, and finally, double-click the Site folder.

The Site folder contains the contents of the website that you'll be working with.

5　Right-click (Windows) or Control-click (Mac OS) the home.html file, and choose Open With from the context menu. Choose a web browser to open the HTML file.

6　Move the pointer over the topics on the left side of the web page and over the images. When the pointer hovers over a link, it changes from an arrow to a pointing hand.

● Note: Depending on the settings in your browser, it may display security warnings. You are working with files on your hard disk, not on the Internet, so you can safely display the content.

7 Click the image of the angel in the lower right area of the page. The Zoomify window opens. Click the Zoomify controls to see how they change the magnification and reposition the image.

8 To return to the home page, close the Zoomify tab or window.

9 Click the image of the boy with the lightbulb to get a closer look at it in its own window. Close its browser window when you have finished.

10 On the home page, click the topics on the left side to jump to their linked pages. To return to the home page, click the "Museo Arte" text just below the logo in the upper left corner of the window.

11 When you have finished viewing the web page, quit the web browser, and return to Bridge.

12 In Bridge, click the Lesson13 folder in the breadcrumbs (the navigation path) at the top of the window to display the Lesson13 folder contents. Double-click the 13Start folder in the Content panel, and then double-click the 13Start.psd thumbnail to open the file in Photoshop.

13 Choose File > Save As, and rename the file **13Working.psd**. Click OK in the Photoshop Format Options dialog box. Saving a working copy preserves the original start file in case you need to return to it later.

In the preceding steps, you used two different types of links: slices (the topics on the left side of the page) and images (the boy and the angel).

Slices are rectangular areas in an image that you define based on layers, guides, or precise selections in the image, or by using the Slice tool. When you define slices in an image, Photoshop creates an HTML table or Cascading Style Sheet (CSS) layers to contain and align the slices. You can generate and preview an HTML file that contains the sliced image along with the table or cascading style sheet.

You can also add hypertext links to images. A website visitor can then click the image to open a linked page. Unlike slices, which are always rectangular, images can be any shape.

Creating slices

When you define a rectangular area in an image as a *slice*, Photoshop creates an HTML table to contain and align the slice. Once you create slices, you can turn them into buttons, and then program those buttons to make the web page work.

Any new slice you create within an image (a *user slice*) automatically creates other slices (*auto slices*) that cover the entire area of the image outside the user slice.

Selecting slices and setting slice options

You'll start by selecting an existing slice in the start file. We created the first slice for you.

1 In the Tools panel, select the Slice Select tool (⌐), hidden under the Crop tool (¤).

When you select the Slice or Slice Select tool, Photoshop displays the slices, with their slice numbers, on the image.

The slice numbered 01 includes the upper left corner of the image; it also has a small icon, or *badge*, that resembles a tiny mountain. The blue color means that the slice is a user slice—a slice we created in the start file.

Also notice the gray slices—02 to the right, and 03 just below slice 01. The gray color indicates that these are auto slices, automatically created by making a user slice. The symbol indicates that the slice contains image content. See "About slice symbols" for a description.

2 In the upper left corner of the image, click the slice numbered 01 with the small blue rectangle. A gold bounding box appears, indicating that the slice is selected.

About slice symbols

The blue and gray slice symbols, or *badges*, in the Photoshop image window and Save For Web And Devices dialog box can be useful reminders if you take the time to learn how to read them. Each slice can contain as many badges as are appropriate. These badges indicate the following:

⬛ 01 The number of the slice. Numbers run sequentially from left to right and top to bottom of the image.

⬛ The slice contains image content.

⬛ The slice contains no image content.

⬛ The slice is layer-based; that is, it was created from a layer.

⬛ The slice is linked to other slices (for optimization purposes).

3 Using the Slice Select tool, double-click slice 01. The Slice Options dialog box appears. By default, Photoshop names each slice based on the filename and the slice number—in this case, 13Start_01.

● **Note:** You can set options for an auto slice, but doing so automatically promotes the auto slice to a user slice.

Slices aren't particularly useful until you set options for them. Slice options include the slice name and the URL that opens when the user clicks the slice.

4 In the Slice Options dialog box, name the slice **Logo**. For URL, type #. The pound sign (#) lets you preview a button's functionality without programming an actual link. It's very helpful in the early stages of website design, when you want to see how a button will look and behave.

5 Click OK to apply the changes.

Creating navigation buttons

Now you'll slice the navigation buttons on the left side of the page. You could select one button at a time and add navigation properties to it. But you can do the same thing a faster way.

1 In the Tools panel, select the Slice tool (✐), or press Shift+C. (The Crop tool, Perspective Crop tool, Slice tool, and Slice Select tool share the C key as their keyboard shortcut. To change which of the four tools is selected, press Shift+C.)

Notice the guides above and below the words on the left side of the image.

2 Using the guides on the left side of the image, drag the Slice tool diagonally from the upper left corner above the first line of text, to the bottom guide below the last line of text, so that all five lines are enclosed.

A blue rectangle, similar to the one for slice 01, appears in the upper left corner of the slice you just created, numbered slice 05. The blue color tells you that this is a user slice, not an auto slice. The gold bounding box indicates the bounds of the slice and that it's selected.

The original gray rectangle for auto slice 03 remains unchanged, but the area included in slice 03 is smaller, covering only a small rectangle above the text. Another auto slice, numbered 07, appears below the slice you created.

3 With the Slice tool still selected, press Shift+C to toggle to the Slice Select tool ( ). The options bar above the image window changes to include a series of alignment buttons.

Now you'll slice your selection into five separate buttons.

4 Click the Divide button in the options bar.

5 In the Divide Slice dialog box, select Divide Horizontally Into, and type **5** for Slices Down, Evenly Spaced. Click OK.

You'll name each slice and add a corresponding link.

6 Using the Slice Select tool, double-click the top slice (containing the words "About Museo Arte").

7 In the Slice Options dialog box, name the slice **About**; type **about.html** for URL; and type **_self** for Target. (Be sure to include the underscore before the letter *s*.) Click OK.

The Target option controls how a linked file opens when the link is clicked. The _self option displays the linked file in the same frame as the original file.

● **Note:** Type the HTML filenames in the URL box exactly as shown, to match the names of the existing pages to which you will link the buttons.

8 Repeat steps 6 and 7 for the remaining slices in turn, starting from the second slice, as follows:

- Name the second slice **Tour**; type **tour.html** for URL; and type **_self** for Target.

- Name the third slice **Exhibits**; type **exhibits.html** for URL; and type **_self** for Target.

- Name the fourth slice **Members**; type **members.html** for URL; and type **_self** for Target.

- Name the fifth slice **Contact**; type **contact.html** for URL; and type **_self** for Target.

9 Choose File > Save to save your work so far.

▶ **Tip:** If you find the indicators for the auto slices distracting, select the Slice Select tool and then click the Hide Auto Slices button in the options bar. You can also hide the guides by choosing View > Show > Guides, because you won't need them again in this lesson.

About creating slices

Here are other methods for creating slices that you can try on your own:

- You can create No Image slices, and then add text or HTML source code to them. No Image slices can have a background color and are saved as part of the HTML file. The primary advantage of using No Image slices for text is that the text can be edited in any HTML editor, saving you the trouble of having to go back to Photoshop to edit it. However, if the text grows too large for the slice, it will break the HTML table and introduce unwanted gaps.

- If you use custom guides in your design work, you can instantly divide up an entire image into slices with the Slices From Guides button on the options bar. Use this technique with caution, however, because it discards any previously created slices and any options associated with those slices. Also, it creates only user slices, and you may not need that many of them.

- When you want to create identically sized, evenly spaced, and aligned slices, try creating a single user slice that precisely encloses the entire area. Then, use the Divide button on the Slice Select options bar to divide the original slice into as many vertical or horizontal rows of slices as you need.

- If you want to unlink a layer-based slice from its layer, you can convert it to a user slice. Select it with the Slice Select tool, and then click Promote in the options bar.

Creating slices based on layers

In addition to using the Slice tool, you can create slices based on layers. The advantage of using layers for slices is that Photoshop creates the slice based on the dimensions of the layer and includes all its pixel data. When you edit the layer, move it, or apply a layer effect to it, the layer-based slice adjusts to encompass the new pixels.

1   In the Layers panel, select the New Wing layer. If you can't see all of the contents of the Layers panel, drag the panel from its dock, and expand it by dragging the lower right corner downwards.

2   Choose Layer > New Layer Based Slice. In the image window, a slice numbered 04, with a blue badge, appears over the image announcing the new wing. It is numbered according to its position in the slices, starting from the top left corner of the image.

3   Using the Slice Select tool (⌖), double-click the slice, and name it **New Wing**. For URL, type **newwing.html**. Type **_blank** for Target. The _blank Target option opens the linked page in a new instance of the web browser. Click OK.

Be sure to enter these options exactly as indicated, to match the pages you'll be linking the slices to.

Now you'll create slices for the Image 1 and Image 2 layers.

4   Repeat steps 1–3 for the remaining images, as follows:

   •   Create a slice from the Image 1 layer. Name it **Image 1**; for URL, type **image1.html**; and type **_blank** for Target. Click OK.

   •   Create a slice from the Image 2 layer. Name it **Card**; type **card.html** for URL, and type **_blank** for Target. Click OK.

You may have noticed that the dialog box contains more options than the three you specified for these slices. For more information on how to use these options, see Photoshop Help.

5 Choose File > Save to save your work so far.

Exporting HTML and images

You're ready to make your final slices, define your links, and export your file so that Photoshop creates an HTML page that will display all of your slices as one unit.

It's important to keep web graphics as small (in file size) as possible, so that web pages open quickly. Photoshop has built-in tools to help you gauge how small each exported slice can be without compromising image quality. A good rule of thumb is to use JPEG compression for photographic, continuous-tone images and GIF compression for broad areas of color—in the case of this lesson's site, all of the areas around the three main art images on the page.

You'll use the Save For Web dialog box to compare settings and compression options for different image formats.

1 Choose File > Save For Web.

2 Select the 2-Up tab at the top of the Save For Web dialog box.

3 Use the Hand tool (🖐) in the dialog box to move the image within the window so that you can see the portrait of the boy.

4 Choose the Slice Select tool (🔪) in the dialog box, and select slice 17 (the portrait of the boy) from the slices in the image on the left. Note the file size displayed beneath the image.

5 On the right side of the dialog box, choose JPEG Medium from the Preset pop-up menu. Notice the file size displayed beneath the image; the file size changes dramatically when you choose JPEG Medium.

Now you'll look at a GIF setting for the same slice in the image on the right.

6 With the Slice Select tool, select slice 17 in the image on the right. On the right side of the dialog box, choose GIF 32 No Dither from the Preset pop-up menu.

Notice that the color area in the portrait in the lower image looks flatter and more posterized, but the image size is roughly the same.

Based on what you've just learned, you will choose which compression to assign to all of the slices on this page.

7 Select the Optimized tab at the top of the dialog box.

8 With the Slice Select tool, Shift-click to select the images of the boy, the angel, and the new wing announcement in the preview window. From the Preset menu, choose JPEG Medium.

9 Shift-click to select all of the remaining slices in the preview window, and then choose GIF 64 Dithered from the Preset menu.

10 Click Save. In the Save Optimized As dialog box, navigate to the Lesson13/13Start/Museo folder, which contains the rest of the site, including the pages that your slices will link to.

11 For format, choose HTML And Images. Use the default settings, and choose All Slices from the Slices menu. Name the file **home.html**, and click Save. If you're prompted to replace images, click Replace.

12 In Photoshop, choose File > Browse In Bridge to switch to Bridge. Click Lessons in the Favorites panel. Double-click the Lesson13 folder in the Content panel, double-click the 13Start folder, and then double-click the Museo folder.

13 Right-click (Windows) or Control-click (Mac OS) the home.html file, and choose Open With from the context menu. Choose a web browser to open the HTML file.

14 In your web browser, move around the HTML file:

- Position your mouse over some of the slices you created. Notice that the pointer turns into a pointing finger to indicate a button.

- Click the portrait of the boy to open a new window with the full image.

- Click the New Wing Opening link to open its window.

- Click the text links on the left to jump to other pages in the site.

15 When you have finished exploring the file, close your browser.

Optimizing images for the web

Optimizing is the process of selecting format, resolution, and quality settings to make an image efficient, visually appealing, and useful for web browser pages. Simply put, it's balancing file size against good looks. No single collection of settings can maximize the efficiency of every kind of image file; optimizing requires human judgment and a good eye.

Compression options vary according to the file format used to save the image. JPEG and GIF are the two most common formats. The JPEG format is designed to preserve the broad color range and subtle brightness variations of continuous-tone images such as photographs. It can represent images using millions of colors. The GIF format is effective at compressing solid-color images and images with areas of repetitive color, such as line art, logos, and illustrations with type. It uses a panel of 256 colors to represent the image and supports background transparency.

Photoshop offers a range of controls for compressing image file size while optimizing the onscreen quality. Typically, you optimize images before saving them in an HTML file. Use the Save For Web dialog box to compare the original image to one or more compressed alternatives, adjusting settings as you compare. For more on optimizing GIF and JPEG images, see Photoshop Help.

Using the Zoomify feature

With the Zoomify feature, you can publish high-resolution images on the web that viewers can pan and zoom to see more detail. The basic-size image downloads in the same time as an equivalent-size JPEG file. Photoshop exports the JPEG files and HTML file that you can upload to your website. The Zoomify capabilities work with any web browser.

1 In Bridge, click the 13Start folder in the breadcrumbs at the top of the window. Then, double-click the card.jpg file to open it in Photoshop.

The card is a large bitmap image that you'll export to HTML using the Zoomify feature. You'll convert the angel image into a file that will be linked to one of the links that you've just created in the home page.

2 Choose File > Export > Zoomify.

3 In the Zoomify Export dialog box, click Folder, select the Lesson13/13Start/ Museo folder, and click OK or Choose. For Base Name, type **Card**. Set the quality to **12**; set the Width to **800**, and set the Height to **600** for the base image in the viewer's browser. Make sure that the Open In Web Browser option is selected.

4 Click OK to export the HTML file and images. Zoomify opens them in your web browser.

5 Use the controls in the Zoomify window to zoom in and out of the angel image.

6 When you have finished, close the browser.

Creating a web gallery

Using Bridge, you can easily showcase your images in an online gallery, so that visitors can view individual images or a slide show of your work. You'll create a media gallery linked to the exhibits.html file in the museum website.

1 In Bridge, double-click the Watercolors folder (in the Lesson13/13Start folder).

You'll create a slide show from the images in the Watercolors folder.

2 Select the first image, and then Shift-select the last, so that all the images are selected. Remember that you can use the Thumbnails slider at the bottom of the Bridge window to reduce the size of the thumbnails, so that more fit in the Content panel at a time.

3 Click Output at the top of the Bridge window to display the Output workspace. If there is no Output button, choose Window > Workspace > Output.

4 In the Output panel, click the Web Gallery button.

5 Click the triangle next to Site Info if its contents aren't already displayed. In the Site Info area of the Output panel, enter **Watercolors** for the Gallery Title, **Paintings from the Watercolors exhibit** for the Gallery Caption, and **Now showing at Museo Arte** in the About This Gallery box. You can also add a contact name and information if you want to.

6 Click the triangle next to Site Info to collapse its contents. Scroll down to the Create Gallery area. Expand its contents if they aren't already visible.

7 Name the gallery **Watercolors**. Click Browse, and navigate to the Lesson13/13Start/Museo folder. Click OK or Open to close the dialog box, and then click Save at the bottom of the Output panel in Bridge.

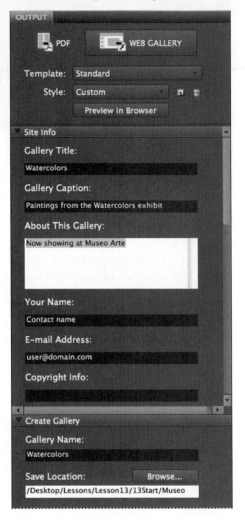

Bridge creates both a gallery folder named Watercolors that contains an index.html file and a resources folder containing the watercolor images.

8 Click OK when Bridge reports that the gallery has been created. Then, in Bridge, click the Essentials button at the top of the window to return to the default workspace.

9 Navigate to the Lesson13/13Start/Museo folder. Double-click the Watercolors folder, which is the gallery folder Bridge just created. Right-click or Control-click the index.html file, choose Open With, and select a browser.

10 If you see a security warning, click OK, or follow the instructions to change settings.

The gallery opens. One image is displayed on the right side, and thumbnails of the others are shown on the left.

11 Click the View Slideshow button beneath the larger image to start the slide show. Click the View Gallery button beneath the featured image to return to gallery view.

12 Close the browser application.

The exhibits.html file already contains a link to the folder you created, as long as you named the folder exactly as specified in step 7. Now you'll open your website and use the link to view the gallery.

13 In Bridge, navigate to the Lesson13/13Start/Museo folder. Right-click (Windows) or Control-click (Mac OS) the home.html file, and choose Open With from the context menu. Choose a web browser to open the HTML file.

14 In the website, click the Exhibit Schedule link in the navigation area. Then, on the Exhibit Schedule page, click the link to the Watercolor slide show. The gallery opens.

15 Explore the gallery and the website further, if you'd like. When you're finished, close the browser application, Bridge, and Photoshop.

You're on your way to building engaging websites from Photoshop images. You've learned how to create slices, optimize images for the web, use Zoomify, and create media slide shows in Bridge.

Review questions

1 What are slices? How do you create them?

2 What is image optimization, and how do you optimize images for the web?

3 How can you create a slide show for the web?

Review answers

1 Slices are rectangular areas of an image that you define for individual web optimization. You can add animated GIFs, URL links, and rollovers to slices. You can create image slices with the Slice tool or by converting layers into slices using the Layer menu.

2 Image optimization is the process of choosing file format, resolution, and quality settings for an image to keep it small, useful, and visually appealing when published to the web. Continuous-tone images are typically optimized in JPEG format; solid-color images or those with repetitive color areas are typically optimized as GIF. To optimize images, choose File > Save For Web.

3 To create a slide show for use on the web, use Bridge. Select the files you want to include, and then select Web Gallery in the Output panel in Bridge. Set the appropriate settings, and save the gallery. Bridge creates an index.html file with slide show and gallery controls that link to the files you selected.

14 PRODUCING AND PRINTING CONSISTENT COLOR

Lesson overview

In this lesson, you'll learn how to do the following:

- Define RGB, grayscale, and CMYK color spaces for displaying, editing, and printing images.

- Prepare an image for printing on a PostScript CMYK printer.

- Proof an image for printing.

- Save an image as a CMYK EPS file.

- Create and print a four-color separation.

- Understand how images are prepared for printing on presses.

 This lesson will take less than an hour to complete. Copy the Lesson14 folder onto your hard drive if you haven't already done so. As you work through this lesson, you'll preserve the start files. If you need to restore the start files, copy them from the *Adobe Photoshop CS6 Classroom in a Book* DVD.

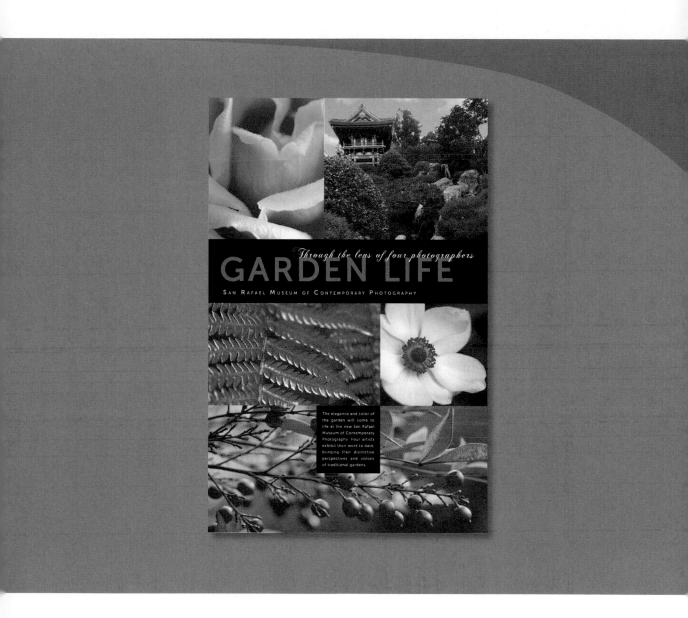

To produce consistent color, you define the color space in which to edit and display RGB images, and the color space in which to edit, display, and print CMYK images. This helps ensure a close match between onscreen and printed colors.

About color management

● **Note:** One exercise in this lesson requires that your computer be connected to a PostScript color printer. If it isn't, you can do most, but not all, of the exercises.

Colors on a monitor are displayed using combinations of red, green, and blue light (called RGB), while printed colors are typically created using a combination of four ink colors—cyan, magenta, yellow, and black (called CMYK). These four inks are called *process colors* because they are the standard inks used in the four-color printing process.

RGB image with red, green, and blue channels

CMYK image with cyan, magenta, yellow, and black channels

Because the RGB and CMYK color models use different methods to display colors, each reproduces a different *gamut*, or range, of colors. For example, RGB uses light to produce color, so its gamut includes neon colors, such as those you'd see in a neon sign. In contrast, printing inks excel at reproducing certain colors that can lie outside the RGB gamut, such as some pastels and pure black.

A. Natural color gamut
B. RGB color gamut
C. CMYK color gamut

RGB color model

CMYK color model

But not all RGB and CMYK gamuts are alike. Each monitor and printer model differs, and so each displays a slightly different gamut. For example, one brand of monitor may produce slightly brighter blues than another. The *color space* for a device is defined by the gamut it can reproduce.

RGB model

A large percentage of the visible spectrum can be represented by mixing red, green, and blue (RGB) colored light in various proportions and intensities. Where the colors overlap, they create cyan, magenta, yellow, and white.

Because the RGB colors combine to create white, they are also called *additive* colors. Adding all colors together creates white—that is, all light is transmitted back to the eye. Additive colors are used for lighting, video, and monitors. Your monitor, for example, creates color by emitting light through red, green, and blue phosphors.

CMYK model

The CMYK model is based on the light-absorbing quality of ink printed on paper. As white light strikes translucent inks, part of the spectrum is absorbed, while other parts are reflected back to your eyes.

In theory, pure cyan (C), magenta (M), and yellow (Y) pigments should combine to absorb all color and produce black. For this reason, these colors are called *subtractive* colors. But because all printing inks contain some impurities, these three inks actually produce a muddy brown, and must be combined with black (K) ink to produce a true black. (K is used instead of B to avoid confusion with blue.) Combining these inks to reproduce color is called four-color process printing.

The color management system in Photoshop uses International Color Consortium (ICC)-compliant color profiles to convert colors from one color space into another. A color profile is a description of a device's color space, such as the CMYK color space of a particular printer. You specify which profiles to use to accurately proof and print your images. Once you've selected the profiles, Photoshop can embed them into your image files, so that Photoshop and other applications can accurately manage color for the image.

For information on embedding color profiles, see Photoshop Help.

Before you begin working with color management, you should calibrate your monitor. If your monitor doesn't display colors accurately, color adjustments you make based on the image you see on your monitor may not be accurate. For information about calibrating your monitor, see Photoshop Help.

Getting started

First, start Photoshop and restore its default preferences.

1 Start Photoshop, and then immediately hold down Ctrl+Alt+Shift (Windows) or Command+Option+Shift (Mac OS) to restore the default preferences. (See "Restoring default preferences" on page 4.)

2 When prompted, click Yes to delete the Adobe Photoshop Settings file.

Specifying color-management settings

In the first part of this lesson, you'll learn how to set up a color-managed workflow in Photoshop. Most of the color-management controls you need are in the Color Settings dialog box.

By default, Photoshop is set up for RGB as part of a digital workflow. If you are preparing artwork for print production, however, you'll want to change the settings to be more appropriate for images that will be printed on paper rather than displayed on a screen.

You'll begin this lesson by creating customized color settings.

1 Choose Edit > Color Settings to open the Color Settings dialog box.

The bottom of the dialog box interactively describes each option.

2 Move the pointer over each part of the dialog box, including the names of areas (such as Working Spaces), the menu names, and the menu options. As you move the pointer, Photoshop displays information about each item. When you've finished, return the options to their defaults.

Now, you'll choose a set of options designed for a print workflow, rather than an online workflow.

3 Choose North America Prepress 2 from the Settings menu. The working spaces and color-management policy options change for a prepress workflow. Then click OK.

Proofing an image

You'll select a proof profile so that you can view a close onscreen representation of what an image will look like when printed. An accurate proof profile lets you proof on the screen (*soft-proof*) for printed output.

1 Choose File > Open. Navigate to the Lessons/ Lesson14 folder, and double-click the 14Start.tif file. Click OK if you see an embedded profile warning.

An RGB image of a scanned poster opens.

2 Choose File > Save As. Rename the file **14Working.tif**, keep the TIFF format selected, and click Save. Click OK in the TIFF Options dialog box.

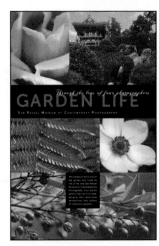

Before soft-proofing or printing this image, you'll set up a proof profile. A proof profile (also called a *proof setup*) defines how the document is going to be printed, and adjusts the onscreen appearance accordingly. Photoshop provides a variety of settings that can help you proof images for different uses, including print and display on the web. For this lesson, you'll create a custom proof setup. You can then save the settings for use on other images that will be output the same way.

3 Choose View > Proof Setup > Custom. The Customize Proof Condition dialog box opens. Make sure Preview is selected.

4 From the Device To Simulate menu, choose a profile that represents the final output device, such as that for the printer you'll use to print the image. If you don't have a specific printer, the profile Working CMYK–U.S. Web Coated (SWOP) v2 is generally a good choice.

5 Make sure that Preserve Numbers is *not* selected.

The Preserve Numbers option simulates how colors will appear without being converted to the output device color space.

● **Note:** The Preserve Numbers option is not available when the U.S. Web Coated (SWOP) v2 profile is selected.

6 From the Rendering Intent menu, choose Relative Colorimetric.

A rendering intent determines how the color is converted from one color space to another. Relative Colorimetric, which preserves color relationships without sacrificing color accuracy, is the standard rendering intent for printing in North America and Europe.

7 If it's available for the profile you chose, select Simulate Black Ink. Then deselect it, and select Simulate Paper Color; notice that selecting this option automatically selects Simulate Black Ink. Click OK.

▶ Tip: To display the document with and without the proof settings, choose View > Proof Colors.

Notice that the image appears to lose contrast. Paper Color simulates the dingy white of real paper, according to the proof profile. Black Ink simulates the dark gray that actually prints to most printers, instead of solid black. Not all profiles support these options.

Normal image

Image with Paper Color and Black Ink options selected

Identifying out-of-gamut colors

Most scanned photographs contain RGB colors within the CMYK gamut, so changing the image to CMYK mode converts all the colors with relatively little substitution. Images that are created or altered digitally, however, often contain RGB colors that are outside the CMYK gamut—for example, neon-colored logos and lights.

Before you convert an image from RGB to CMYK, you can preview the CMYK color values while still in RGB mode.

1   Choose View > Gamut Warning to see out-of-gamut colors. Adobe Photoshop builds a color-conversion table, and displays a neutral gray in the image window where the colors are out of gamut.

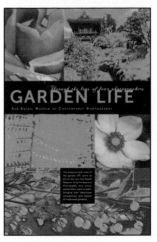

Because the gray can be hard to spot in the image, you'll convert it to a more visible color.

2   Choose Edit > Preferences > Transparency And Gamut (Windows) or Photoshop > Preferences > Transparency And Gamut (Mac OS).

3   Click the color sample in the Gamut Warning area at the bottom of the dialog box. Select a vivid color, such as purple or bright green, and click OK.

4   Click OK to close the Preferences dialog box.

5   Click anywhere on the image with the Move tool. The bright new color you chose appears instead of the neutral gray as the gamut warning color.

6 Choose View > Gamut Warning to turn off the preview of out-of-gamut colors.

Photoshop will automatically correct these out-of-gamut colors when you save the file in Photoshop EPS format later in this lesson. Photoshop EPS format changes the RGB image to CMYK, adjusting the RGB colors as needed to bring them into the CMYK color gamut.

Adjusting an image and printing a proof

The next step in preparing an image for output is to make any color and tonal adjustments that are necessary. In this exercise, you'll add some tonal and color adjustments to correct an off-color scan of the original poster.

So that you can compare the image before and after making corrections, you'll start by making a copy.

1 Choose Image > Duplicate, and click OK to duplicate the image.

2 Choose Window > Arrange > 2 Up Vertical so you can compare the images as you work.

You'll adjust the hue and saturation of the image to move all colors into gamut.

3 Select 14Working.tif (the original image).

4 Choose Select > Color Range.

5 In the Color Range dialog box, choose Out Of Gamut from the Select menu, and then click OK.

The areas that were marked as out of gamut earlier are now selected, so you can make changes that affect only those areas.

6 Click the Hue/Saturation button in the Adjustments panel to create a Hue/Saturation adjustment layer. (Choose Window > Adjustments if the panel isn't open.) The Hue/Saturation adjustment layer includes a layer mask, created from your selection.

7 In the Properties panel, do the following:

- Drag the Hue slider until the colors look more neutral (we used -5).

- Drag the Saturation slider until the intensity of the colors looks more realistic (we used -40).

- Leave the Lightness setting at the default value (0).

8 Choose View > Gamut Warning. You have removed most of the out-of-gamut colors from the image. Choose View > Gamut Warning again to deselect it.

9 With 14Working.tif still selected, choose File > Print.

10 In the Print dialog box, do the following:

- Choose your printer from the Printer menu.

- In the Color Management area of the dialog box, choose Printer Manages Colors from the Color Handling menu.

- Choose Hard Proofing from the pop-up menu.

- For Proof Setup, choose Working CMYK.

- If you have a color PostScript printer, click Print to print the image, and compare the color with the onscreen version. Otherwise, click Cancel.

Saving the image as a CMYK EPS file

You'll save the image as an EPS file in CMYK format.

1 With 14Working.tif still selected, choose File > Save As.

2 In the Save As dialog box, do the following, and then click Save:

- Choose Photoshop EPS from the Format menu.

- Under Color, select Use Proof Setup. Don't worry about the warning icon; you'll save a copy.

- Accept the filename 14Working.eps.

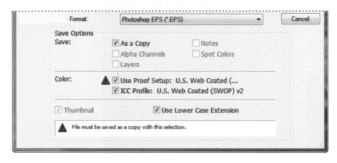

3 Click OK in the EPS Options dialog box that appears.

4 Save and then close the 14Working.tif and 14Working copy.tif files.

5 Choose File > Open, navigate to the Lessons/Lesson14 folder, and double-click the 14Working.eps file.

Notice in the image file's title bar that 14Working.eps is a CMYK file.

Printing

When you're ready to print your image, use the following guidelines for best results:

- Print a *color composite*, often called a *color comp*, to proof your image. A color composite is a single print that combines the red, green, and blue channels of an RGB image (or the cyan, magenta, yellow, and black channels of a CMYK image). This indicates what the final printed image will look like.

- Set the parameters for the halftone screen.

- Print separations to make sure the image separates correctly.

- Print to film or plate.

When you print color separations, Photoshop prints a separate sheet, or *plate*, for each ink. For a CMYK image, it prints four plates, one for each process color.

In this exercise, you'll print color separations.

1 With the 14Working.eps image open from the previous exercise, choose File > Print.

By default, Photoshop prints any document as a composite image. To print this file as separations, you need to explicitly instruct Photoshop in the Print dialog box.

2 In the Print dialog box, do the following:

- In the Color Management area, choose Separations from the Color Handling menu.

- Click Print.

3 Choose File > Close, and don't save the changes.

This lesson has provided an introduction to printing and producing consistent color from Adobe Photoshop. If you're printing on a desktop printer, you can experiment with different settings to find the best color and print settings for your system. If you're preparing images for professional printing, consult with your print service provider to determine the best settings to use. For more information about color management, printing options, and color separations, see Photoshop Help.

Review questions

1 What steps should you follow to reproduce color accurately?

2 What is a gamut?

3 What is a color profile?

4 What are color separations?

Review answers

1 To reproduce color accurately, first calibrate your monitor, and then use the Color Settings dialog box to specify which color spaces to use. For example, you can specify which RGB color space to use for online images, and which CMYK color space to use for images that will be printed. You can then proof the image, check for out-of-gamut colors, adjust colors as needed, and—for printed images—create color separations.

2 A gamut is the range of colors that can be reproduced by a color model or device. For example, the RGB and CMYK color models have different gamuts, as do any two RGB scanners.

3 A color profile is a description of a device's color space, such as the CMYK color space of a particular printer. Applications such as Photoshop can interpret color profiles in an image to maintain consistent color across different applications, platforms, and devices.

4 Color separations are separate plates for each ink used in a document. Often, you'll print color separations for the cyan, magenta, yellow, and black (CMYK) inks.

INDEX

SYMBOLS

3D Axis widget 313, 320, 325
   resizing 321
3D features 310–337
3D files, importing 316
3D layers
   creating 3D postcards 314–315
   creating from imported files 316–317
   merging 318
   overview 312
3D objects
   applying materials to 329
   moving 320
   positioning 319–326
   rotating 325
   scaling 325
3D panel 322
3D postcards 314
3D scenes
   lighting 332
   rendering 334
3D shape presets 310, 315–316
3D text 317
   extruding 326–327
3D tools 312

A

actions 258–266
   batch-playing 261–262
   creating new 259
   creating new sets 258
   naming 259
   overview 258
   playing 260
   recording 259

Actions panel 258–264
   Play button 260
Adaptive Wide Angle filter 264–265
Add Audio option 282
adding
   borders 256
   canvas 255
Add Media button 272
Add To Path Area option 212
adjustment layers 113–114
   Black & White 63, 277
   Curves 19, 147
   defined 20
   Hue/Saturation 114, 183
   Levels 141, 181, 183
   using in video 276
   Vibrance 162
adjustments
   Invert 76, 182
   Match Color 259
Adobe Application Manager 37
Adobe Bridge
   adding favorites 13
   creating a slide show in 355–357
   Favorites panel 13
   installing 3
   opening files in Camera Raw
      from 48, 130
   opening files in Photoshop from
      13–14
   starting 48
Adobe Camera Raw
   adjusting white balance in 49, 131
   Basic panel 50, 133
   Detail panel 135
   dialog box 130
   HSL/Grayscale tab 63

opening images in 48, 129
Open Object button 139
saving files in 140
synchronizing settings across
    images 136
workflow 130
Adobe certification 7
Adobe Illustrator
    Glyphs panel 202
    importing Smart Objects
        from 227
    importing text from 227–228
Adobe InDesign 62
Adobe Photoshop CS6
    closing an image file in 12
    installing 3
    new features 2
    resetting the default
        preferences for 10
    resources for learning 6–7
    starting 4, 10
    updating 37
    work area 10–43
*Adobe Photoshop CS6 Classroom
    in a Book* 1
    copying lesson files 4–5
    disc contents iii
    installing lesson files 4
    new features covered in 2
    prerequisites 3
Adobe Photoshop CS6
    Extended 2
    3D features 310–337
Adobe Photoshop Lightroom
    148–149
Align Bottom Edges button 324
aligning
    layers 120
    objects 324
    selections 239
    slices 346–347
alpha channels 168, 178
    about 180, 184
anchor points 210, 211
animating
    a zoom effect 277
    lighting in a 3D scene
        335–336

position 280
style effects 278–279
text 274
anti-aliasing 87
application frame, in Mac OS 12
Apply Layer Comp box 119
arrow keys
    nudging selections with 73–74
    using the Shift key with 73
assets
    importing for video 271
    resizing for video 274
audio
    adding to a video timeline 282
    fading 283
    muting 283–284
    shortening clips 282
Audio track 282
Auto-Align Layers 120, 159
automating tasks 258–266
auto slices 343
    hiding 347
axes, 3D 313

B

background layer 92
    converting to regular layer 94
    erasing 97
    overview 94
badges, on slices 343, 344
barrel distortion, correcting 155
Basic panel (in Camera Raw) 133
Batch command 261
bitmap images
    overview 10, 208
    vector graphics vs. 208–209
black and white
    converting color images in
        Photoshop 63
    converting images in Camera
        Raw 63
black point 133
Black & White adjustment layer
    63, 277

_blank Target option 348
blending colors with a
    photograph 300
blending modes
    achieving different effects with
        101
    applying to layers 102
    Lighten 247
    Multiply 102
    Overlay 102, 251
    overview 100
blurs
    interactive 161
    Iris Blur 161
    Surface Blur 150
borders
    adding 97, 116, 256
    discarding 52
breadcrumbs 342
Bristle Brush Preview 293
bristle tips 290
browsing files in Adobe Bridge 13
brushes
    loading with color 297
    settings 291
    Shape Dynamics options 303
Brush panel 291
    special effects 250
Brush Pose settings 303
brush presets 298
Brush Presets panel 299
Brush tool, setting options
    27–28, 175
buttons, website 345

C

calibration, monitor 363
camera lens flaws, correcting
    155–157
Camera Raw. *See* Adobe
    Camera Raw
camera raw images
    cameras supported by Adobe
        Camera Raw 129

creating 129
file formats for saving 140
histogram 135
opening 129–130
overview 129
proprietary 126
saving 138–139
sharpening 135
white balance and exposure
adjustment 131–132
cameras, in 3D layers 312
changing the angle of 314
camera views 314, 319
Camera widget 314
canvas
adding 255
rotating 228
Canvas Size dialog box 255
center point, selecting from 74
channel masks 184
channels
adjusting individual 180–182
alpha channels 178, 180
applying filters to
individual 243
correcting noise in 154
loading as selections 182
overview 168, 178
Channels panel 168
Character panel 32, 106
checkerboard
pattern 224–226
transparency indicator 97
chromatic aberration 155
Chrome filter 243
Classroom in a Book. *See Adobe
Photoshop CS6 Classroom
in a Book*
Clean Brush After Every Stroke
icon 296
clean brush (Mixer Brush
tool) 296
Clear Override button 201
clipping masks 27
about 184, 189
creating 191–193

indicator 192
in placed video assets 277
shortcut 192
Clone Source panel 56
Clone Stamp tool 55–57
closed paths 209, 211
closing a Photoshop file 12
Clouds filter 104
CMYK color mode, converting
to 366
CMYK color model 363
defined 362
gamut 362
color
additive 363
adjusting overall 49
changing in the Photoshop
interface 38
converting to black and
white 63
correcting skin tones 257
default text 191
editing masks and 174
inverting 76
lightening 144–145
managed workflow 364–365
matching across images
256–258
mixing with the Mixer
Brush 295
out-of-gamut 366
previewing CMYK values in
RGB mode 367
replacing 53–55
sampling 291
selecting by 68
selecting using the Swatches
panel 24–25
softening edge transitions 87
color casts, removing 49
color comp 371
color management 364–365
selecting when printing 369
color modes
changing 61
retouching for 46
Color panel 32

color profiles 363
Color Range, Skin Tones
option 146
Color Replacement tool 53–55
color settings
restoring 5
saving 5
Color Settings dialog box
364–365
color space 363
device profile 363
combining images
montage 234
panorama 262–266
Commit Any Current Edits
button 116
Commit Transform button 227
compression settings 353
Content-Aware fill 264
Content-Aware Move tool 160
Content-aware Patch tool 58
context menus
annotations 203
overview 30–31
type 193, 196
web browser 340
continuous-tone images 353
Contrast slider in Camera
Raw 133
Control Timeline Magnification
slider 273
Coordinates in the Properties
panel 323
copying
and anti-aliasing 87
and transforming 77
at same resolution 78
Classroom in a Book lesson
files 4–5
commands 78
images 118, 368
images, and centering 95
layers 95–97
selections 76, 78
settings in Camera Raw 136
Copy Merged command 78

corner points 211, 213

Create Video Timeline 272

Crop And Straighten Photos command 84

cropping
  adjusting crop area 84
  and straightening automatically 84
  images 51–52, 235–236, 263

cropping shield 51

Crop tool 235, 263

Cross Fade transition 281

curved paths 211, 213–214

Curves adjustment layer 20–21, 147

customizing
  keyboard shortcuts 34
  user interface 38
  workspaces 33

Custom Shape tool 224, 225–226

Cutout filter 243

cutouts 222–223

D

defaults
  resetting 4, 10
  resetting foreground and background color 25

Deform widget 327

depth of field, adding 158

desaturating 247–248

deselecting 18
  paths 223

Detail panel in Camera Raw 135

Direct Selection tool 211, 221

discretionary ligatures 202

displaying
  document size 118
  layers 96
  multiple documents 95

distortions, correcting 155–158

dividing portions of an image into multiple files 84

DNG file format 140

docking panels 31

document size, displaying 118

Dodge tool 144–145

dragging image files to add layers 105

Drag The 3D Object tool 313

drop shadows 109–110, 112, 254

duplicating
  areas of a scene 160
  images 368

duration of video clips, changing 273

E

editing images
  adjusting highlights and shadows 151–153
  correcting distortions 155–157
  nondestructively 174
  reducing noise 153–155
  removing red eye 153–154

editing shapes 221

effects, animating 278–279

Elliptical Marquee tool , 17
  centering selection 75
  circular selections with 72

Environment, in the 3D panel 322

EPS file format 370

Erase Refinements tool 173

Eraser tool 85, 120

erodible tip 294

exporting
  HTML pages 349–351
  video 284

extruding 3D text 326–327

Eyedropper tool 291

eye icon, in the Layers panel 93

F

Fade With Black transitions 282

fading audio 283

Favorites panel, in Bridge 13

Feather command 87

feathering 87

file formats
  from Camera Raw 140
  image quality and 235
  three-dimensional 2
  transferring images between applications and platforms 140
  type 202

files
  reverting to unchanged version 20
  saving 20, 118–121

file size
  compressing for the web 353
  flattened vs. unflattened 118
  reducing 118

fills, Content-Aware 264

film. See video

Filter Gallery 244

filtering layers in the Layers panel 115

filters 243–246
  Adaptive Wide Angle 264
  adding clouds with 104
  improving performance 243
  overview 245
  shortcuts 245

Fit On Screen command 75

focus, adjusting 158

fonts
  alternates 202
  selecting 190

Foreground color swatch 24, 104
  resetting to default 25

four-color printing 61–62, 362

fractions 202

Freeform Pen tool 209

freehand selections 80–81

G

gamut 362
    colors outside of 366–367
Gamut Warning 367–368
Geometry Options menu 212
GIF compression 349, 350
Glass filter 243
Go To First Frame button 281
Gradient Overlay layer style 242
Gradient Picker 108
gradients, listing by name 108
Gradient tool 108
guides
    adding 189, 237
    for creating slices 347
    hiding 238
    overview 237
    Smart Guides 239
    snapping to 237

H

hand-coloring selections 246
Hand tool 83
Healing Brush tool 57, 143
hiding
    layers 96
    selection edges 73–74
High Dynamic Range (HDR)
    images 163
highlights, adjusting 151–153
high-resolution images 47
    filters and 243
histogram, in Camera Raw 135
History panel
    changing number of states 30
    clearing actions 259
    undoing multiple actions
        28–31
Horizontal Type tool , 106, 190
HSL/Grayscale tab
    (Camera Raw) 63

HTML pages

HTML pages
    exporting 349–351
    naming 347
hue, adjusting for printing 368
Hue/Saturation adjustment
    layers 183
hypertext links 343
    about 342
    adding 347, 348

I

illustrations with type 353
images
    centering and copying 191
    continuous-tone 353
    copying 118
    cropping 235
    determining scan
        resolution 48
    duplicating 368
    fitting on-screen 83
    flattening 118–120
    matching color schemes
        256–258
    optimizing for web
        349–351, 353
    resizing for web 138
    resolution 47–48
    sharpening 135
    size and resolution 47–48
    solid-color 353
Image Size command 78
image window 12, 15, 15–16
    fitting image to 75
    scrolling 21
importing 3D files 316–317
Infinite Light 332
Inner Shadow layer style 192
interactive blurs 161
interface. *See* user interface
Inverse command 19
Invert command 76, 182
Iris Blur filter 161

J

JPEG compression 349, 351
JPEG file format
    camera raw images and 129
    image degradation and
        149, 235

K

keyboard shortcuts
    creating 34–36
    customizing 298
    duplicating 76
    filters 245
    finding 19
    for tools 17
    Move tool 72
Keyboard Shortcuts And Menus
    dialog box 34–36
keyframes
    appearance of 275
    moving to the next or
        previous 278
    using to animate text 274

L

Lasso tool 68, 80–81, 81
lasso tools 80–81
layer comps 119
layer effects
    adding 109
    updating 115
layer groups 238
layer masks
    defined 184
    turning on and off 174
layers
    3D shapes from 310
    adding 104–105
    aligning 120
    background 94
    blending modes 100–101
    converting to background 94

copying 95–97

copying and centering 95, 99, 102, 202

copying and merging 78

creating by copying 217

deleting 214

deleting hidden 230

effects 108–111, 109–112

erasing 97–99

filtering in the Layers panel 115

flattening 118

flattening visible 118

hiding 93, 96

hiding all but selected 97

linking 102–104

locking 93

matching colors 257

merging 3D layers 318

merging visible 118

opacity 100

overview 92

rearranging 98–100

removing pixels from 97–99

renaming 95

resizing 102–104

showing 97

slices from 348

template 219, 230

thumbnails, hiding and resizing 93

transforming 102

transparency 100–101

type 106

Layers panel

deleting hidden layers 230

overview 93–94

Quick Mask mode indicator 175

searching for layers in 115

layer styles

adding to type 192

applying 108–111, 109–112

copying to other layers 255

Drop Shadow 109, 112, 242, 254

Gradient Overlay 242

Outer Glow 241

overview 108, 109

Satin 112–113

Stroke 111

Layer Via Copy command 217

length of video clips, changing 273

Lens Correction filter 155–157

Levels adjustment layers 141, 181, 183

Lighten blending mode 247

Lighting Effects filter 243

lightness, adjusting for printing 369

Lightroom. See Adobe Photoshop Lightroom

lights, in 3D layers

adding 333

animating 335–336

changing the color of 332

moving 332

overview 312

linear gradients 104–106

line art 353

linking masks to layers 174

loading brushes with color 297

loading channels as selections 182

Load Path As Selection option 216

low-resolution images 47

M

Mac OS, differences in work area 12

Magic Wand tool 68, 215

combining with other tools 78–79

Magnetic Lasso tool 68, 82–83

magnification 14. See also Zoom tool

magnifying glass. See Zoom tool

Make Selection dialog box 216

Make Work Path From Selection option 215

marquee tools 68

masks

color values for editing 168, 174

creating 169–172

overview 168

refining 170

terminology 184

Masks panel 174

Match Color dialog box 257

materials, in 3D layers 312, 326

adding to 3D text 326–329

applying to 3D objects 329–331

Merge to HDR Pro 163–164

Merge Visible command 118

merging

3D layers 318

images 120, 158

layers 118

meshes, in 3D layers 312

merging into the same 3D layer 318

Mini Bridge

opening the Mini Bridge panel 22

overview 22

viewing a full-screen preview in 22

mistakes, correcting 26–33

Mixer Brush tool

about 290

cleaning the brush 296

mixing colors 295

with a photograph 300

mobile authoring 46

Mode command 61

monitor calibration 363

monitor resolution 47–48

montages, assembling 234–243

Motion dialog box 274, 277

Motion workspace 272

Move tool 24, 217

moving selections 70

scissors icon 75

moving
   3D objects 313, 320
   panels 31
   selections 70–71
Multiply blending mode 102
muting audio 283–284

N

navigating
   using Scrubby Zoom 16
   using the Navigator panel 21
   with the Zoom tool 14–15
navigation buttons, website 345–347
   previewing function 344
Navigator panel 21
Negative Image style 279
New Layer Based Slice command 348
No Image slices 347
noise, reducing 153–155
nondestructive filters 252
Notes panel 198

O

online galleries 355
opacity, changing 100–101
opening images in Camera Raw 129
Open Object button (in Camera Raw) 139
open paths 209, 211
OpenType file format 188, 202
optimizing images 353
options bar 22
   compared to panels 32–33
   overview 23–24
   setting type options in 23
organizing photos 148–149
Outer Glow layer style 241
out-of-gamut color 366–367

output resolution, determining 47
Overlay blending mode 102, 251
overrides, clearing in text 201

P

page layout, preparing images for 61–62
painting
   effects 246, 250
   wetness options 292
   with an erodible tip 294
   with the Mixer Brush tool 288–303
pan and zoom effects, adding to video 280–281
panel dock 31
panels
   3D panel 322
   Brush panel 291
   compared to options bar 33
   docking 31
   expanding and collapsing 32–33
   floating 219
   moving to another group 31
   overview 31–32
   resizing 32
   Styles panel 279
   Timeline panel 271
   undocking 31
   working with 24–26
panoramas, creating 262–266
Pan & Zoom option 274, 281
Paper Color option 366
paper, simulating white 366
Paragraph panel 32
paragraph styles 199–201
paragraph type 190
Paste Into command 78
pasting
   and anti-aliasing 87
   at same resolution 78
   commands 78

Patch tool 58
paths 209–210
   adding type to 194–195
   closing 211, 214
   converting smooth points to corner 213
   converting to selections 214–215, 216–218
   deselecting 221–222, 223
   drawing curved 211
   drawing straight 211
   guidelines for drawing 210
   naming 215
   saving 211, 214
path segments 211
Path Selection tool 221
Paths panel 211, 212
   vector mask 222
patterns, creating 224–226
Pencil tool 209
Pen tool 219
   as selection tool 210
   drawing paths 210–214
   keyboard shortcut 209
   overview 209–210, 211
   setting options 212–213
perspective, changing 264
photo correction
   automatic 60–61
   replacing colors 53–55
   resolution and size 47–48
   retouching strategy 46
   unsharp masking 60–61
Photomerge dialog box 262
Photoshop EPS file format 368
Photoshop file format 235
Photoshop Help 37
Photoshop Raw file format 129
pincushion distortion 155
pixels
   defined 10, 47, 208
   image and monitor 47–48
placing files 227–228
playhead, in the Timeline panel 276

plug-ins 10
Point Light 333
point type 190
    distorting 196–197
    paragraphs vs. 197
Polygonal Lasso tool 68
Polygon tool 222
position, animating 280
positioning 3D objects 319–326
    with the Properties panel 322
PostScript fonts 188, 202
pound sign (#) 344
preferences
    gamut-warning color 367
    restoring defaults 4, 10
Preserve Numbers option 365
presets
    brush 298
    film and video 271
Print dialog box 369, 371
printing 361–373
    adjusting tone and color
        368–370
    CMYK model and 362–363
    guidelines 371
    identifying out-of-gamut color
        366–367
    proofing images on screen
        365–368
    proofs 368
    resolution 47
    saving image as
        separations 370
printing inks, simulating 366
process colors 46, 362
Proof Colors command 366
proofing images 365–368
proof profiles 365
proof setup 365
Properties panel, using to position
    3D objects 322
PSD format 140
    camera raw images and 129
Puppet Warp 177
Purge command 243

Q

Quick Mask mode 175
quick masks 168, 174
    painting color 176
Quick Selection tool 68, 69–70

R

Radius slider, Unsharp Mask
    filter 60
RAM, filters and 243, 245
raster images, overview 208
rasterizing vector masks 174
Rectangular Marquee tool 68, 79
Red Eye tool 153–154
Reduce Noise filter 153–155
Refine Edge 87, 179
Refine Mask dialog box 171
Refine Radius tool 172
rendering
    3D scenes 334
    video 284, 336
repositioning selections 71
Resize To Fill Canvas option 274
resizing
    layers 102
    panels 32
    video assets 274
resolution 47–48
retouching/repairing
    by cloning 55–57
    overview 46
    removing blemishes 57–58
    setting correct resolution
        47–48
    with the Healing Brush
        tool 143
    with the Spot Healing Brush
        tool 57, 143–144
RGB color mode, converting to
    CMYK 367
RGB color model 362–364, 363
    about 363
    gamut 362

Ripple filter 243
Roll The 3D Object tool 313
Rotate View tool 229
rotating 218
    3D objects 313, 325
    selections 81
    the canvas 228
ruler guides 189, 237
rulers 189
    displaying 218
    setting unit of measure 237

S

Sample Aligned option 57
sampling colors 291
sampling ring 291
Satin layer style 112–113
saturation, adjusting in
    Photoshop 54–55, 144–145
Saturation slider (in
    Camera Raw) 133
Save For Web And Devices dialog
    box 349–350, 353
saving
    images as separations 370
    optimized images 353
    Photoshop files 21
scaling 77, 191
    3D objects 313, 325
scan resolution 48
scene, 3D 318, 322
scrubbing 23
Scrubby Zoom 16
searching for layers in the Layers
    panel 115
Secondary View window 319
selecting
    a layer in a multilayer file 71
    from center point 74–75
    high-contrast edges 82–83
    inverse selection 79–80
    layers 97
    overview 68
    skin tones 146

slices 343
text 116
selections
  by color 68
  circular 75
  constraining 18
  converting to paths 214–215
  copying 78
  copying to another image 217–218
  deactivating 18
  duplicating 76
  elliptical 71–79
  feathering existing 87
  freehand 68
  geometric 68
  hiding edges of 74
  inverting 19
  moving 18, 70–71, 72, 75–76, 77
  precise 216
  recognizing 17
  rotating 81–82
  showing edges 74
  softening 87
  subtracting from 79, 216
  subtracting from while loading 249
selection tools 68–69
  Pen tool 210
_self Target option 347
separations
  printing 371–373
  saving image as 370
sepia effect, creating 277
shaders, in 3D layers 312
Shadow/Highlight adjustment 152–154
shadows, adjusting 151–153
Shape Dynamics options, for brushes 303
shape layers 221–222
shapes
  custom 224–227
  editing 221
sharpening images
  in Camera Raw 135–136

using the Unsharp Mask filter 60
shortcuts. See keyboard shortcuts
shortening video clips 273
Show/Hide Visibility column 97
Show Transform Controls option 227
sidecar XMP files 136
Single Column Marquee tool 68
Single Row Marquee tool 68
skewing an object 180
skin tones
  correcting 257
  selecting 146
Slice Options dialog box 344
slices 343–350
  aligning 346–347
  creating buttons from 345
  defined 342
  dividing 347
  layer-based 348–349
  methods for creating 347
  naming 346
  optimizing for web 350
  selecting 343
  selection indicator 343
  symbols 343, 344
  targeting 346
  unlinking from layer 347
Slice Select tool 343, 344, 350
Slice tool 345
slide shows 355
Smart Filters 252–255
Smart Guides 239
Smart Objects
  automatic update on editing 227
  editing 248
  layer thumbnail 227
  linking vector masks to 228
  overview 227
  Smart Filters and 252
smooth points 211, 213
snapping to guides 237

soft-proofing 365–368
solid-color images 353
Spatter filter 243
special effects brushes 250
spell checking 193
Split at Playhead button 282
Sponge tool 54
Spot Healing Brush tool 57–58, 143–144
Sprayed Strokes filter 243
stacking order, changing 98–100
Stained Glass filter 243
Standard mode 175
starting Photoshop 10
status bar 15
sticky notes 198
stopwatch icon in the Timeline panel 275
straightening images 51
Stroke layer style 111
Styles panel 279
styles, paragraph 199–201
Subtract From Selection button 79
Surface Blur filter 150
swashes 202
Swatches panel 25–26
swatches, selecting 24
synchronizing settings in Camera Raw 136

T

Target option 347
temperature, image 131
template layers 219
  deleting 230
text. See also type
  3D 317, 326
  adding 190, 239–243
  animating 274
  applying styles 199–201
  coloring 24–26

creating 106–107
default color 191
deselecting 24
moving 24, 107
placing from Adobe
    Illustrator 227–228
selecting 116
textures, in 3D layers 312
Threshold slider, Unsharp Mask
    filter 60
thumbnails
layer 93
layer mask 174
shape layer 223
Smart Object 227
TIFF (Tagged Image File Format)
    62, 365
camera raw images and 129
overview 140
timeline, creating 272
Timeline panel 335–336
about 271
changing the
    magnification 273
returning to the first
    frame 281
time ruler, in the Timeline
    panel 273
tint, defined 131
tints, in Black & White
    adjustment layers 277
Tolerance option for the Magic
    Wand tool 78
tools
constraining 18–19
Content-Aware Move
    tool 160
Eyedropper 291
keyboard shortcuts for 17,
    209
selecting hidden 16–17
selection 68–69
using 14–20
Tools panel
compared to other panels
    32–33
double-column view 15

selecting and using tools from
    14–20
tool tips, displaying 15
tracks, in a timeline 272
transformations
bounding box 77
freeform 102–103, 218–219
transforming
layers 102–104
Smart Objects 227
transitions
adding to video 281
changing the length of 282
Cross Fade 281
Fade With Black 282
transparency
adjusting 100–101
indicating 97
in web-optimized images 353
Transparency And Gamut dialog
    box 367
TrueType fonts 202
type. *See also* text
aligning 190
clipping mask 189, 191–193
creating 190–191
glyphs 202
on a path 194–195
overview 188
resizing 188
resolution-independent 188
selecting 203
setting options 190, 203
swashes 202
tricks 193
true fractions 202
vertical 202–203
warping 196–197
typefaces
formats 188
selecting 190
type layers 106
creating new 193
selecting contents 193
updating 210
Type tool 23–24

U

undocking panels 31
Undo command 28
undoing actions 26–33
Unsharp Mask filter 60–61
updates for the Photoshop CS6
    application 37
user interface, changing settings
    for 38
user slices 343
USM (unsharp masking) 60–61
U.S. Web Coated (SWOP) v2
    profile 365

V

vector graphics
bitmap images vs. 208
defined 10
drawing shapes 218–220
overview 208
subtracting shapes from
    221–222
vector masks
converting to layer
    masks 174
defined 184
selection indication 223
unlinking from layers 174
vertical type 202–203
Vertical Type tool 202
Vibrance adjustment layer 162
video
adding audio to 282
adding pan and zoom effects
    280–281
adding transitions 281–282
exporting 284
importing assets for 271
overview 271
rendering 284, 336
resizing assets for 274
using adjustment layers
    in 276

video groups 273

vignetting 155

W

Wacom tablets 303

warping type 196–197

web

    browsers 340

    color mode for content 46

    galleries 355

    optimizing images for
        349–351, 353

wetness options, in painting 292

white balance, adjusting 49,
    131–132

White Balance tool (in Camera
    Raw) 49, 131–132

white point 133

widgets, 3D 313, 314, 327,
    332–333

Windows, differences in work
    area 12

work area 10–43

    differences between Mac OS
        and Windows 12

workflows

    color-managed 364–365

    for retouching images 46

    organizing files 148–149

    prepress 364

Working CMYK - U.S. Web
    Coated (SWOP) v2
    profile 365

Work Path

    naming 215

    overview 211

workspaces

    customizing 33–37

    default 11

    Motion 272

    preset 33–34

    saving 36

X

x axis 313

XMP files 136

Y

y axis 313

Z

z axis 313

Zoomify feature 354

zooming

    in to a video through
        animation 277

    in to the Timeline panel 273

    out 72

Zoom option in video 277

Zoom tool 14–15

    shortcuts 170

    using Scrubby Zoom 16

Production Notes

The *Adobe Photoshop CS6 Classroom in a Book* was created electronically using Adobe InDesign CS5.5. Art was produced using Adobe InDesign, Adobe Illustrator, and Adobe Photoshop. The Myriad Pro and Warnock Pro OpenType families of typefaces were used throughout this book.

References to company names in the lessons are for demonstration purposes only and are not intended to refer to any actual organization or person.

Images

Photographic images and illustrations are intended for use with the tutorials.

Lesson 4 pineapple and flower photography © Image Source, www.imagesource.com

Lesson 6 and 7 model photography © Image Source, www.imagesource.com

Typefaces used

Adobe Myriad Pro and Adobe Warnock Pro, as well as other Adobe typefaces are used throughout the lessons. For more information about OpenType and Adobe fonts, visit www.adobe.com/type/opentype/.

Team credits

The following individuals contributed to the development of this edition of the *Adobe Photoshop CS6 Classroom in a Book*:

Project Manager: Elaine Gruenke

Writer: Brie Gyncild

Illustrator and Compositor: Lisa Fridsma

Copyeditor and Proofreader: Wendy Katz

Indexer: Brie Gyncild

Keystroker: Jo Davies

Cover design: Eddie Yuen

Interior design: Mimi Heft

Art Director: Andrew Faulkner

Designers: Elaine Gruenke, Megan Lee, Angela Tolosa

Adobe Press Executive Editor: Victor Gavenda

Adobe Press Project Editor: Connie Jeung-Mills

Adobe Press Production Editor: Katerina Malone

Contributors

Jay Graham—began his career designing and building custom homes. He has been a professional photographer for more than 22 years, with clients in the advertising, architectural, editorial, and travel industries. He contributed the "Pro Photo Workflow" tips in Lesson 5. http://jaygraham.com

Mark Johann—is a photographer based in San Francisco. He contributed photography for Lesson 5. http://www.markjohann.com

Special Thanks

We offer our sincere thanks to Christine Yarrow, Daniel Presedo, Pete Falco, Stephen Nielson, and Zorana Gee for their support and help with this project. We couldn't have done it without you!

Adobe**Press**

LEARN BY VIDEO

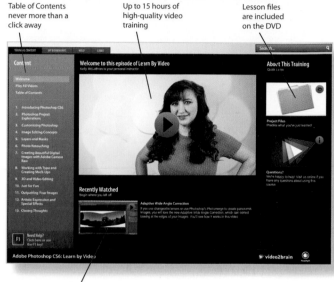

Table of Contents never more than a click away

Up to 15 hours of high-quality video training

Lesson files are included on the DVD

The **Learn by Video** series from video2brain and Adobe Press is the only Adobe-approved video courseware for the Adobe Certified Associate Level certification, and has quickly established itself as one of the most critically acclaimed training products available on the fundamentals of Adobe software.

Learn by Video offers up to 15 hours of high-quality HD video training presented by experienced trainers, as well as lesson files, assessment quizzes, and review materials. The DVD is bundled with a full-color printed booklet that provides supplemental information as well as a guide to the video topics.

For more information go to
www.adobepress.com/learnbyvideo

Video player remembers which movie you watched last

Watch-and-Work mode shrinks the video into a small window while you work in the software

Titles

Adobe Photoshop CS6: Learn by Video: Core Training in Visual Communication
ISBN: 9780321840714

Adobe Illustrator CS6: Learn by Video
ISBN: 9780321840684

Adobe InDesign CS6: Learn by Video
ISBN: 9780321840691

Adobe Flash Professional CS6: Learn by Video: Core Training in Rich Media Communication
ISBN: 9780321840707

Adobe Dreamweaver CS6: Learn by Video: Core Training in Web Communication
ISBN: 9780321840370

Adobe Premiere Pro CS6: Learn by Video: Core Training in Video Communication
ISBN: 9780321840721

Adobe After Effects CS6: Learn by Video
ISBN: 9780321840387